D1210190

Bel Canto
in Its Golden Age

Da Capo Press Music Reprint Series

MUSIC EDITOR

BEA FRIEDLAND

Ph.D., City University of New York

Bel Canto
in Its Golden Age

A STUDY OF ITS TEACHING CONCEPTS

by
PHILIP A. DUEY

DA CAPO PRESS · NEW YORK · 1980

Library of Congress Cataloging in Publication Data

Duey, Philip A
Bel canto in its golden age.

Reprint of the ed. published by King's Crown Press, New York.
Bibliography: p.
Includes index.
1. Singing. I. Title.
[MT820.D92 1980] 784.9 79-28302
ISBN 0-306-76021-5

This Da Capo Press edition of *Bel Canto in its Golden Age* is an unabridged republication of the first edition published in New York in 1951 by King's Crown Press, a division of Columbia University Press. It is reprinted by arrangement with the author.

Published by Da Capo Press, Inc.
A Subsidiary of Plenum Publishing Corporation
227 West 17th Street, New York, N.Y. 10011

Manufactured in the United States of America

Bel Canto
in Its Golden Age

Bel Canto in Its Golden Age

A STUDY OF ITS TEACHING CONCEPTS

by
PHILIP A. DUEY

KING'S CROWN PRESS
Columbia University, New York 1951

King's Crown Press is an imprint established by Columbia University Press for the purpose of making certain scholarly material available at minimum cost. Toward that end, the publishers have used standardized formats incorporating every reasonable economy that does not interfere with legibility. The author has assumed complete responsibility for editorial style and for proofreading.

Published in Great Britain, Canada, and India
by Geoffrey Cumberlege, Oxford University Press
London, Toronto and Bombay

Manufactured in the United States of America

PREFACE

Among the opinions presently held by music psychologists in regard to singing there are three that are of paramount interest both to the teacher and student of singing. The first is that no evidence exists that anatomical and physiological studies of voice production help in any way the process of learning to sing. The second is that attempts to consciously control a certain muscle or muscles become pitfalls for voice students. And the third is that it is unnecessary for students of singing to go beyond the problem of mechanics such as pose, breathing, mouth position, and so forth. These opinions are not generally shared by singing teachers and writers of singing methods.

It is common experience for voice students to be met with a different set of rules and vocabulary in whatever studio they chance to enter. Nor is much agreement to be found in the printed pages of those who write on "How to Sing." Nearly all of them go more or less into detail concerning the function of the muscles, nerves, cartilages, and bones involved in voice production. Even physicists and anatomists have come forth boldly in the past hundred years to dogmatize on the whys and wherefores of proper singing techniques. Scientific methods of voice production from the hands of persons of little or no professional and artistic ability have appeared regularly in print and enjoyed considerable popularity largely because of the esoteric claims made therein. All of which has led one psychological authority to say that there are few areas "where one finds a greater profusion of impossible ideas, or wilder clouds of mythology." [1]

However, there is one period when the art of singing became epitomized into a style and a technique that set the model for correct singing throughout the Western World. This era was that of the so-called *bel canto,* a term now generally used to denote that flowering of vocal lyricism which reached its peak during the course of the eighteenth century in Italy. From her conservatories this "Land of Song" poured forth a flood of singers and teachers that not only made Italian musical terminology official in all languages, but also established the Italian "maestro" as the *sine qua non* wherever music was the subject of serious study, both of which developments have persisted with remarkable tenacity to our own day. Italian opera was their stock in trade and together they placed that peculiarly unnatural exponent of the whole system, the "castrato," in a state of eminence that reached at times a point approaching veneration, and made the castrati the favorites of court and salon throughout Europe. *Bel canto* was king and generously lavished its vocal affluence upon all who came to be astounded by its technical accomplishments or to be overcome by the sheer beauty of its tone.

Why should this subject be investigated? There are adequate reasons. In the first place the story of singing has never been told.[2] This chapter of the history of music has yet to be carefully investigated and chronicled. And since the history of all vital human activity, in which singing is certainly to be included, has long since been justified, we may safely assume that the history of singing deserves telling. Besides, the term *bel canto* has been given a rather loose application. One of America's most highly regarded voice teachers has defined it as "that magic system which every self-respecting teacher of singing professes to teach and which every self-respecting newspaper critic says is an extinct art." [3] An English authority says, "In modern usage the phrase has become studio cant, for there is no school of *bel canto*." [4] The term does not appear in the dictionaries until after 1900, and those that do define it usually say that it denotes the method of singing developed in Italy in the seventeenth and eighteenth centuries which emphasized beauty of tone and vocal technique. Yet the expression as a specialized term, with particular meaning apart from context, does not seem to appear in print until after 1850.

The most important reason for investigation, however, is the fact that the two cardinal principles of *bel canto,* virtuosity and beauty of tone, still remain among the prime requisites of good singing today. Therefore an investigation which would throw light on how they achieved these ends should be of value to student and teacher alike.

As mentioned above, our own manuals on singing usually devote a goodly share of their pages to the physiology and hygiene involved in the vocal processes. Research which would reveal how and to what extent these factors were integrated in the singing method of the period under consideration should in turn reveal pertinent guides for our own times. Artists and teachers involved in creative endeavours have always returned again and again to the masters to seek guidance and inspiration from the things they said and did. In some respects, at least, *bel canto* is singing's finest model. This study is an effort to find out some of the things that were said and done about the art of singing during the period of its greatest virtuosity.

ACKNOWLEDGMENT

IT is a pleasure to express my gratitude to those who have been so helpful during the course of this study. I am especially indebted to Professors James L. Mursell, Harry R. Wilson, Howard Murphy, Jane Dorsey Zimmerman, Herbert Walker, and Erling M. Hunt, all of Teachers College, Columbia University. Doctors Ross Golden, Samuel R. Detwiler, and Raymond C. Truex of the College of Physicians and Surgeons, Columbia University, gave valuable specialized assistance, while Professors Paul Henry Lang and Erich Hertzmann of the Department of Musicology, Columbia University, were generous counselors. The library staffs at Teachers College, the Columbia University Music Library, the New York Public Library Music Division, and the New York Academy of Medicine were all of great service. In addition to these, I am grateful to teachers, classmates, and friends whose assistance, interest, and good will have been the sustaining influence in making this project a reality.

CONTENTS

PART I: INTRODUCTION

I. THE PROBLEM

ONE reads much and hears more about the vocal secrets of the old Italian School of singing, commonly called *bel canto.* It invariably is described as the Golden Age of Song, a period when the art of singing was supposed to be more highly developed than at any time before or after. Its *floruit* is usually regarded as the seventeenth and eighteenth centuries, with a special Rossinian flavor being added during the second and third decades of the nineteenth century, followed by a rather rapid descent as Romanticism triumphantly gained the upper hand and forced into limbo all that remained of classic and rococo elements. The aura of legend and mystery that has surrounded it since has served to confound rather than assist in understanding it.

Another element of great significance in singing has been the scientific study of the voice. An analysis of all the physiological functions involved has been widely held to be not only useful but also to be the only means to achieve vocal mastery. There is no question that we know more today than ever before about the mechanics of voice production, but instead of being an aid, this knowledge appears only to have broadened the field of controversy where the problem of correct singing is involved.

This leads us to an interesting hypothesis. If the singers of two or more centuries ago commanded and used a technique which challenges or surpasses the abilities of our own performers, then the present emphasis on the mechanical study of voice production is beside the point. The problem then becomes one of finding out the extent to which physiological factors were studied by those learning to sing according to this old Italian method. Because of the close relationship of the care and preservation of the voice to the study of singing at all times, it has been considered desirable to include vocal hygiene within the scope of this study. Therefore within the limits as defined below (Chapter II), available sources will be examined with the purpose of finding out to what extent physiological and hygienic factors were emphasized in the old Italian method of singing known as "Bel Canto."

II. DEFINITION OF TERMS

PHYSIOLOGY will be regarded in the strict sense of the word, as having to do only with the function of the organs and tissues used in the process of phonation. This is to insure the reader against the introduction of anatomical matters concerned with the structure of these organs or pathological considerations concerned with their diseases.

Hygiene will be used in the sense of the care and preservation of the voice. The object is to discover what means were taken to insure a healthy state of the vocal processes.

Bel canto is not so easily defined. It will be necessary to place some arbitrary limitations on our use of the term. There is no standard definition although there does seem to be a usage which has gradually found favor not only in music dictionaries but in general lexicons as well. It runs like this: "*Bel canto* (It. 'beautiful singing'), denotes the Italian vocal technique of the 18th century with its emphasis on beauty of tone and brilliant virtuosity, rather than dramatic expression or romantic emotion." [1] This style of singing, along with the teaching methods used, are regarded by many to have been lost in the myriad musical cross currents of the nineteenth century. On the other hand it is not uncommon to find teachers today who claim their method is that of *bel canto*,[2] and the popular musical journals sometimes discuss the term with no reference whatever to eighteenth century Italian vocal style.[3] The voice student today reads or is told that the *bel canto* style is the only way to sing and many a teacher will say with assurance that his method is that of *bel canto*, but when pressed for explanation, he adds many words but throws little light upon the subject.

Some definitions speak of its application to the seventeenth and eighteenth century Italian style of singing and add that in the nineteenth century it came to be distinguished from the Wagnerian declamatory style of dramatic vocalism.[4] It is of no little interest to note that the definitions of *bel canto* in the present German lexicons extend a somewhat wider application to the term. They admit that its standards of tone quality and vocalization have been an integral part of the Italian methods of singing from the seventeenth century to date. They also admit that the German style of singing has placed more emphasis on dramatic and declamatory elements. However they make the point that the German style of singing also calls for beautiful tone and virtuosity.[5]

All of these shades and varieties of opinions naturally invite etymological investigation. Here, the first thing that strikes with force is the fact that the term does not appear as a particularized expression, out of context, during the period with which it is most often associated, i.e., the seventeenth and eighteenth centuries. It becomes more astonishing to find that neither the musical nor the general dictionaries see fit to include it until after 1900. Even after this date, Grove's, the most comprehensive music dictionary in the English language, does not list the term, nor does Vannes,[6] most comprehensive of all dictionaries of musical terminology. Baker's dictionary [7] includes it in the supplement of the 1905 edition, although it is not to be found in the 1899 edition, and the first date given by Murray's (Oxford) dictionary for its use is 1908. Riemann's *Musik-Lexicon,* considered by many to rank first among all music dictionaries, does not give it a listing until the eighth edition, in 1916.

These facts have led us to a considerable investigation of books, periodicals, and dictionaries of the nineteenth century, the results of which are clarifying, especially when set against the great diversity of popular conceptions of *bel canto.* This research is by no means complete, since it lies beyond the scope of this study. Yet it seems not only useful but also pertinent to offer a résumé of these findings.

As is to be expected, Italy was the first country in which a particularized connotation was given to *bel canto.* Already in 1819, Benelli speaks of the various ornamentations as being "le bellezze del canto" ("the beauties of song").[8] Costa says of the Italian language that it is "la più addatta al bel canto" ("the best adapted to beautiful singing." The accompanying English translation renders "bel canto" as "vocal music.").[9]

He does not use the words *bel canto* except in a general sense nor does he use them anywhere else in the text. In a testimonial letter to the author,[10] Crescentini speaks of "il vostro bel metodo di canto" and "bell'arte del canto." [11] Likewise Florino uses identical expressions as well as others, viz., "la bell'arte del canto," [12] "un bel metodo di canto," [13] "il bel metodo di cantare," [14] and "nell'arte bella del canto." [15] Here again these expressions are not used in a special sense but only in the course of the text.

A more indicative use of the term turns up in the title given to a collection of songs by Nicola Vaccai,[16] *Dodici Ariette per Camera per l'Insegnamento del Bel-canto italiano.* But even here the author evidently is not concerned with the singing style of previous centuries since all the songs are by Vaccai himself. Indeed the title of this publication could very well be the inspiration of the publishers or of Vaccai himself to aid in its promotion. This may have been the first time *bel canto* was used in a marked way. Speculation makes us wonder if this may not have been the start of its specialized usage just as Caccini's *Le Nuove Musiche* and Viadana's *Centi Ecclesiastici Concerti . . . per Basso Continuo,* etc., furnished the nomenclature for new vocal and accompanying styles two and a half centuries earlier. Vaccai's publication enjoyed considerable popularity in Italy, a second edition appearing in 1855. The twelve songs were written during his stay in London, 1833–1838.[17]

By the 1860's the Italians began to realize the decadent state of their singing and from here on they spoke with increasing alarm about the deterioration of their old and honored vocal traditions. Even though the words *bel canto* appear frequently, still they are used only in a general sense. Lamperti writes at the beginning of his Preface,[18] "It is a sad but undeniable truth that singing is to be found today in a deplorable state of decadence." Later he tells us that he is offering his treatise in order to counterbalance present-day music, "used to the detriment of bel canto." [19] The words *bel canto* are not set off in any way, and it is interesting to note that in the edition translated into English [20] these words are rendered simply as "good singing."

Biaggi [21] uses the term "colle grazie del nostro bel canto," and again, "per la scuola complimentare e di bel canto," [22] but still the words seem to have no specialized significance. In a review of Lamperti's *Nuova Guida,* Ventura calls Italy "quest'alma mater del bel canto," and says that Lamperti gives the causes "del decadimento del bel canto." [23] The *Dizionario della Lingua Italiana* [24] offers what may be the first definition of the term. Under the word "bello" there are several hundred uses given and among them is to be found the following: "Del vostro bel cantar, me n'innamoro. . . . Il bel canto è lode special del canto condotto con finita ornatura e con esattezza delicata." ("I am enamoured of your beautiful singing. . . . *Bel canto* is special praise of singing performed with finished ornamentation and sensitive exactitude.") Here we are given a rather clear idea of what beautiful singing meant to the Italians in 1865. Although there is still no particularized usage indicated, the words "finita ornatura" and "esattezza delicata" are significant in that they seem to point to a style of vocalism more often associated with previous centuries.

This sort of thinking, hinting at retrospection, is uppermost in the mind of Perini, [25] who is very much concerned over the inroads of the declamatory style of singing and suggests that the way to restore beautiful singing to its former state of supremacy is to reunite "il canto *fiorito* e *brillante* a quello declamato e parlante." He points out that this was done in the seventeenth century when vocal virtuosity was integrated with the monodic declamatory style of the Florentine Camarata. Polidoro [26] goes further, complaining that hardly anyone is interested in maintaining and propagating the real traditions of beautiful singing.[27] He says that there are many more teachers than before, but they spend their time teaching composition and the piano rather than in the education of the voice. D'Arcais [28] says that in the days when "il bel canto italiano" was at its height the attention of the pupils and the teachers was turned to voice training rather than to the science of music itself.[29] All of these last three, Perini, Polidoro, and D'Arcais, present a common point of view which associates "beautiful singing" with a past era and express a conviction that the style of singing of their own day is inferior to that which obtained in former times.

There is the implication that the words *bel canto* no longer describe contemporary vocal practices, but that it would be desirable to restore such qualities to their singing.

The evidence we are seeking turns up in another article by Biaggi.[30] The author says that in *William Tell* Rossini combines the dramatic feelings of the French and the instrumental theories of the Germans with "il *bel canto* e la melodia degli italiani" ("the *bel canto* and the melodic sense of the Italians"). The words *bel canto* are here set off in italics showing conclusively that by this time they were beginning to have a particularized connotation. Subsequent to this Biaggi italicises these words in an article [31] bitterly criticising the vocal style of Wagner's *Lohengrin.* In distinction to some of the others noted above, he does not say anything about previous or lost vocal traditions. Rather he sets off *bel canto* as a contemporary style of singing peculiar to Italy and in which the Italians may justifiably take pride.

It is important to note the growing concern of Italian authors over the aggressions of the German *stile parlante* and the corresponding fate of their own *bel canto.* The decadence of singing appears to be a most popular subject to write about and the Wagnerian style comes in for mounting criticism. Baci [32] says that the musical theatre in Italy is in a dreadful state because of the deterioration in singing and because it has become saturated with melodrama, causing it to lose its essential vocal character. He concludes that Italy can no longer be called the first land of music.[33] Lamperti [34] becomes sarcastic, saying that whereas the celebrated masters of other lands always used to come to Italy to study, now the Italians go to Germany, where they are taught a pantheistic, chaotic, mathematical music based on instrumentation which may be all right for the Germans, but when written in Italy by Italians it becomes disfigured, hybrid, and altogether incompatible to those who have been nourished by the noble and chaste Italian melody. Carozzi [35] says, "Today these traditions of our *bel canto* are overthrown, not only by the new direction of a dramatic opera based on declamation, but by the deplorable condition of lyric art held in the clutches of ignorance and of those 'in the trade.' " [36]

German manuals on singing of the nineteenth century reveal unmistakably a heritage that came from the South. Not until late in the century do the words *bel canto* appear but the German equivalents are frequently in evidence before this time. Mannstein [37] pays high tribute to the old Italian method (which he says reigned from 1590 to 1790) and adds that there is little hope that it will be revived either in Germany or Italy.[38] Mannstein's eighth chapter is headed by these words: "Vom schönen Tone," and the first words are, "Beautiful tone is the only material out of which the singer can construct his art." [39] The Italians are called "the creators of beautiful sounds," [40] which the present generation of singers, even in Italy, has neglected to cultivate. In an article on *Gesangs-methode,*[41] Gassner discusses the merits of the Italian method and places considerable emphasis on the Italian ideal of beautiful sound [42] as the basis of their method. He says also that now Italy lacks both singers and teachers.[43] Nehrlich [44] says that beauty of sound is the "one" and "all" of the old Italian method [45] and that it must be admitted that the best German singers are trained according to the Italian method which is the basis of all true voice building.[46] Wieck,[47] the father of Clara Schumann, often mentions the beauties of singing, beauty in tone, and supports the old Italian method of singing over that of the present day, especially in Germany.[48] In the Preface, Wieck says, "When I speak generally of singing, I mean only beautiful singing, which is the basis for the best and most complete musical performance." [49] Sieber, [50] one of the most renowned of nineteenth century voice teachers, devotes a section of his book to "development of beautiful tones." [51]

We would expect some sharp statements from Hanslick, the confirmed anti-Wagnerian critic, and he does not disappoint us. "While our budding opera singers soon lose their way in dramatic expression, the Italians develop first of all the independent beauty of the voice, the well-rounded technique of singing. Above all they like a beautiful tone." [52] He insists that the independence of "schönen Gesanges" must be established for only after there is complete mastery over the voice is that loftier dramatic expression made possible. Then, and only then, may one speak of the art of singing.[53] Beauty of sound, "Tonschönheit," is also considered the primary means of effective singing by Haertinger [54] and Mendel uses the words "schöne Gesang" several times in his article on "Gesang," although they are not set off from the rest of the text in any way.[55]

In the 1878 edition of *Klavier und Gesang*,[56] Wieck echoes the opinions of Hanslick, even going beyond the latter in his disdain for the German singers and teachers of singing. "There triumphs now in our opera houses mostly lungs, bad taste, monstrous caricatures and foolish exaggerations, hence the most objectionable misuse of the human voices." [57] Especially does his condemnation fall on the teachers who "have no feeling for beauty," and who "do not know a natural, soulful, rich, forward-produced tone from a cold, ugly, tight, forced, and throaty one." [58]

By the time Hugo Riemann, outstanding German musicologist, brought out the first edition of his *Musik-Lexikon*,[59] the words *bel canto* expressed, in epitome, what was meant by the Italian ideals of proper singing to the Germans. While Riemann did not give the term a separate entry, as has been done beginning with the eighth edition, published in 1916, nevertheless in his article on "Gesangskunst" he took over the Italian term and set it off from the German text in Latin type,[60] indicating that it had become by this time, even in Germany, an expression with a particular connotation. It is important to note that Bremer also sets off the words in Latin type in his lexicon, published the same years as Riemann's.[61] While Riemann implies that perhaps the old Italian method was better than those of "our century," Bremer names great teachers of both the eighteenth and nineteenth centuries whose schools were outstanding.

The birth of the Empire in 1870 furnished the wellspring for a torrent of nationalism that succeeded mightily in stemming the flow of cultural cross-currents in Germany. These had served her well in past centuries especially where music was concerned. But chauvinistic bombasts and art are not nurtured in common soil and the course of singing over the past three-quarters of a century has been duly influenced. The colossal music-dramas of Richard Wagner were heaven-sent for those convinced that

Italian vocal style was too effete to express virile German sentiment. Julius Hey, arch-exponent of Wagner's ideas in regard to singing and selected by the latter as being best fitted to promote them, gave expression to the German vocal concepts in an extensive four-volume work on the teaching of singing.[62] He says that the faded traditions of the Italian *bel canto* do not offer the slightest thing for the cultivation of the "Vaterlandischen Sprachgesangs." [63] There are increasing signs from about this time that German singing methods are considered sufficient if not superior, and especially that German opera has supplanted that of Italy. This statement may be read: "The era of Italian opera finally appears to be ended," [64] and the editor of *Allgemeine Musik-Zeitung,* Otto Lessmann, uses the term *bel canto* with increasing frequency albeit with decreasing respect.[65] There were those among the Germans who championed the Italian singing method throughout, viz., Stockhausen, Goldschmidt and Sieber. Stockhausen was a pupil of Garcia and Goldschmidt of Stockhausen, while Sieber studied with Ronconi. Sieber brought out a collection of songs by old Italian masters, one of the last of a great number of his works, under the title *Il Bel Canto.*[66] In the preface Sieber comments on the state of singing in Germany at about the time of Wagner's death. He says, "In our time, when the most offensive shrieking under the extenuating device of 'dramatic singing' has spread everywhere, when the ignorant masses appear much more interested in how loud rather than how beautiful the singing is, a collection of songs will perhaps be welcome which—as the title purports—may assist in restoring *bel canto* to its rightful place." [67]

French opposition to Italian singing style exhausted itself during the Gluck-Piccini controversy of the eighteenth century whereas at this same time Germany was drinking in all that Italy had to offer. The nineteenth century saw just the reverse. We have already noted the slow crystallization of a vocal style diametrically opposed to Italian precepts in Germany, but France accepted them wholeheartedly. Fétis says [68] of the effect of Gluck's operas, that they substituted cries of a monotonous languor instead of promoting among the French "the tradition of the excellent Italian school of this epoch and retarded for nearly thirty years the knowledge of the art of singing in France."[69] Fétis comes pretty close to the French equivalent of *bel canto* when in discussing Tosi's famous manual on singing he calls it "la belle école du chant italien."[70] By the 1880's France had also taken over the term and the French were using it to denote the old Italian school. Boisson says, "The era of Rossini was that when the Italian bel canto cast away its last glory,"[71] while Lavoix in the same year says practically the same thing, but uses the Italian words, "The interpreters of Rossini, Bellini, and Donizetti were the last pupils of the masters of *bel canto,* or the art of singing of the eighteenth century."[72]

The English speaking countries offer little to add to our discussion. It seems important to note however that the term *bel canto* began to appear both in America and England at almost the identical time of its use in France and Germany. Dow makes use of it to describe the Italian manner of singing[73] while Bach calls Adelina Patti "the most eminent representative of *bel canto.*"[74]

This discussion of *bel canto* has run to considerable length. Our efforts to trace its origin and usage have led us to uncover the evidence listed above and since it should help to clarify a number of uncertain facts in this area which has been almost totally void of investigation, we believe it not to be out of order to present the results even though they should have further corroboration. The following conclusions would seem to be justified:

1. The term *bel canto* does not appear as such during the period with which it is most often associated, i.e., the seventeenth and eighteenth centuries; this may be said with finality.

2. The words *bel canto* did not take on a special meaning until the 1860's in Italy.

3. By 1880 the other countries had recognized this special meaning to the extent that it began to appear in print in Germany, France, England, and America.

4. Neither musical nor general dictionaries saw fit to attempt definition until after 1900.

5. The conflict between the German "Sprechgesang" and

Italian *bel canto* was an important factor in the latter's etymology.

6. Present usage favors its application to the Italian singing methods of the seventeenth and eighteenth centuries with its emphasis on beauty of tone and virtuosity. It is in this last sense that we limit our definition for the purposes of this study.

PART II: BACKGROUNDS

III. LARYNGOLOGY

THE most complete historical study of laryngology is that of Holmes,[1] of which extensive use has been made here. The first period that saw the emergence of what might be called a science of anatomy and physiology was that commonly known as the Hippocratic age, i.e., the fifth and fourth centuries B.C. Such scientific knowledge was scanty indeed and in regard to laryngeal action there was almost total ignorance. The fact that air implemented voice was recognized, and that the tongue, palate, teeth and head cavities were instrumental in speech.[2] But even these slender facts were not comprehended beyond the Asclepiadae, a school of Greek physicians on the island of Kos, from whom emanated the famous collection of writings named after their most famous member, Hippocrates. Because of the strong prejudices of priests and medicine-men their anatomical inquiries were limited to the slaughter of animals in preparing food and the incidents of warfare.

Aristotle, who had already begun his omnifarious scientific investigations by the time of Hippocrates' death, did not surpass his distinguished predecessor to any great extent in physiological knowledge, although he pondered long and deeply over the problem of voice production. In the *De Anima* he rationalizes step by step and reaches the following definition:

> Voice, then, is a sound made by a living animal, even then not with any part of it taken at random. But since sound occurs only when something strikes something else in a certain medium, and this medium is the air, it is natural that only those things should have voice which admit the air. . . . The throat is the instrument of respiration; the reason for which this part exists is the lung. . . . So it is necessary that during respiration the air should be breathed in. So the blow given to the air breathed in by the soul in these parts [lungs and throat] against what is called the windpipe causes the voice.[3]

In the *De Audibilibus* we are given a remarkably extended discussion of the physiological phenomena of phonation,[4] including the lungs, windpipe, mouth, breathing, breath control, diction, etc. His comments here as well as in the *Problems* [5] disclose opinions that, although of a speculative nature, are remarkably consonant with those of today.

In order to find precise scientific information we are obliged to traverse nearly five centuries to the prolific writings of the greatest anatomist of antiquity, Galen (130–200 A.D.). Highly educated and widely travelled for his day, this man, who was also a philosopher, gathered into numerous treatises all the anatomical, physiological and pathological knowledge of his time together with many contributions from his own broad experience. His predecessors in the great Alexandrian school had largely neglected the larynx and it is with complete justice that Galen has been called the founder of laryngology.[6] The principal cartilages are described (i.e., the thyroid, arytenoid, and cricoid) as is the external and internal musculature. The pneumogastric and recurrent nerves receive careful attention although the spinal accessory and superior laryngeal nerves are alluded to only vaguely. It was Galen who gave the name *glottis,* or tongue, to the vocal cords and says that it is like the tongue of a pipe (reed) when looked at from above or below.[7] His comments on phonation are of particular interest since his theories were not successfully challenged until barely two hundred years ago. Galen says,[8]

"Voice could not be formed unless the passage is narrowed. For if the whole should lie widely open . . . voice could in no way be produced; for if the breath pass out gently, expiration is made without sound; but should it be sent forward in the volume suddenly and with vehemence, what is called a sigh occurs. In order, however, that the animal may emit voice it requires, no doubt, the motion of the breath, but none the less the narrowing of the channel in the larynx; not a simple narrowing, but one which can by degrees be constricted and by degrees relaxed. Such is what the body we are dealing with effects accurately, and hence I call it the glottis or tongue of the larynx."

Thus we see that Galen conceived changes in pitch and volume to be dependent on the width of space between the vocal cords. As we shall see, it was not until the experiments of Ferrein in 1741 that this theory was dethroned.

There were no contributions worthy of the name made to

laryngology after Galen until the scientific method received regenesis under the stimulus of Humanism. The erudition of the Arabs, while it added little or nothing to anatomical and physiological knowledge, was the primary sustaining and transmitting agent for all that Galen and his predecessors knew. The practice of performing human anatomies was not revived until the fourteenth century, and even then was of rare occurrence.

It was not until after 1500 that progress was resumed. The preceding two hundred years were concerned with making up lost ground, especially that cultivated so thoroughly by Galen long centuries ago. But about 1500 Berengarius of Pavia discovered that the arytenoid cartilages were a pair instead of one as described by the ancients. Vesalius (1514–1564) of Padua made the most careful laryngeal dissections to date and with the aid of nearly thirty woodcuts was able to give the cartilages and muscles an extended description. Fallopius (1523–1563), also of Padua, was the first to establish the nomenclature for the cricoid cartilage (it had previously been called "innominata" since the ancients gave it no name) and described the thyro-arytenoid and crico-thyroid muscles more accurately than his colleague, Vesalius.

The year 1600 has come to be associated with important developments in vocal music, the opera, oratorio, and monody emerging approximately at that time. It is highly interesting to note the simultaneous increased interest in the anatomy and physiology of the larynx, in fact it would be logical to speculate on a common cause for this coincidence. Battista Codronchi,[9] Hieronymus Fabricius[10] (1537–1619), Caspar Bauhinus[11] (1550–1624), and Julius Casserius[12] (1545–1616) formed an illustrious quartet each of whom brought forth, almost concurrently, works dealing in specific detail with the larynx. Codronchi was the least important since his work leaned heavily on Galen and was more in the nature of a popular treatment. Bauhinus' contribution was mostly confined to muscular nomenclature, but the remaining two, both of Padua, made comprehensive studies of the larynx in man and in animals giving details not mentioned before. These were published with engravings, those of Casserius being especially copious and carefully drawn,

There remain only a few names to mention before we turn to the theories of phonation that accompanied these anatomical discoveries. The innervation of the larynx was better understood after the investigation of Thomas Willis (1621–1675) of Oxford. This brilliant English anatomist furnished the first definite description of the superior laryngeal nerve and the spinal accessory, both of which had been almost totally neglected by Galen and all after him. Another remarkable product of Padua, the last and the greatest from this most celebrated seat of medical learning, John Baptist Morgagni (1682–1771), together with Dominic Santorini of Venice, labored to correct the errors of previous anatomists as well as to fill in the final details in a picture that was complete except for some conjectures that remained to be verified by the laryngoscope and high-speed motion picture cameras.

It should not be too surprising that Galen's theories of phonation persisted so stubbornly into modern times. Only unproven hypotheses were possible since no way had been devised to observe the larynx in action. The science of acoustics, too, was stumbling along in its infancy and did not yet know how to be of much assistance. Many were the theories of voice production, some "fanciful and often conflicting," [13] but in general they were concerned with two important principles, first, that of vibration of columns of air as in organ pipes, and second, the vibration of the glottis itself. Even as great a scientific thinker and anatomist as Leonardo da Vinci went far astray in his explanation of pitch, comparing the throat to an organ pipe and concluding "that the pitch of the human voice is dependent upon the length and diameter of the trachea." [14] Although others shared similar opinions, that which was most commonly held was in substance the theory of Galen, viz., that phonation was effected by bringing the vocal bands within a short distance of each other, while the length and breadth of the *rima glottidis* determined the pitch. All of the anatomists mentioned above reasoned, sometimes falsely, on the exact action of the cartilages and musculature of the larynx, but the aberrant dicta of Galen led them to mistaken judgments.

It remained for a musical theorist as well as a scientist to explode the theory that vocal pitch was dependent on the alteration in size of the various respiratory canals. Marin Mersenne (1588–1648) was one of the most erudite scholars of his time. Philosophy could not long monopolize such a prolific mind, and with his knowledge of mathematics, acoustics and musical instruments he was able to set aside once and for all the theory that pitch in singing operated anything like an organ pipe. Knowing that a vibrating column of air has to be doubled to produce a sound an octave lower, and that two octaves or more are common to the singing voice, he reasoned that such changes were manifest impossibilities. He indicated that the solution was to be found in the study of musical reeds and that the edges of the glottis offered the most likely clue.[15]

Perhaps no scientific theory of the ancients was maintained essentially unchanged to such a late date as was Galen's theory of voice production. For more than fifteen hundred years it persisted, and as late as 1706 we find Dodart (1624–1707) presenting a monograph [16] based on Galen. A diagram [17] shows the position of the vocal cords in a wide ellipse which becomes narrower as the pitch of the voice ascends. This is precisely as Galen described glottal action in the second century A.D.

The year 1741 marks an important milestone in the physiological understanding of the larynx, for in that year Antoine Ferrein (1693–1769), professor of anatomy at the Jardin du Roi, Paris, made "the first acoustic experiments on the natural larynx, and by so doing he advanced the physiology of the organ more than any other investigator, not excepting Galen." [18] By a number of experiments on the human larynx as well as those of animals [19] he was able to show, first, that in order to phonate the lips of the glottis had to come together, second, that vibration of the lips was the essential factor since by touching them the sound stopped, and third, that difference in tension of the edges of the glottis caused the changes in pitch. He thus demonstrated that the vocal bands function more like vibrating strings and so he gave the name of *cordes vocales* or vocal cords to the lips of the glottis, which term still remains in common usage. Although these conclusions of Ferrein were debated they gained general acceptance and were by and large verified or corrected in the nineteenth century.

It only remains to say that in 1800 many of the most important functional matters pertaining to the larynx were still very imperfectly understood. We have seen that anatomical discoveries were for all purposes generally complete, but the action of the intrinsic muscles, those most immediately concerned with phonation, were not yet clearly apprehended and the views held rested on no clear demonstration. Nor was the knowledge of the innervation of the larynx any more rounded.

From this brief historical survey of the anatomy and physiology of laryngology two very important conclusions pertinent to our study are brought forward:

1. Any emphasis on the physiological study of phonation in the art of singing before 1800 was based on false or incomplete theories.

2. The successful methods of teaching used were, perforce, entirely empirical in nature.

IV. VOCAL HYGIENE BEFORE 1600

THE ancients went to great pains to preserve and protect their voices. This may have been more the practice of orators even than singers since rhetoric reached the extremes of sophistication among the Greeks and Romans. References to hygienic practices are by no means uncommon, especially to those used by public speakers. We include such references in our study since it is logical to assume that singers made use of the same devices as the orators in the matter of vocal hygiene. Some of our sources make this assumption entirely reasonable.

The art of rhetoric called for voices of the greatest suavity and polish and recourse was made to a variety of emollients and medicines to insure these ends. Servants were wont to accompany the orators, keeping in readiness medicated fluids from which their masters now and then sipped.[1] Galen gives us a clear account of the ingredients of these medicaments, almost all of which are still employed. They include tragacanth, squill, turpentine, styrax, horehound, myrrh, poppy-seeds, pepper, frankincense, cassia, etc. These were mixed with wine or honey and were sometimes boiled down, cooled, and made into lozenges to be held under the tongue and dissolved.[2] Some thought it sufficient merely to sip warm water. An injunction found in St. Jerome [3] would indicate that actors and singers were likewise accustomed to the use of all these medicated fluids to sustain their voices. He accuses certain of the church choirs of bedewing their mouths and throats with sweet medicaments as if they belonged to a theatrical company. That this kind of thing had been taken most seriously in classical antiquity is indicated by the report that a chorus member was poisoned when he sought to increase his vocal ability by taking a fluid for this purpose.[4]

Even in antiquity diet was considered as having a profound effect on the voice. Singing immediately after eating was apparently avoided; thus we read in the *Problemata:* "Why does it spoil the voice to shout after food? We can see that all who practice voice production such as actors, chorus-singers and the like, perform their exercises in the morning and fasting." [5] And again: "Neither choruses nor actors rehearse after breakfast but when fasting." [6] Quintilian mentions the fact that an easy digestion is essential both to the singer and orator.[7] Again in the *Problemata* we read that lack of sleep makes the voice rougher; [8] that drinking makes the voice lower [9] and more cracked than the normal voice of the sober.[10]

As to the precise foods helpful to clear vocalization we are told that leeks, garlic, and even partridge produce smoothness and thus clear out the larynx.[11] Singers were called "bean eaters" because the pulse of leguminous vegetables was considered salutary to the voice.[12] Eels and firm-fleshed fish were beneficial,[13] as was the yolk of an egg.[14] Many kinds of food were thought unwholesome for those dependent on the healthy state of their throats. Various fruits were shunned, notably apples [15] and figs, especially when eaten in the middle of the day.[16] Nuts were held to be peculiarly noxious for singers,[17] and actor and singer alike carefully avoided cold drinks.[18]

Those who used their voices as a means of livelihood were strongly urged to give careful attention to their way of living. We have already noted some opinions on drunkenness and lack of sleep. Fevers and sore throat likewise were mentioned as having ill effects. But that which was especially recommended was a modest and careful way of life. Quintilian is particularly solicitous over the care that one should take in order to preserve vocal powers. Of course he is considered primarily with the orator but he makes pointed comparisons between the latter and singers. He says:

> In both cases physical robustness is essential to save the voice from dwindling to the feeble shrillness that characterises the voices of eunuchs, women and invalids, and the means for creating such robustness are to be found in walking, rubbing-down with oil, abstinence from sexual intercourse, an easy digestion, and, in a word, in the simple life.[19]

The ill effects of diseases of the throat are discussed as well as bodily fatigue. A strong body is placed at a premium, for

> while exercise, which gives strength in all cases, is equally necessary both for orators and singing masters, it is a different kind of exercise which they require. For the orator is too much occupied by civil affairs to be able to allot fixed times for taking a walk. . . . Nor is the same regime suitable as regards food: for the orator needs a strong and enduring voice rather than one which is soft and sweet.[20]

Quintilian informs us that all authorities agree "that the voice should not be overstrained in the years of transition between boyhood and manhood, since at that period it is naturally weak." [21] The implications here are plain. As part of their training routine singers were accustomed to observe the following: regular physical exercise, careful eating habits, avoidance of vocal strain, and simple living. Singing manuals of today prescribe the same.

The medieval writers on music are almost totally void of references to the care of the voice. Johannes de Muris (*ca.* 1290–1351) is the only one to suggest that the circumstances of health affect singing. Under the heading, "What sort of errors arise in singing and in how many ways they arise," we are told that they come

> from incapacity, from carelessness, from obstinacy, or indifference. It is from incapacity that old people, boys, and those who are sick sing badly, and this is pardonable, since natural weakness excuses such people. . . . Due to carelessness, drunken people sing badly. . . . People sing badly from indifference if they are wearied by some labor.[22]

De Muris does not offer advice such as we found in the writings of Aristotle and Quintilian. His observations are limited to generalizations but they indicate plainly that he recognized such things as fatigue, sickness, and drunkenness to be the cause of bad singing and we may infer that the singers of his time were not wholly lacking in suggestions to look after their health. It must be said, however, that more than a thousand years had elapsed between the careful and precise instructions of Quintilian and the passing comments from the hand of De Muris. In the following chapter [23] reasons will be offered to explain this extended void.

The Renaissance offers little or nothing that was not mentioned by the ancients as to special hygienic care recommended for singers. Just as Galen's theory of phonation remained in vogue, so did the theories on physical care of the voice follow the general precepts of Aristotle and Quintilian. Maffei gives us ten rules for coloratura singing, the second of which says: "Practice time is in the morning or four to five hours after a meal, because, when the stomach is full, the windpipe and with it the voice, do not possess the necessary purity and clarity for practicing the 'gorga' [ornaments]." [24]

It has already been mentioned that the treatise on the voice by Codronchi [25] was not only a popularization but was also based on the authority of the ancients. This is especially true of those parts concerned with the care of the voice and because of this "popular" quality, the work is most useful to us, since the author seemingly does not bring his information under careful scientific scrutiny. For this reason his comments may come nearer to representing general beliefs and practices. That his opinions are pertinent for our study we may safely assume since Codronchi himself says, "I may be able somewhat by my skill to benefit the singers themselves." [26] Weakness of the voice is caused by general bodily weakness, fatigue, too much sleep especially after eating,[27] and from weakness of muscles which move the throat.[28] Quintilian is quoted on the importance of bodily health for the conservation and preservation of the voice,[29] by taking walks, temperance, abstinence from love, and the use of ointments; all of which promote digestion, stronger breathing, open passages and good elimination. It is bad to exercise the voice after eating, for the spirit is made hot by food and is disturbed by indigestion.[30] Codronchi is especially careful to warn against overindulgence of cohabitation. He mentions the practice of infibulation among ancient actors in order to prevent sexual indulgence and thus save the voice,[31] and comments that in his time the custom of castration prevails for the same purpose. As an anaphrodisiac he suggests the root of the "Bride of Hercules," [32] which causes cessation of sexual functions, thus conquering the flesh. Besides one should avoid evil thoughts, the sight or company of women, and the reading of evil books.[33]

Food and drink come in for considerable attention. So as not to harm the voice one should refrain from eating caterpillars, chives, headed vine, asparagus, basil, fennel, *cunila,* parsnips, artichokes, ragwort, *Nux myristica,* galangal, pine nuts, *Nux avellana,* pistachios, *Mala insana,* and many more of such. Abstain also from wine, meat and eggs while there is an excess of sexual activity; [34] also, cold drinks are bad and Galen is quoted as saying that it is bad to take wine without food after exercise.[35]

One should sleep on a hard bed but not on the back nor in a reclining position. There is no general agreement about the use of ointments, and Codronchi conjectures as to what kind of ointment Quintilian used.[36] The use of baths among the ancient actors for preservation of their voice is mentioned but the author says that in his own time it would be difficult because of the lack of facilities. There follow a great many details on medicaments and ointments for the care of the voice. Galen, Aetius, Rasis and Avicenna are cited as authorities and we offer one of the prescriptions considered as most important:

3 oz. juice of barley
2 oz. juice of sweet almonds
1 oz. fresh butter
1 oz. of the whitest sugar
6 oz. clear water of barley

Cook all together until a fourth part of it is gone (evaporated). Singers may take six ounces of this in place of dinner (caena) and the same or a smaller quantity in the morning.

In order to get relief from throat indisposition due to catarrh, light, warming, drying medicine is recommended, e.g.: ". . . warm rose honey mixed with myrtle syrup, or licorice in tragacanthus, which can be made into pills. If the matter in the vocal organs is thick and clinging, use dried sedge (*carex*) or grapes with honey added; or yet a stronger medicine, hyssop, pennyroyal (*pulegium*) and licorice." [37]

In his "Histoire du Chant" [38] A. De Martini offers some cardinal points [39] which were observed by the sixteenth century singers. According to this author they ate only light foods and shunned almonds, filberts, and other nuts because of the oils and little irritants they possess. Singers of this time never ate before singing and were always very sober—they ate only vegetables and the name "fabarri" (i.e., grass eaters, eaters of beans) was given to them. Careful advice was suggested for drinking. Falsettists, sopranos, and contraltos should be very temperate because wine makes the voice heavy, thus robbing it of its resonance. Tenors and basses, if young, and above all in the spring, should dilute their wine because wine irritates the stomach and renders the mouth dry and less sonorous. In the winter, on the contrary, it should be drunk just as it comes from the vine-plant. As to the older singers, they should drink only dry wine. Unfortunately De Martini does not document this information.

From this study of vocal hygiene before the era of *bel canto* two things are evident: First, that the essential requirements for the care of the voice were apprehended by the ancients, especially by the time of Quintilian (first century A.D.). These included a careful diet, regular physical exercise, and a modest way of living, all resulting in a strong, healthy body. Even many of their therapeutic agents are still considered efficacious for the treatment of vocal indispositions. Second, little or nothing of value was contributed by the Medieval and Renaissance eras, that which was added being more in the nature of unscientific popular theories and remedies.

V. DEVELOPMENT OF SINGING TECHNIQUE PRIOR TO 1600 [1]

THE musical treatises of the ancients have very little to say about singing technique. Since our own theorists are likewise remiss we should not hold them too strictly to account. Philosophers, grammarians, essayists, poets and the like are more likely to comment here or write a paragraph there, and it is to such sources that we turn.

Singing was an improvisatory art in the time of Homer and Hesiod. The eighth book of the Odyssey gives us considerable information on the singer.[2] The first lines of *The Battle of the Frogs and Mice* [3] and the famous *Contest of Homer and Hesiod* [4] show clearly the *ex tempore* nature of singing at that time.

Both Plato and Aristotle imply that there was a considerable vocal art in their day, i.e., fifth and fourth centuries B.C. The former complains of the deterioration of music in the hands of the professional musicians [5] due to their "disorderly tastes." [6] He will not have them in his perfect state [7] since they must cater to the prevailing vulgarities of the multitude.[8] The following quotation not only is strong evidence of a considerable virtuosity but also shows how strongly Plato disapproved:

> For they (the muses) behold all these things jumbled together, and how, also the poets rudely sunder rhythm and gesture from the tune, putting tuneless words into meter, or leaving tune and rhythm without words, and using the bare sound of harp or flute, wherein it is almost impossible to understand, what is intended by this wordless rhythm and harmony. . . . Such methods, as one ought to realize, are clownish in the extreme in mechanical accuracy and the imitation of animal sounds, and consequently employ the pipe and the harp without the accompaniment of dance and song; for the use of either of these instruments by itself is the mark of the mountebank or boor.[9]

Aristotle is no less a source of evidence for the existence of virtuosity. In the *Politics* [10] he too complains of the undesirable effects of elaborate performance technique. While he recommends that the young should learn to sing because it will keep them out of mischief and teach them to judge good music, yet the practice of music should never interfere with the ideal of becoming a good citizen. Says Aristotle: "Professional musicians we speak of as vulgar people, and indeed we think it not manly to perform music except when drunk or for fun." [11] Those who study music should not "go on toiling at the exercises that aim at professional competitions, not the wonderful and elaborate performances which have now entered into the competitions." [12]

In his *Poetics,* Aristotle takes care to define minutely the elements of tragedy with the exception of "melopoeia" [13] or "song-making," which term he says "I use in the full, obvious sense of the word." [14] He calls it the "most delightful" of all the "pleasurable accompaniments and embellishments of the Tragedy." [15] Overacting and vulgarity are condemned,[16] and as for *delivery* he says: "It only made its appearance late in tragedy and rhapsody, for at first the poets themselves acted their tragedies. . . . Now delivery is a matter of voice, as to the mode in which it should be used for each particular emotion; when it should be loud, when low, when intermediate; and how the tones, that is, shrill, deep and intermediate should be used; and what rhythms are adapted to each subject. For there are three qualities that are considered—volume, harmony, rhythm. Those who use these properly nearly always carry away the prizes in dramatic contests . . . as at the present day actors have greater influence on the stage than the poets." [17] When actors (artists) have greater influence than poets (composers), it is an age of virtuosity.

In the *De Audibilibus* [18] there is considerable evidence that vocal technique received more than passing attention. First of all he explains the differences in voice quality:

We all breathe the same air, but we emit different sounds owing to the difference in the organs involved through which the breath passes to the region outside. These are the windpipe, lungs and the mouth. But the greatest difference in sound is produced by the blows of the air and the shapes assumed by the mouth. This is evident, for all the differences of voice arise from this cause, and we see the same people imitating the voices of horses, frogs, nightingales, cranes, and almost every other kind of living creature, using the same breath and the same windpipe, by driving the air from the mouth in different ways.[19]

This is a very clear and concise explanation of why each voice has its own particular quality. Different shapes and sizes of the throat modify the voice, but

It is not merely the difference in the organs but all the accidental properties which cause a difference in the voices . . . [such as] in cases of catarrh and drunkenness . . . or if the breath is quite dry the voice becomes harder. . . . The differences of organs and of accidental properties which belong to them each produce corresponding voices.[20]

This last sentence sums up the entire question. By "difference of organs" he means physical or inherent differences, i.e., in size and shape of lungs, throat, mouth, etc., and by "accidental properties" he refers to disease, climate, drunkenness, rest, and other things of circumstance. All of these are considered today the most important things contributing to difference in voice quality. The fact that the same voice will vary from one day to the next is also noted. "The same people have not only sometimes a shriller and sometimes a deeper voice, but also one harder or softer." [21]

Breath control is noted: "If the lung is large and pliable it can admit much air, and expel it again husbanding it as it wishes, because of its softness and because it can easily contract." [22] Again, "For the swiftness of the breath makes the voice sharp and its violence makes it hard." [23] Also,

And yet some people suppose that voices become hard owing to the harshness of the windpipe, but they are in error. This no doubt makes some small contribution, but so does the breath violently expelled by the lung. . . . Consequently the breath in some cases comes out softly, and in others hard and violent, since it is easy to see that the windpipe itself supplies only a small force. . . . Some pipe softly and some harshly. This is clear from sensation itself; for if one strains the breath more violently, the voice immediately becomes harsher because of the violence, even if it is inclined to be soft.[24]

In Book XI, "Problems of the Voice," and Book XII, "Problems Connected with Harmony," of the *Problemata* [25] there are numerous comments that indicate a high development of virtuosity. Aristotle explains that in the olden days the songs were sung by citizens, but in his time there were professional artists who varied their songs continually,

> for it is easier for one person alone to execute variations than for a number, and for a professional artist than for those who have to preserve the character of the music. That is why they composed simpler chants for the latter. . . . For the actor is a professional artist and imitator, but the chorus is less capable of filling an imitation role.[26]

This obtains, by and large, today, in our own choral organizations where the choruses of the operas, oratorios, etc., are performed by comparatively less trained singers while highly trained soloists sing the more difficult parts.

From the above citations attributed to Aristotle it is evident that vocal technique had received no little attention as early as the fourth century B.C. in Greece. By the beginning of the Christian era virtuosity was apparently even more important. Dionysius of Halicarnassus was a highly esteemed scholar of his time (fl. 30 B.C.–10 B.C.). In his remarkable work on literary criticism and composition, *De Compositione Verborum*,[27] he makes pointed comments and comparisons concerning vocal practices. In Chapter XI he mentions the high degree of skill demanded of professionals, the great variety of intervals used in vocal music and very significantly says: "Music, further, insists that the words should be subordinated to the tune, and not the tune to the words." [28]

This is stout evidence of an advanced state of virtuosity. He speaks of the "perfect mastery" that comes from long training and which produces "effects with the utmost ease from sheer force of habit." [29] And as a final warning to would-be artists, in the final paragraph of the treatise he suggests daily exercises, for "No rules . . . can suffice to make experts of those who are determined to dispense with study and practice. They who are ready to undergo toil and hardship can alone decide whether such rules are trivial and useless, or worthy of serious consideration." [30]

These observations of Dionysius may be considered highly

pertinent. They indicate the existence of a highly specialized technique of such nature that its mastery required long and arduous training. His statement that the words were to be kept subordinate to the tune is most revealing. There have been periods in the history of modern singing, especially that of *bel canto,* when the same might be truly said, and it is not nonexistent at the present time. It also shows that a great change had taken place since the earlier centuries when the text was considered far more important in representation than the music.

Plutarch (46–120 A.D.), a widely travelled and liberally educated Greek of noble character and high ideals is a further source for the existence of singing technique. His *De Musica* [31] is an interesting and curious collection of facts, theories and comments on mythology, philosophy, science, history, etc., all in relation to music.[32] According to this author music has undergone a notable regression and he complains bitterly of its degeneration from its once high and noble estate: "But our men of art, contemning its ancient majesty, instead of that manly, grace, heaven-born music, so acceptable to the Gods, have brought into the theatres a sort of effeminate musical tattling, mere sound without substance." [33]

Plutarch relates how music declined in the hands of various musicians, how they became "bewitched with the theatre's new fangles and the innovations of multiplied notes," and "were most depraved with diversity of notes and baneful innovations." [34]

He follows with further discussions of the difficulties in acquiring the skill necessary for becoming a "most accurate musician" which, along with other statements of his, speak for themselves.

A notable contemporary of Plutarch, Quintilian (A.D. 35–95) places much emphasis on musical and vocal training in preparation for an oratorical career. He says:

> The good qualities of the voice, like everything else, are improved by training and impaired by neglect. But the training required by the orator is not the same as that which is practised by the singing master, although the two methods have many points in common.[35]

Also,

> while exercise which gives strength in all cases, is equally necessary both for orators and singing-masters, it is a different kind of exercise which they require. For the orator . . . cannot tune his voice through all the notes of the scale nor spare its exertion . . . [he] needs a strong and enduring voice rather than one which is soft and sweet, while the singer mellows all sounds even the highest, by the modulations of his voice. . . . Consequently, we [the orators] must not attempt to mellow our voice by coddling it.[36]

The implications here are that singers regularly practiced scales and avoided straining the voice. Our own singing manuals invariably prescribe the same.

The medieval centuries do not offer evidence of much virtuosity in singing. Entertainments, in which singing was preeminent, had discredited itself to such a thorough extent in the waning of the Roman Empire that the rising might of the Church made the subservience of the performer to the music philosopher complete. The early Church Fathers, notably St. Augustine and Boethius, devote almost exclusively their rather lengthy treatises on music to mathematical and abstract considerations of harmony, prosody, meter, and rhythm "in which the mind is raised from the consideration of changeable numbers in inferior things to unchangeable numbers in unchangeable truth itself." [37]

Subsequent theorists fall in line, the performers being unflatteringly described as blind and ignorant beasts of habit while the real musicians are the philosophers of music.[38] Already with Boethius (*ca.* 524) the philosopher is the real musician, the composer second and the performer a very poor third. When we read, "But he is a musician who, in the light of reason, has acquired the science of singing not through the servitude of performing, but through the command of contemplation," [39] it is clear why the not inconsiderable vocal art and virtuosity of later antiquity passed into limbo. Any art ruled over by such a dictum must wither.

And wither it did. Nearly a thousand years passed before the singing artist regained his position of importance. For at least half of this time nothing worthy of the name of virtuosity is evident. It is highly interesting to note that as the spirit of Humanism began to assert itself, the art of singing starts on its long regenesis. Expression is the first of the integral elements of singing art to show itself. John Cotton who flourished about 1100, at the beginning of the so-called "Twelfth Century Renaissance" says under the heading, "Precepts for the Composing of a Song":

The first precept which we add for the making of a melody is that the song should vary according to the sense of the words. . . . If you wish to compose a song at the request of young people, let it be youthful and sportive, but if for elderly people, let it be slow and express gravity. . . . The composer can be reproached if he brings in a mood of jollity in material that is sad, or a mood of lamenting in happy material.[40]

Also Johannes de Muris (*ca.* 1290–*ca.* 1351) says:

If one recognizes the proper nature of a song, one will see that it is not enough to sing what has already been devised by others, but either, perchance by zeal of his own nature, or persuaded by the requests of other people, he will be careful to set the text of the song with suitable notes.[41]

And Marchettus of Padua (fl. 1270–1310) in his *Lucidarium:* "The things that appear in the voice are signs of the feelings that are in the mind." [42] By the time of Arnulfo of San Gilleno (fifteenth century) the artist is again in command. Says he: "He [the gifted singer] even takes music that was rough and inelegantly forged on its composer's anvil and . . . reduces it to a more pleasing form, like one reminting money. . . . True felicity distinguishes these men who excel in both ways, in nature and in art." [43] Arnulfo represents a complete about-face from Boethius and is a prophet of even still greater vocal triumphs to come.

In these latter centuries there was recognition of the fundamentals of voice production. In his *Lucidarium,* Marchettus of Padua says that the voice is formed by the natural instruments of the body of which there are six, i.e., the lungs, the throat, the palate, the tongue, the front teeth and the lips:

First, the breath proceeds from the lungs; second, it passes through the throat; third, it strikes the palate; fourth, it is divided by the tongue so that it may be diversified; fifth, what a man pronounces is determined by the touching of the tongue itself against the teeth; sixth, it is controlled by the lips.[44]

Theodoricus de Campo (fl. 1450) says that nine parts produce the voice, viz., the two lips, the four principal teeth, the plectrum (which may mean the uvula), the tongue, and the palate. Adam de Fulda (*ca.* 1490) says, "Voice is the sound formed by striking the teeth with the tongue as a plectrum, by striking the two lips like cymbals, by the hollow of the throat and the lungs which aid in the formation, and which, like a pair of bellows take in and send out air." [45]

In our evaluation of these quotations we must keep in mind that the function of the vocal bands as we now know it to be was not yet discovered. However by this time the restrictions of inhibitions against anatomies performed on the human body were beginning to be brushed aside, which may account for the greater anatomical interest manifest here. Also, since northern Italy was the birthplace of modern anatomy in the early *trecento,* Padua being famous for its medical school, it is not too surprising to find Marchettus and Theodoricus writing as they did. It is altogether possible that they witnessed some of the anatomies that took place there.

There is evidence that these medieval theorists appreciated the qualities of the human voice in the same general meanings that we use today. Writing in the early years of the seventh century, Isadore of Seville (570–636) has this to say about them: "They are light and delicate, i.e., sharp, clear and penetrating, as those of women, children and sick people, or full and ample, as those of men . . . because of much breath coming out."

He classifies voices as (1) *acuta,* sharp, like a stringed instrument, (2) *dura,* hard, like thunder or a hammer against an anvil, (3) *aspera,* raucous and not smooth (uneven and broken up), (4) *cocca,* blind, i.e., it stops as soon as it is sounded (it is dull and unresonant), (5) *vinnola,* delightful, i.e., sweet, soft, and flexible, and (6) *perfecta,* high, sweet, and clear. "The perfect voice is high, sweet and clear; it is high so as to be adequate in the upper range; it is clear so as to fill the ears amply; it is sweet so as to delight the spirits of the listeners. If any of these is lacking the voice is not perfect." [46]

Regino Prumensis speaks of the "vox perfecta" in the same terms.[47] Unpleasant voices are often mentioned, and in highly uncomplimentary terms. Such expressions as "neighing of horses," "bellowing of bulls," and "braying of asses" are frequently encountered and are strong indications that the medieval audience was keenly aware of voice quality.

While breath control was not directly considered, there are a number of references to the necessity of pausing for breath and the problems of phrasing that arise therefrom.[48]

Both the singing teacher and the pupil will take particular interest in the fact that vocal registers were not only recognized but discussed intelligently. John of Garland (*ca.* 1193–*ca.* 1270) says:

> It must be known that the human voice exists in three forms: it is a chest voice, throat voice, or head voice. If it is a chest voice, then it is in the low register; it ought to be placed in the lowest part of a piece. If it is a throat voice, it is in a middle position in relation to each, that is to the low and the high. And just as far down the chest voice is in the low register, so the head voice is high in the upper register. And, in regard to the way of singing, chest voices ought to be placed in their proper place, that is in the lower part, throat voices also ought always to have the middle place in the upper sections.[49]

Jerome of Moravia (*ca.* 1250), a younger contemporary of Garland, says in effect very much the same thing:

> Speaking popularly, not of their real nature, certain voices are of the throat, certain of the chest and certain actually of the head itself. We call chest voices those that form the notes in the chest; throat voices, those that form notes in the throat, and head voices, those that form them in the head. Chest voices are good for low tones; throat voices for high tones; head voices for very high tones. For generally heavy and low voices are in the chest, light and very high voices are in the head; and medium voices between these, are from the throat.[50]

Similar classifications are in vogue today. It is quite usual to speak of low, middle and high registers, or chest voice, middle voice, and head voice. But the first two words of this last quotation, "Speaking popularly," would seem to have special importance for us as they certainly indicate that such a division of the singing voice was well known and was generally accepted.

The personal appearance and manner of the singer was often

discussed. The singer is told that it is not necessary to move the body around while singing. He should stand devout, humble and erect. Some singers bend and extend themselves, while others look around to see if people are looking at them, but this is dishonest.[51]

As the spirit of the Renaissance emerged, the singer, along with his contemporaries in the other arts, shared fully in the urge for greater self-expression. This was of the greatest importance and had been in mounting evidence throughout the Gothic period. Singing artists have never been content to do just what was set before them and no more, and the centuries under discussion were no exception. Ecclesiastics were continually complaining about the corrupt practices of the singers. Already Hucbald (*ca.* 840–930) objects to overdone suaveness even though the performer is sincere in his praise of the Lord.[52] John Cotton (*ca.* 1100) remonstrates that many songs are spoiled by bad singers of which there are so many "we can't count them," [53] and adds that they introduce extraneous elements or elaborations which are extremely annoying. John of Salisbury (1115–1180) apparently finds nothing but evil in contemporary performances. He says:

> Music defiles the service of religion. For the admiring simple souls of the congregation are of necessity depraved—in the very presence of the Lord, in the sacred recesses of the sanctuary itself—by the riot of the wantoning voice, by its eager ostentation, and by its womanish affectations in the mincing of notes and sentences.[54]

Johannes Gallicus (late twelfth century) writes about the execrableness of "modern singers," [55] and later adds that they are all committed to vain practices and do not catch the sweet and angelic strains with the ear of the mind.[56] Johannes de Muris has some very hard words to say about singers who do not know enough to make a discant correctly but who try all the same to sing in church and in so doing offend both the senses and the intellect.[57] Elsewhere de Muris elaborates under the heading, "What sort of errors arise in singing and in how many ways they arise." [58] Adam de Fulda speaks of the necessity for rules because "the practice of the performer has come to be extremely bad." [59] Also, "They must take upon themselves certain grandiose things in practice. Furthermore, some of them who hardly understand the form of the notes, or have only the slightest skill in the art, amend every song, mutilate, corrupt it, and make false everything that is composed correctly." [60]

But it remains for Arnulfo to hurl the last word in invective against certain inept singers.

In the barking of their brawls they roar higher than the ass's braying, and blare out more terrible than the uproar of beasts, and spew out bedlam. Discanting opposite the rules, they never fail to create barbarism in music. . . . They impudently offer themselves as able to make corrections, or to give directions with authority. . . . In an educated group of musicians they spoil everything that is done very regularly because of their lack of training. . . . It is impossible to force silence on these men, for even though they become very unpopular they make more noise than ever. . . . These are truly they whom the kingdom of music has irrevocably exiled from her boundaries, —or rather they in whose faces the favor of outraged music has spat.[61]

The *bête noir* responsible for much of this malpractice so unanimously criticized by these ecclesiastics was the use of descant in the divine service. Not that simple descant was objected to, but the elaborations of these opposing melodies—elaborations that were to reach unexpected complexities—were quite naturally opposed by the Church, which was bent on preserving music as a most helpful adjutant to divine worship. Opposed were the singers, who saw and felt music primarily as an art, and without their gradual assertion of independence nourished by secularism, it is quite unlikely that the world would have seen the great musical cultures which flowered during the Gothic and Renaissance period. Woolridge says:

On the one hand was the great and powerful body of the clergy, endeavoring by all means to preserve intact in public worship that elementary expression of the congregational spirit which is contained in the music of the Church. . . . On the other hand were the composers and descantors, at first of one mind with the clergy, but later becoming by degrees more and more preoccupied by the artistic problem, and employing more and more in their enrichments of the service material essentially different in character from plain song.[62]

Paul Henry Lang says it more succinctly: "The Church began to realize that its monopoly on music was being seriously challenged as the development of polyphony went forward on a more universal basis than strictly liturgic aims could afford." [63]

There was hardly an ecumenical council that did not prescribe the limits of music and proscribe many of its practices. There were not infrequent papal pronouncements to the same end, one of the most notable being that of Pope John XXII (1324–1325), in which the singers are described as "preferring to devise methods of their own rather than to continue singing in the old way," and consequently "their voices are incessantly running to and fro, intoxicating the ear, not soothing it, while the men themselves endeavor to convey by their gestures the sentiment of the music which they utter." All of these things they have decided to "cast entirely away, far from the house of God," and no one henceforward "shall think himself at liberty to attempt those methods, or methods like them." [64] This is summary language but its influence was short-lived.

Mankind has always tried to beautify and ornament his efforts at self-expression, and although much of it has tended toward the tawdry, its true and sound qualities have remained either as masterpieces or as framework upon which masterpieces find expression. Even the might of the Church could not withstand a stronger power which as Nietzsche says comes from "the folk as a unity," and from which all cultures stem. The impotence of any manner of opposition to such inherent primal forces is clearly shown by the fact that vocal ornamentation not only continued in vogue, but expanded in usage and increased its demand on the skill of the performers. Writing of the time of Pope Urban V, *ca.* 1362, Ambros says: "The singer could no better display his art than, when asked to improvise a descant to a tenor at sight, to render it as richly and as expensively as he was able." [65] Apparently after scarcely one generation, Pope John's bull was already in limbo.

All languages of Western Europe had a word for it. In Latin it was "cantus super librum" or "cantus a mente"; in Italian it was "contrapunto alla mente"; in French "chant sur le livre"; in German "Verzierungskunst." The English equivalent has been variously rendered as "art of ornamentation," "improvization," "diminution," "coloration," or "embellishment." By the time of Tinctoris (*ca.* 1435–1511) these practices had been sufficiently stylized so that he was able to define the term and explain its uses with accompanying examples. In order to get an idea of the techniques of the day we quote substantially from his *Liber de Arte Contrapuncti:*

> Now both the simple and the diminished counterpoint occur in two ways, that is, either written or mentally supplied. Counterpoint which is written is generally called "resfacta." But the kind we supply mentally we simply call "counterpoint" and those who perform it are popularly said to be singing "over the book." The *resfacta* differs from the *counterpoint* especially in this respect: that all parts of the *resfacta,* whether they are three or four or more, are connected, so that the order and principle of the consonances of any part must be observed with respect to the others, singly and altogether, as is clear from the following example, which is in five parts, for of these, plainly, first three, then four, and finally all five parts are in accord. [A five part example follows.] But when two or three, four or more sing together "over the book," one is not subject to another. But for any one of them, so far as the principle and the arrangement of the consonances are concerned, it is sufficient to make a consonance with a tenor. I do not think it blameworthy, however, but extremely laudable, if, as they sing together, they produce similar placing and progressions of consonances among themselves. For thus they make an ensemble which is very full and smooth.[66]

While the *resfacta* is of no little interest, that which commands our attention is the "cantus a mente" which the singer improvised as the music progressed and which provoked all the ecclesiastical protestations and circumscriptions. As Tinctoris describes the practice we cannot escape comparing it to the twentieth century dixieland jazz bands, jam-sessions and even boogie-woogie. Moreover it is here that our own vocal technique in the narrow sense of skill and virtuosity finds its genesis.

This brings us to the sixteenth century which saw the Renaissance vocal idioms reach their synthetic culmination. That there was a concomitant growth in the art of singing must be accepted since the music demanded more and more of the singer and participation grew both intensively and extensively. While these vocal idioms placed the greatest emphasis on choral ensemble there is a plethora of evidence at hand to show that toward the end of the century at least, more and more emphasis was being placed on the art of the individual performer.[67]

The outward general appearance and conduct of the singer while performing received increasing attention. "The singer must sing with his voice, not with movements of the body," said Lanfranco.[68] Maffei may be quoted to the same effect: "Nothing should move while singing except the arytenoid cartilage. . . . People look ugly if they shake their heads while singing from the throat. . . . The singer should keep a mirror in front of him so as to know of any ugly gesture (accents) which he has made while singing." [69]

Also Zarlino: "The singer should not sing with movements of the body or actions or gestures which produce laughter from those who see and hear them—as some do, moving so much that they really seem to be dancing." [70] Zacconi, writing about two decades later, goes into full detail. After offering advice on dress and cleanliness, he says:

> The singer must be young, refined, well-dressed, not entirely ignorant, not hesitant of speech, nor sharp in speaking; but gentle, courteous, clean, and adorned [adorno]. He should not be a jester, given to ridiculing the company, or marked by any notable defect, for these things cause contempt for a person.[71]

After explaining why elderly people should not sing, he adds:

> First the singer must be careful not to make gesticulations not only with his body but with his mouth, turning now one way and now another, and not to roll his eyes like a person bewitched . . . and good manners always please more than anything else, for which reason I say that the straightforward and modest singer always pleases the hearer more than the artificial and pretending one. If a person has a straight and beautiful mouth, or clean and sincere eyes, does he wish to spoil these beauties by twisting them around? Every one ought to exhibit all the beautiful physical qualities which he has. . . . Secondly, singers should be careful not to fall into the error into which many do fall—in accommodating the voices and uttering musical figures with the tremolo, as if this tremolo came from the head, although it has nothing to do with the head. . . . There are some singers who don't know how to sing if they do not hold the book with the head turned to the right or the left, and others who handle their beards or clean their noses with their fingers, or lean

over with their hands on their faces. . . . It is not well for the person who is singing to play with his hands, with his feet, or with whatever is on the table, or to handle them purposelessly or thoughtlessly. Some when they cannot reach the figures in certain chords stretch their necks and arch their eyebrows, so that it is apparent that they are pulled there by force. Some put their faces down under their throats and look as if, while they are singing, they want to hide their beards in their chests. After a singer has sung something . . . he should not yawn or turn the pages, or count how many things have now been sung, or otherwise show that he wants to be off for some affair of his.[72]

Generally speaking, this advice is still pertinent nowadays.

The problems concerned with breathing and breath control were noted and discussed. Rossetti [73] is quite dogmatic in his advice. The singer must breathe easily and not with anxiety, the breath must not seem to be drawn in violently. Breath must not be taken before the final syllables of a two-syllable word except where there are too many notes to a syllable. The breath must strike the palate fully and the voice and breath must be emitted uniformly. Johann Frosch (d. 1533) says that one purpose of rests in music is to give the singer a chance to catch his breath.[74] Ganassi says that the voice should proceed with a medium amount of breath which can be increased or diminished at will.[75] Maffei describes the proper handling of the breath as "little by little pushing the breath with the voice, and taking care that it shall not go out through the nose or the palate." [76] Zacconi says that "many singers have not large enough breathing capacity, lose out trying to catch breath and are obliged to stop before the end of the passage." [77] Bovicelli also objects to audible breathing "making more noise with the drawing of the breath than with the voice," and speaks of "those who through weakness or fright take a breath every few notes." He adds that breath must not be taken in the middle of a "passaggio" or cadenza and must be taken in time and with judgment.[78]

There is no evidence at hand that the importance of ear-training as such was recognized before the sixteenth century. But the statements we find here leave no doubt that the services rendered to a singer by a good ear were held to be of great use. By the middle of the century Coclicus writes: "He [the singer] will always bring to bear the judgment of his own ears also. For the ears readily understand what is done correctly or otherwise, and are the mistress of the true art of singing." [79] About the same time Vicentino, after discussing the difficulty and importance of singing wide intervals with correct intonation, says: "The music would be especially excellent if the singers could utter the notes and the words at the same time in tone and sing a composition as true as the organ plays it." [80] Now if the singer cannot employ such exact intonation (*tal giusta intonatione*), at least they will spare no effort to agree as much as they can in their ensemble (*concerti*).[81]

Zarlino advises that "Singers should be careful to sing correctly those things which are written . . . intoning the notes well, and putting them in their proper places, seeking to suit them to the consonance." [82] In the list of requirements for perfection in music "perfection of hearing is presupposed," [83] and he adds that "hearing when it has been purified, cannot easily be deceived as to sound." Zacconi [84] discusses the difficulty of singing wide intervals with just intonation and offers examples from Josquin, Obrecht, and the madrigal *Solo pensoso* of Werth which is shown as containing some strikingly difficult leaps, e.g., two successive fifths downward, a fifth followed by a sixth upward, and a downward tenth with the melody then continuing in downward direction. His remark that these intervals require a skillful singer would seem to preclude the suggestion that they were played and not sung. As to ornaments [85] they are much easier learned from hearing than from written examples. Chest voices are never off pitch like head voices or dull voices and Zacconi prefers those who sing sharp rather than flat although all voices with too false intonation must be rejected.[86]

Just as we found vocal registers generally recognized among the later medieval theorists, so in the sixteenth century there are a substantial number of references to the same subject and with the same general substance, i.e., there exist three practical registers, high, middle, and low. The falsetto voice, however, comes in for increasing mention and consideration. References exist that Saint Bernard (1091–1153) said to sing "not with high, lax voices in a womanish fashion, but, masculine in sound and feeling." [87] His contemporary, Saint Raynard, Abbot of Citeaux, 1133–1151, writes to the same end: "It becomes men to sing with a masculine voice, and not in a feminine manner, with tinkling, or as is popularly said, with false voices to imitate theatrical wantonness." [88] Gerbert reports a dialogue between the Cistercian and the Clunian in which the former censures the latter for having emasculated voices at Cluny; he says that these voices are too light and effeminate and make for luxury contrary to the canon.[89]

Ulrich gives us several references to what must be considered as the use of the falsetto. Ornithoparcus speaks of descant as harmony which must be produced with a voice like a girl's. [90] Fink, Hermann, says, "Let the descant be sung with a light and penetrating voice." [91] Beurhusius describes descant as "the highest voice, melodiously turned to the very high sounds, and consequently light and childlike." [92] And Maffei mentions the use of a feigned voice "called falsetto" when there was a dearth of sopranos.[93] Vicentino says that frequently sopranos are lacking and suggests in that event for the soprano to "be dropped an octave and become tenor and the contralto be like soprano with changed voice [come soprano à voce mutata]." This author goes on to suggest that one may compose masses, motets, madrigals, etc., so that they can be sung "a voce piena," or "à voce mutata." In the light of Vicentino's discussion, "à voce mutata" can only mean "with falsetto voice." [94] Zacconi advises that when singing in the high register, the voice should not be forced if the singer cannot reach it comfortably. It is better, he adds, to sing notes falsetto or to omit them.[95]

These references all point up a problem that faced the choir directors of the Renaissance and became more acute as the sixteenth century advanced. Every self-respecting court, monastery, and church had its choir of singers which varied in sumptuousness and quality with the fortunes of the sponsoring individual or institution. As music flourished both more widely and more intensely, the supply of choir boys fell far short of the demand and we read of incidents such as that of Orlando di Lasso who after being abducted three times was allowed by his parents to go into the service of Ferdinand Gonzaga, viceroy of

Sicily, as a boy soprano. The chapel masters were forced to turn to other sources, these being first the Falsettists, especially those from Spain, and then, of far greater importance, the castrati.[96]

There is a wealth of evidence to indicate the necessity for and the existence of a considerable degree of vocal pedagogy in the sixteenth century, even in the strict sense of the term, i.e., over and beyond the ability to read the notes. The facility to handle passages and intervals of wide range and with good tone quality was an established precept for good performance. But means used by the singing teachers to acquire the physical ability to perform these elaborated and ornamented vocal melodies are scarcely in evidence. We know that the singers were told when and where to breathe but not how. There are no manuals showing how the flexible voice was acquired. We can only say *ipso facto* that the methods existed. Kuhn tries to show what these methods were; [97] however most of his sources to this point postdate 1600. His quotation from Coclicus is only a general statement to the effect that any boy who wishes to sing well must find a teacher who also sings well. His other two sixteenth century sources, Maffei and Conforto, assert that students may learn to sing without the aid of a teacher by the use of their books. Chrysander is more successful with his study of Zacconi,[98] in showing what actual methods may have been used, for as this author says, Zacconi suggests that singers should practice on all the vowels the various examples of ornamentation that he gives as an aid to flexibility. But Zacconi's work comes at the end of the century, and its circulation was not wide. For the most part he offers only generalities and these tell what should be done rather than what was done. Singers should not sing too high, not too low, too loud nor too soft, too fast nor too slow. They should have a satisfactory appearance and manners, should not be entirely ignorant, should have a good chest for sufficient breath, vocal agility, a good ear, know when and where to perform the colorations with good taste and these should not be too simple nor too complex. The practice of the ornamented passages, he suggests, will not be considered necessary by some since nature has disposed the fortunate ones for such things, but the less fortunately endowed can also become skilled singers by hard study and much practice. While Zacconi remains our best source for this period, yet the other writers cited above offer general advice concerning the same points and usually to the same end as has already been noted. Zacconi describes the situation at the end of the sixteenth century thus: "Music has always been, and still more with every hour is, embellished by the diligence and effort of singers. It is made new, or changed, not by means of figures which are always the same but with graces and accents it is made to seem ever more beautiful." [99]

Here in essence we find described what was expected of the skilled singer at the end of the sixteenth century. It was a highly sophisticated art which afforded the means for technical display but by the very nature of the music itself individual emotional expression was lacking, or at least, was well circumscribed. The next century was to see a complete change.[100]

VI. THE CASTRATI

Their History in Singing

This study of *bel canto* would not be complete without giving due consideration to the most important element in its development, i.e., the castrato voice. The practical value of such a study may be questioned since such a vocal phenomenon no longer exists. But the misunderstandings, legends, and prejudices that prevail in this general area are so notable as to deserve and demand careful appraisal. Moreover the effect on the vocal soloistic art of these unnatural voices was most notable, an influence we experience every time we hear a Händel opera or oratorio, or a Bach cantata. Since the immediate source was physiological, albeit artificial, it is pertinent to present a brief résumé of the subject.[1]

The institution of castration has always been of more or less importance in human affairs. Taboo and false modesty especially in periods and countries under the influence of Christianity have stood in the way of its frank and unbiased appreciation and understanding. This particular aspect of the problem cannot be discussed here for it would lead us into unrelated fields. What is essential, however, for a true appraisal of the castrati is a realization that the approach to this subject has been usually unsympathetic resulting in superficial and unfair judgments. Of the great many criticisms levelled at the castrati as to character, mentality, initiative, and even morality, their history shows that they are seldom more open to criticism in these respects than "normal" people and especially than those who would discredit them. Critics have never held a corner on the desirable human virtues nor has criticism ever likely been free of bias.

The trail of mutilation, self or inflicted by others, appears far back in myth and saga, and as the stream of history broadens it assumes at times considerable influence. The *Iliad* of Homer and the *Theogeny* of Hesiod both relate incidents relating to its status in the affairs of both men and the gods. The religious cults of Asia Minor such as those headed by Mylitta, Astarte, Artemis, and Attis all gave high standing to their eunuch priests. The cult of Cybele, whose famous self-mutilated priests, called "Galli," indulged in frenzied, orgiastic dances of unbelievable intensity, was established in Greece by 400 B.C., and in Rome about two hundred years later. Here it joined hands with the established Roman religion but retained its wild ritualistic practices, especially that part played by the priests. As the Roman empire crumbled this religion degenerated into fantastic ritualistic depths.

Eunuchry found an established place at an early date in Christianity, the eunuchs always holding a position of respect. In Matthew, chapter 19, verse 12, Jesus says: "For there are some eunuchs which were made eunuchs of men; and there be eunuchs, which have made themselves eunuchs for the kingdom of heaven's sake." In Luke, chapter 23, verse 29, we read, "For behold the days are coming in which they shall say, Blessed are the barren." Here as also in Matthew, chapter 18, verses 8–9, we find justification for, if not approval of, self-mutilation and these scriptural lines were in all likelihood the basis for this rather common practice in subsequent centuries among the Christian religious zealots. Origen, one of the most famous of the early teachers of Christianity was a victim of self-mutilation because of complete dedication to his religious duties. Many others followed his bizarre example. However, Christian dogmas, with their championship of the opposite principle of "Be ye fruitful and multiply," soon began to hedge regarding castration, and at the council of Nicea, 325 A.D., definite measures were taken to curb the practice, allowing it to be done only by qualified physicians. These decrees were never strictly enforced, but still later only priests were allowed to perform or take part in such an operation. The names of such prominent Church Fathers as Saint Augustine, Gregory of Nazianus, Theodore (teacher of Constantine), and Tertullian are to be found among those opposing castration.

There have been many studies of castration in modern times from every conceivable point of view.[2] It has not always been easy to get at the facts, and the period of *bel canto* is no exception. The best known first-hand investigation was that of Burney, made during his memorable travels to Italy and elsewhere in 1770 and later. He was intent to get at the real situation, but after following many leads he was always told he could get precise information elsewhere. Burney writes:

> I inquired throughout Italy at what place boys were chiefly qualified for singing by castration, but could get no certain intelligence. I was told at Milan that it was Venice, at Venice that it was Bologna, but at Bologna the fact was denied, and I was referred to Florence; from Florence to Rome, and from Rome I was sent to Naples. The operation is most certainly against law in all these places, as well as against nature; and all the Italians are so much ashamed of it, that in every province they refer it to some other.[3]

But Burney was not entirely unsuccessful in getting at least a general conception of the situation. From reputable physicians, British consuls, friends, and other sources including personal observations, he was able to report that the conservatories never actually performed the operations. However, beforehand, the boy possessing a promising voice was brought to the conservatory for a professional opinion concerning his talents and, if favorable, he was taken elsewhere for the actual operation. Veterinarians were a common agency and travellers report seeing signs in Naples and other places, "Qui si castrano ragazzi," and in Rome "Qui si castrano li soprani per li cappella papali." The number of boys castrated has been estimated as high as four thousand yearly during the heights of the professional production of castrati in eighteenth century Italy.[4]

In the affairs of state and society castration has always been a fact with which to be reckoned. Its effect upon the individual was soon learned and it was considered advantageous not only to have docile slaves but also to prevent a warlike enemy from propagation, especially those in line for enemy thrones. The supervision of the harem was a strong reason for eunuchry and this confidential position frequently enabled eunuchs to attain great influence and power including promotion to the highest offices. Herodotus says that they were especially prized for their fidelity.[5] At any rate, the sordid profession of selling mutilated African boys to Moslem harems has persisted to the present generation.

But it would seem that they enjoyed their greatest political triumphs in the last centuries of the Western Roman Empire. After Constantine they appear everywhere. They meddled in the business of the Church and were vigorously attacked by the Church fathers. Their influence upon Julian the Apostate caused him to return to the Oriental cult of Astarte. Eutropius and Scholasticus were among the more noted eunuchs to gain high places of state while Narses, Hermias and Bagoas became military leaders of renown. Claudianus is especially bitter against them because of their trickery, wantonness and power while Lucian in his *Eunuchus,* Petronius in his *Satyricon,* and Ovid in *The Art of Love* are sources giving us vivid pictures of the times and the role played by eunuchs. But the barbarian invasions put an end to many of these customs and, with the final triumph of Christianity, were considered a purifying influence. During the medieval centuries scarcely a trace of eunuchry is to be found in the Western World and not until the Renaissance do they make a consequential reappearance. Here again it is interesting to note that though their realm was musical, they often served as confidants or emissaries of popes, kings, cardinals and ministers.

We come now to that area of our subject with which we are particularly concerned, viz., castration for the purpose of retention of a high voice. While it was recognized at a very early time that a eunuch usually possessed a voice of high range, yet it is to be doubted if the motive of the operation was ever for singing in these early times. On the other hand, eunuch slaves were often called upon to entertain especially if they possessed musical talent, and it is only natural to assume that their unusual vocal qualities were soon observed. Besides the term "eunuch voice" was a common one from remote antiquity, the connotation of which is not difficult to conjecture. But that this result was ever the reason for anyone becoming a eunuch is to be almost completely discounted until a somewhat later period. It is of interest to note that the first use of castration for the purpose of art was in the realm of the dance and pantomime instead of singing. Saint Cyprian (200–258) says that the operation was performed in late boyhood in order to retain a lithe and supple body, but since according to Petronius these dancers and pantomimists also sang, its effect on the voice must have been evident. Infibulation was a much more widely practiced custom in Rome both among heathen and Christians to delay maturity among youthful singers, cytharists, and actors.[6]

Bearing in mind the important part played by castration in the Near Eastern religious cults as well as in their domestic and civil life, it is not surprising to find eunuchs singing in the Eastern Church long before they appeared in the Western branch. Origen was probably the first castrated singing teacher to appear in the Christian Church although we know that his act was not motivated by musical ambition. But according to Sosomen (*ca.* 400–450) and the church historian Socrates (*ca.* 380–450), Briso, a eunuch of the Eastern emperor, was director and teacher of singing in Constantinople in the fourth century and instructed the eunuchs in the singing of hymns. Also according to the testimony of Balsamon, a learned canonist, who wrote his *Commentaries* in 1170, eunuch singing was established in the Eastern Church by that date. Balsamon's revealing statement is as follows: "First of all it must be noted . . . that the body of singers of former times consisted not only of eunuchs, as is the case today, but also of those not of this sort." [7]

Most of these eunuchs came from Constantinople and went as singers and teachers wherever the Eastern Church was established. Russian annals tell of the eunuch Manuel who, with two other eunuchs wandered to Smolensk where they established themselves as music teachers in 1137. From the twelfth century on we can safely say that eunuch singing was the rule in the Eastern Church.[8]

The first date of their appearance in the Western Church is not definitely established nor do we know whether they came by way of Constantinople, Spain, or directly from the Near East. The growth of self-mutilation among Christian monks is thought by some to have made their entrance easier. There is definite evidence that castrati were used to sing in certain religious celebrations in Spain about 1557 and afterward,[9] and Fantoni [10] definitely hands the palm to Spain as being the first to use them.[11] As to the Sistine Chapel we know that at least by 1562 the castrato voice could be heard in its public performances, as Padre Soto, a Spanish castrato, was entered on June 8 of that year. The edict of Pope Paul IV, on July 30, 1555, paved the way since it dismissed and excluded all married men from the Sistine ranks.[12] A few years later the word "eunuch" begins to appear regularly after the names of newly admitted singers. Pope Clement VIII, 1592–1602, has been widely quoted as justifying their presence by the words, "ad honorem Dei." [13] After 1609 only Italian castrati were trained as sopranists for the Sistine Chapel and by 1625 the last falsettist in the choir had died.

Already in the latter half of the sixteenth century the castrati had begun to consider their careers as that of singers and because of more careful study and training soon ousted the boy singers and falsettists from the Italian choirs. When the opera appeared they were already prepared, technically, and this "Dramma per Musica" was not laggard in realizing that the extraordinary vocal gifts of these "unnatural" ones were made to order for its essential baroque characteristics. Together they gave to the world a calibre of vocalism such as had never been heard. Nor can it be heard today and probably never will again, at least as long as society is controlled by its present religious and moral precepts. Although their accomplishments were considered sensational, there was yet another side to the story and it is a sordid one. For every one that gained fame and fortune, hundreds were sacrificed by conscienceless guardians, teachers, agents, and even parents, to drag out the rest of their days in a drab and dreary world, usually of prejudice and unfriendliness.

At the very moment of their greatest achievements, forces were at work which were to destroy the castrati. Here we can only consider in barest outline how this came about. The greatest upsurge in natural sciences which followed close upon the Renaissance brought forth a new era of rationalism in philosophy with the thinking of Descartes, Locke, and Leibnitz in the van. This led in turn to new conceptions of individual liberty and freedom in which spirit the Enlightenment flourished and which the eighteenth century philosophers carried forward to the French Revolution. Part and parcel with the times was a widespread growth of naturalistic sentiments summed up in Rousseau's popular slogan "Return to Nature." This produced a climate of opinion and feeling quite unwholesome for these artificial and "unnatural ones" in which they rapidly lost favor. Even more directly the Opera Seria, the musical genre which provided them their greatest opportunities, was nurturing in the "Intermezzo" what proved to be a veritable fifth column for the castrati. Introduced between the acts as comic relief, it received such wholehearted approval that soon it achieved independence and stood on its own feet as the "Opera Buffo." Dealing with subjects of natural interest instead of the unrealities and superficialities of the Opera Seria, it had no place for such voices, and as its popularity increased the castrati were relegated more and more to the sidelines. After some of Mozart's early operas there were no more roles of consequence written for them and their disappearance from the theatre was only a matter of time.

The Italian church choirs continued to use the castrati all through the nineteenth century and even into the twentieth, and though they made their finest contributions to the Church in the seventeenth century before the opera took away the better singers, the written testimony of those who heard the great choirs in Rome is almost universal in heaping praise upon their performances. Even the hypercritical, such as Burney, Mendelssohn, and Spohr, while taking them to task for carelessness, indifference, and at times faulty intonation, had to admit the superb effects of the Passion Week music, especially the renditions of the widely famed "Miserere" of Allegri and the "Improperia" of Palestrina. They were the chief factor in making the Sistine choir world famous.

However, there can be no gainsaying the fact that definite deterioration had begun by 1800. Even in 1770 Burney was warned not to expect too much from the papal singers and while their performances moved him because of their delicacy and profound expressiveness, yet he felt they lacked spirit and he seemed to see signs of disintegration. Ludwig Spohr, writing in 1816,[14] unfavorably criticized their appearance, age, intonation, and carelessness, while Mendelssohn writes both favorably and unfavorably.[15] Under the leadership of the devoted but retrospective

Baini there was a renaissance of former excellence, but his death in 1844 marks the beginning of the final descent of the castrati and with them the glories of the Roman Church music.

Castration of young boys continued, although with increasing rarity, up to 1870. In this year the emerging nationalism of a seething continent culminated in the capture of Rome by the Italian troops, the fall of the Napoleonic empire and the establishment of the Third Republic in France, while in January of the next year the German Empire was established. The long and bitter struggle of the Church for temporal power thus came to a close in total defeat and Pope Pius IX who was destined to suffer this humiliation discontinued all papal functions including services in the Sistine Chapel. His successor, Leo XIII (1878–1903), called upon the soprano-castrato Mustafa to restore the choir but the diminishing supply of singers was an insurmountable obstacle. Moreover the moral sensibilities even in Italy itself revolted against the renewal of castration which alone could have saved the day. So strong was the feeling that existing castrati tried desperately to hide their true circumstances by getting doctor's certificates to prove that they were born eunuchs or were otherwise the victim of accidents beyond their control. Some insisted that they were really falsettists and through influence obtained permission to marry.

But the facts were common knowledge among the Romans and these efforts only brought down such derision upon them that the Church was obliged to take a hand through its official publications. It is not without pathos to find the last real resistance to their abolition among the old singers themselves. Perhaps it was an innate, well-founded pride in the vanished glories of their once proud profession which made a few of these rally around their last really great artist and leader, Mustafa, in spite of an opposition that included Pope Leo himself.

Perosi took over the Sistine choir from Mustafa in 1898 and it was he who administered the "coup de grace." He strengthened the soprano and contralto sections by the addition of boys and falsettists as the castrati gradually passed out of the picture. Most of the old ones were pensioned off; only three, Salvatori, Sebastianelli, and Moreschi remained singing in both the Sistine and the Cappella Giulia. Moreschi, the last to survive, died in 1922, and therewith ended once and probably for all time an art which was so extraordinary in method as well as in results obtained. Their end was ignominious when one considers the splendors once lavished upon them and, far more important, their great contribution to our musical heritage.

Physiological Characteristics Uniquely Adaptable to Singing

Consideration of the castrati has usually been colored with a mixture of curiosity, facetiousness, contempt and superiority. This is due, first, to the fact that they cannot live up to the Christian ideal of "be ye fruitful and multiply," [16] and second, to the physical development which resulted from their particular circumstances. As to the former we need to say only, in their defense, that so-called "normal" human beings who have ever been guilty of the entire gamut of moral irregularities are in exceeding ill-grace to condemn the castrati for their abnormalities. But the physical changes that come about as a direct result of castration are of the utmost importance since these are the phenomena with which we are concerned.

When castration occurs before the glandular functioning of the testicles has begun, certain abnormal physical developments result. The body grows somewhat larger than otherwise and the bony structure takes on feminine characteristics. The chest becomes round, measuring approximately the same from front to back and side to side, while the muscles become softer, the skin sallow and flabby, the body hairless, the hair on the head thicker and the face beardless. Moreover, the mammary glands, ordinarily dormant in the male, develop in a marked way which fact accounted much for the castrati being able to assume feminine roles with such success on the stage. But of all the changes resulting from such an operation, that which occurs in the larynx is the most remarkable and the most pertinent to our study. Due to the delay in ossification of the entire skeleton the larynx remains for a long time cartilaginous and along with this, as in women, there was no growth comparable to the normal male Adam's apple. This is not to say that there was no mutation whatever, but rather that it was a very slow and gradual change that extended throughout most of their life. Moreover this mutation was only a fraction of what would normally have occurred during the comparatively short period of puberty. As this gradual change took place the lower range of the boyish voice was extended, taking on a tenor quality which due to greater physical strength was capable of far greater volume and brilliance than the female voice. It was usual for the *soprano* to change to *mezzo* and the *mezzo* to *contralto* as they turned into middle and old age. Their uncommon flexibility was due to continuous and careful training begun usually at a tender age and extending throughout this period of very slow mutation. Their phenomenal capacity in singing long *bravura* passages and producing their famous *messa di voce* or "swell tone" (i.e., crescendo and diminuendo) was due first to their abnormal chest dimensions which allowed them to inhale a great amount of air and second to the fact that the larynx was considerably smaller than normal, thus allowing the voice to be produced with much less expenditure of breath. Of course, the long years of continuous study without any distracting outside influences or interests had much bearing on their astounding faculty for performing their fantastic vocal feats, but the fundamental facts concerning their special physical qualifications, i.e., small larynx and large chest capacity must be given prime consideration in accounting for their vocal accomplishments.[17]

As to their physical appearance, it is more or less true that as Charles de Brosses says, "Most of them grew to be big and fat like capons, with hips, buttocks, arms, breast, and neck round and plump like women. When one meets them at a party, it is astonishing, when they speak, to hear a small childish voice coming forth from such giants." [18] Even Brosses who is not particularly prejudiced in their favor had to admit in the next sentence that some of them were very attractive in appearance and that they often possessed real talent.

During the period of their popularity little objection is found to their assumption of feminine roles and there are many statements indicating that they accomplished remarkable results in costume and make-up. The majority of the famous castrati made their debuts in feminine impersonations: Farinelli, Gizziello,

Caffarelli, Carestini, Marchesi, Pachiarotti, Crescentini, Rauzzini, etc., while all the others enacted such parts frequently.[19] The castrati singers in Saint Mark, Venice, were much in demand to play female characters in the Venetian opera houses. Caffi praises their appearance on the stage, especially that of the soprano, Angeletti, "because of the beauty of his figure in feminine dress." [20] Raguenet praises in glowing phrases the voices and the singing of the castrati. He insisted that the chief advantage the Italian Opera held over the French rested with the castrato voice. He heard Ferini in the part of Sibaris in *Themistocles* at Rome in 1698, and said that there had probably never been a more beautiful woman in the world.[21] Perhaps no more interesting evidence as to their ability to delineate the weaker sex can be found than in the memoirs of Casanova. In the fascinating account of the "False Bellino," he recounts the very unusual circumstance in which a female soprano, Theresa, realizing that greater opportunities existed for male sopranos, took the name of the young castrato, Bellino, who had died very suddenly, and masqueraded successfully for many years, singing with considerable acclaim in various opera houses in Europe as "Castrato-primadonna." According to Haböck [22] this was done by a number of female singers seeking theatrical careers. Another convincing piece of evidence as to their ability as well as acceptability in feminine roles turns up in a novelette, *Sarrasine* by Balzac. Here the author chooses to make a castrato the "heroine" of the piece in which a young sculptor becomes enamored of a castrato whom he has only seen on the stage in feminine attire. Urged by friends to encourage him for its humorous implications, the castrato carries on a flirtation which gives rise to such a state of passion in the victim that the true state of affairs has to be revealed. Whereupon the young lover in a fit of anger tries to kill his deceiver but is killed instead by the guards of the castrato's patron. The spectacle of men masquerading as women both on and off the stage was not uncommon during the seventeenth and eighteenth centuries. For the most part women were taboo in the theatre and men were obliged to perform in their stead. The "harmless" tendency on the part of both sexes to disguise themselves in the garb of the other is discussed by Goethe in his "Römischen Carnival." [23]

In masculine roles the castrati were less successful. Their general physical characteristics marked them as too effeminate, and their tendency to corpulence was decidedly against them. But as Haböck notes,[24] the present opera singers have little room to talk since the husky dramatic sopranos, the buxom contraltos, the smiling fat-faced tenors, and the all too corpulent basses are the cause of many a funeral dirge among directors, agents and critics. Very seldom does nature combine beauty with great talent, and we are obliged to put up with youth and age, slimness and heft, beauty and ugliness in our singers. Music is paramount and fantasy is able to and does overcome reality.

Haböck gives us a long list of quotations by eighteenth century critics concerning the castrati that are both favorable and unfavorable.[25] Here it seems pertinent to note some of these opinions. Marcello (1720) was very scornful and derisive, but he wrote in a satirical manner concerning all singers both men and women. Grosley (1764) preferred women's or boys' voices and could never understand why the Italians liked the *evirato* voice, yet he relates how he was favorably impressed with the performance of a castrato in Hasses' opera *Demofoonte* at Naples in 1758. Rousseau [26] opposed them on moral grounds; he liked their singing but said they were the most miserable actors in the world. Algarotti (1775) found fault with them in general. Volkmann (1770) discussed to some extent their unconventional life outside the theatre but he took all singers and dancers to task for their unorthodox ways. Sonetti (1777) observed that male roles should be played by men and female roles by women and not by a creation that is neither man nor woman.

But that there were some excellent actors among them is amply proven by some of their most vociferous critics. Sir Richard Steele [27] describing a performance of Nicolini said that he "was fully satisfied with the sight of an actor [Nicolini] who, by the Grace and Propriety of his Action and Gesture, does Honour to an Human Figure," and "sets off the Character he bears in an Opera by his Action, as much as he does the Words of it by his Voice. Every limb and every Finger, contributes to the Part he acts, insomuch that a deaf man might go along with the Sense of it." [28] Addison said,[29] "I am sorry to find by the Opera bills for this day, that we are likely to lose the greatest performer in dramatic Music, that is now living, or that perhaps ever appeared upon the stage. I need not acquaint my readers that I am speaking of Signor Nicolini." Galliard wrote,[30] "Nicolini who came the first time into England about the year 1708 had both qualities [i.e., singing and acting] more than any other that have come here since. He acted to perfection and did not sing much inferior." Marpurg,[31] concerning Senesino, Carestini, Romani, and Porporino, said "that they had gained their position of esteem not only because of their singing art but also on account of their stage deportment." Burney's account of individual singers often mentions their stage performances and their reputations as actors, and Goethe [32] reports, "The castrati, disguised as ladies, play their part ever better, to ever more satisfaction. . . . They play with uncommon naturalness and good humor." [33] Schopenhauer heard Crescentini in Vienna in 1804 and wrote, "This opera held a great attraction in Crescentini, perhaps the most famous of all castrati . . . he sings with very much expression and, what one would not expect, he is a good actor." [34] This phenomenal singer was heard by Napoleon at Vienna during his campaign of 1805. He so impressed the Emperor that after very substantial inducement he went to Paris and had brilliant successes for the next six years. Fétis gives us a vivid description of his singing the role of Romeo in *Romeo et Juliette* and its profound effect upon his audience including Napoleon. "Never was song and dramatic art carried to such heights. The entrance of Romeo in the third act, his prayer, his cries of despair, the aria *Ombra adorata, aspetta,* all this made such an effect that Napoleon and all the spectators gave way to tears and not knowing how to express his pleasure the Emperor sent to him the decoration of the order of the cross of iron, rank of chevalier." [35]

Perhaps no fairer judgment of the case for and against the castrati can be found than that of Burney. Says he, "I must, however, in justice, as well as humanity, endeavor to remove some prejudices which throw an unmerited contempt upon beings, who, as they are by no means accountable for that imperfection under which they labor, are entitled to all the pity and alleviation we can bestow." From here he goes on to make the following points:

They are not cowards and do not lack fortitude in times of danger; they are not devoid of interest in literature or other serious study; they are not deficient in mental ability, and, as for composition, and the theory of Music, not only the best singers of the Pope's chapel ever since the beginning of the last century [1600], but the best composers are among the soprani in that service.[36]

Such statements should go a long way to disabuse us of any prepossessed estimates concerning the character and artistic ability of the *evirati*. Burney offers a wealth of historical, literary, and musical data to bolster his opinions and the very fact that they were expressed at the time (*ca.* 1770–1780) when the popularity of the castrati was well on the wane and the moral indignation at such an institution was about at its height,[37] they bear eloquent testimony to the tolerance and open-mindedness of this eminent musicographer.

Haböck himself, after twenty years of research, came to the following conclusions: the castrati were not above the average in thoughtlessness and foolishness; there is essentially no difference in intellectual powers between them and normal men, nor is there any indication of a loss of intellectual keenness after castration, the cases of Origen, Narses, Abelard, etc., being cited; they have often indicated unusual sagacity in diplomacy and on the field of battle as well as great personal courage in duels; as to the charge of vanity, avarice, and cowardice, these are common to all men everywhere although it must be said that as the castrati became aware of their uniqueness they developed a keener sense of shrewdness and oftentimes superiority.

Singers as a whole have never been considered paragons of histrionics. One evening at the opera will convince even the neophyte of the low estate of the singers' acting ability. This has ever been the case and there are two important reasons accountable. First, vocal skill is stressed throughout training, especially in the earlier formative years. Oftentimes the histrionic aspect of his art is not considered until the singer is ready to step upon the concert stage or assume the responsibilities of an operatic role. Second is the fact that singing is at best an artificial means of emotional expression and is singularly inadequate for the broad spectrum of human feelings that are part and parcel of successful dramaturgy. It is self-evident that very few passions lend themselves easily and naturally to such a formalized art as song. An actor has a bag of tricks of great variety to which he can resort at all times. He may shout, scream, growl, coo, or even reduce his voice to a whisper. But the singer, regardless of the situation in which he may find himself, must sing and sing correctly else his voice may not last to the final curtain, not to mention the implications of continued vocal abuse with regard to his future career. Tosi says,[38] "I don't know if a perfect Singer can at the same time be a perfect Actor; for the Mind being at once divided by two different operations, he will probably incline more to one than the other; it being, however, much more difficult to sing well than to act well, the Merit of the first is beyond the second. What a Felicity would it be to possess both in a perfect Degree!"

By way of summation it can certainly be contended that from these opinions expressed by a great variety of individuals, the castrati were likely not far below nor much above the average in personable, artistic, and intellectual qualities. For each case of low morals, bad manners, inferior intelligence, lack of courage, poor artistry, or any other uncomplimentary attributes, parallels are easily noted among so-called "normal" human beings.

The Influence of the Castrati on Singing

At the present day the acquirements of flexibility is not in great esteem, and were it not, perhaps, for the venerable Händel, declamatory music would reign alone. This is to be regretted for not only must the art suffer but also the young fresh voices, to which the brilliant florid style is the most congenial. . . . It would not be difficult to trace the causes for the decline of the florid style. . . . Let it suffice, however, to mention, as one of the most important, the disappearance of the race of great singers who, besides originating this art, carried it to its highest point of excellence.[39]

This statement by the most famous voice teacher of the nineteenth century, in the fullness of years (he was in his eighty-ninth year), is appropriate praise for the art of the castrati. Moreover, it gives credit where credit is due when it comes to establishing responsibility for the precepts underlying *bel canto*. For it cannot be denied that the castrati both as teachers and as singers were almost entirely the direct and motivating agents in the foundation of everything that is meant by "the old Italian singing methods." There is hardly a single vocal ornamentation that does not find its genesis and development at their hands. All of seventeenth and eighteenth century Europe looked to Italy for singers as well as singing teachers and it has only been in the past quarter of a century that singers have been able to attain consequential success without the stamp of Italian training. It is true that during the past century the Wagnerian declamatory style threatened for a time to turn the tide against Italy, but even the mighty musical colossus of the North abetted by a considerable amount of self-criticism on the part of the Italians was at last turned back as the forces of vocal lyricism rallied around their banner "Bel Canto." And this was the struggle that made the term famous. We have already seen how it was never used in or associated with the centuries and musical styles usually considered its own until after the middle of the nineteenth century in Italy and the 1870's in the rest of Europe. It may be said without hesitation that the castrati built their vocalism on a singularly firm basis to have withstood the test of nearly four centuries of changing musical styles. We still look to Italy as the Madonna of Song. The castrati provided her with a halo.

PART III: BEL CANTO PHYSIOLOGICAL AND HYGIENIC FACTORS IN ITS DEVELOPMENT

VII. APPEARANCE AND POSE

What dignity and charm is contributed by the countenance which has a role second only to the voice.[1]

Physical uncouthness may be such that no art can remedy it.[2]

Italian Sources

The older music histories were accustomed to emphasize the development in music genres in the period around 1600 as being a sudden change, in fact a musical revolution. As long as musicology shunned the scientific historical method such conclusions were to be expected as superficial investigation shows monody, opera, and oratorio to have made a meteoric appearance at the beginning of the seventeenth century. Happily for us, present-day research is such that we are now well disabused of such ingenuousness. While it is not to be denied that this was a time of transition, the flux was natural and orderly. The medieval liturgical dramas, mystery plays, *balletti, intermedi, sacre rappresentazioni,* etc., all give us a direct line of descent to oratorio and opera while the lute accompanied solo song and later the solo madrigal were well established before the freer monodic style of Caccini.[3] Says Grout:

> The mere composing of songs for solo voice with instrumental accompaniment was nothing revolutionary. Not to mention the medieval troubadours and minnesingers or the composers of the Ars Nova, the whole sixteenth century furnishes examples. . . . Even in Italian polyphonic music of the sixteenth century there was a constantly increasing tendency to give the highest voice the character of a solo and to reduce the others to the function of accompaniment.[4]

The need for a more sophisticated soloistic art brought out more and more refinements in vocal practices as the century progressed. As the *bel canto* period began there were no sudden changes but rather greater emphasis placed on those things which stressed the dramatic elements of solo song.

As to the exterior physical attributes of singing the Italians continued to emphasize in general the same factors observed in earlier centuries. Durante says, "Do not make gestures with the body." [5] In his recommendations for the performance of his opera, *Dafne,* Da Gagliano asks that every step be with the music and every gesture be in keeping with the nature of the music.[6] Diruta suggests that the singer stand straight and with pleasing posture avoiding improper movements of the mouth.[7] Cerone's advice is as follows: "I say that a genuine and simple singer who is modest will always please an audience better than one who is skillful and apt but artificial." [8]

Scaletta urges pupils not to make ugly motions with the eyes, mouth or body,[9] while Doni observes that some singers "make so many affectations and prim movements with the mouth and the eyes that it really seems that they are swooning with sweetness." [10]

Donati counsels the singer always to hold the head high and not arch the eyebrows [11] and a half century later Penna includes among his rules to follow and snares to escape for those learning the *Canto Figurato:* Rule 3, Singers should not twist around the body, head, eyes, mouth, etc.[12]

Our next source is one of the most important and one to whom we shall have frequent recourse, viz., Pietro Francesco Tosi.[13] Being a castrato and famous both as singer and teacher we should take special note of his advice. He says:

> He [the master] should always make the scholar sing standing, that the Voice may have all its organization free. Let him take care, whilst he sings, that he get a graceful posture, and make an agreeable Appearance. Let him rigorously correct all grimaces and tricks of the Head, of the body, and particularly of the mouth; which ought to be composed in a manner (if the sense of the words permit it) rather inclined to a smile, than too much gravity.[14]

In singing divisions, i.e., *bravura* passages, "let him [the pupil] be corrected if he marks them with the tongue, or with the chin, or any other grimace of the head or body." [15] The pupil should never be allowed "to hold the musick-paper, in singing, before his face, both that the sound of the voice may not be obstructed, and to prevent him from being bashful." And the scholar should sing often before people of distinction, "that by gradually losing his fear, he may acquire an Assurance, but not boldness. Assurance leads to a Fortune, and in a singer, becomes a Merit. On the contrary, the Fearful is most unhappy. . . . A timorous singer is unhappy, like a Prodigal, who is miserably poor." [16]

For practice apart from the teaching studio Tosi has this to say:

When he [the scholar] studies his Lesson at Home, let him sometimes sing before a looking glass, not to be enamoured with his own person, but to avoid those convulsive motions of the Body, or of the Face (for so I call the Grimaces of an affected Singer) which, when once they have took Footing, never leave him.[17]

Ecclesiastical singers were given more rigid advice, being told "to avoid everything which can be offensive to others as peculiar movements of the body, of the head, of the lips, of the throat." [48]

If there is a better source for the singing methods of *bel canto* than the work of Tosi already mentioned, it is the highly important book of Giovanni Battista Mancini.[19] At the age of fourteen he was a pupil of Leonardo Leo [20] and then studied in Bologna with Bernacchi whose singing school has always been considered one of the best. He went to the celebrated Padre Martini for counterpoint studies and in 1757 was called to the imperial Austrian court as singing teacher where he remained until his death in 1800 at the age of eighty-four. His practical approach to singing as revealed in his *Riflessioni* is the most voluminous and detailed in existence for the *bel canto* period and we quote from him at length, not only here but later.

Naturally pleasing physical features are a most important asset according to Mancini.

A singer possessing a noble, sweet and pleasing face will be well received by the public, though he may have a small degree of talent; while on the contrary, an expressive face with homely or harsh features will not be tolerated unless the person is unexcelled in the art of singing.[21]

That he taught by personal illustration is evident from the following:

As for myself I always acted with my pupils like a dancing master. I used to call my pupils one by one in front of me and after having placed them in the right position, "Son," I would say, "Look, observe, . . . raise your head . . . don't lean it forward . . . nor backwards . . . but straight and natural." In that position your vocal organs remain relaxed and flexible, because if you lean your head forward it [the neck] will suddenly become tense; also if the head is leaned backwards.[22]

And further,

The student does not only correct the defects of the voice through the teacher's exposition, but also all the other defects. Defects of this second kind are bad position of the mouth, wrinkling of the forehead, twisting of the eyes, contortions of the neck and of the whole body, and things of this kind. To correct these defects, I would have my student stand in front of me and sing his lesson by heart. Such a position afforded two good results, one for me and one for the pupil. For me it was easier to observe his defects, and it was exercising his memory also. Singing in this way, it was easier to correct his faults because his mind was not occupied in reading his notes.[23]

The singer is continually warned against incorrect facial expression and bodily movements. Again we read,

He [the singer] should be careful not to make contortions with his mouth, and thus make himself look convulsed, and much less make contortions with his body, like some singers, who in reaching a high tone, stand on their toes, thinking this will help them. Instead it makes them appear ridiculous, and they acquire unmendable habits. . . . Now if the faulty position of the mouth, as I said, mars the beauty and expression of the voice, how much more will it spoil the amiable features of the singer? Features which are exposed at that moment to a public which is there ready to praise or censure him?[24]

Mancini writes with such direct simplicity and offers such common sense advice that one can hardly refrain from quoting him in entirety. He insists that although a singer may have received from nature "a good appearance and graceful movements of the arms and hands," yet the use of these must be learned through study and are

dictated by sane and mature judgment, or copied from actors of renown by observing them in those special roles we are learning. The first thing of importance is to learn to walk gracefully and naturally on and off the stage. The best place to learn this is at a dancing school. Dancing teaches one to move the feet and to carry the arms gracefully, to turn the head with ease and move the whole body with elasticity and grace.

Fencing and horseback riding are strongly recommended by him since they make the body strong, agile and robust.[25] The mask should be cultivated because it is essential that the singer be able to show any emotion or mood at will with the face.

One must have ease in changing from a sweet expression to a harsh one, from tenderness to madness, from affection to disdain, etc. This is the most beautiful part of the art of acting. The important thing is that these changes of expression must succeed each other with naturalness and at the exact moment.[26]

In his counsel to the student of singing Mancini gives us a rare blend of psychological and practical advice. He, in turn, seems to have gotten his point of view from his own teacher whom he does not identify but who was in all likelihood the great Bernacchi. He says,

In closing this chapter [XII], it strikes me that I would prove my sincere affection for studious youth, if I give them the advice given to me by a valiant and loving teacher, a "souvenir" of the love and affection of the way he taught me to sing and which I shall never forget as long as I live. "Never allow yourself to be timid; never be lazy; never permit yourself to be stage frightened when singing in public. One must have spirit, dash and life, otherwise everything will be tame and lifeless." I know it is natural for a beginner to be timid but the teacher should take care that when a pupil is able to sing by himself, to allow him to sing once in a while in public. First let him sing before a few friends, then little by little, have him sing before a more exacting audience.[27]

A word of caution against temerity, impetuousness, and forwardness is offered to those who might misunderstand his suggestions concerning spirit, dash, and life, for modesty along with art and knowledge will enable the singer "to earn a serious consideration" from his audience.

Never forget to keep self-possession while you are singing. Never allow yourself to wander or be careless. Since man is not always in the same mood, but will sometimes feel joyful and vivacious, and other times sad and lowly, he must be able to overcome the mood in which he finds himself, when the moment comes for him to sing in public. He must make an effort to cheer himself, and make himself pleasing by virtue if not by nature. Careless singing is languid and uninteresting. Often we hear an audience wishing that such a singer would end his song soon. On the other hand, when singing is vivacious and jocund, it gives pleasure to the audience and such an atmosphere makes both the singer and the audience happy and cheerful. Then we hear the words *da capo, da capo*. An atmosphere of joy reflects more upon the heart of a singer than upon the audience. It makes his rendition easier, because he has gathered within himself all his thoughts. When his mind is in a happy mood, he feels like singing, and takes such an interest in what he is doing, that his mind runs always in advance of the following phrase, and it is just that excellent prevision which prepares him for the execution and makes his rendition easier and more graceful and appeals to the ear and heart of his audience.[28]

There remains one further useful Italian source, viz., Vincenzo Manfredini (1737–1799). His *Regole Armoniche* was first published in 1775 but this edition contains little or nothing about singing. However in the second edition [29] there was included an important section on singing.[30] In essence the author echoes previous writers. Many singers have beautiful voices but lack the ability and the means to move their hearers, for they sing "without spirit, and without color, and they recite with such indolence that they resemble plaster figures." [31] He suggests that the mouth should be opened not too much nor too little, and the correct way is to keep it open "as in the act of smiling; neither should one put out his tongue on to one's lips." [32] Manfredini is quite precise in his directions for correct posture.

When singing, one should always hold one's head firm and straight; neither should one make any unbefitting motions with one's shoulders, arms, or any other part of one's body; on the contrary, one should hold oneself in a noble posture, and sing while standing in order that the voice might come out more easily, particularly when studying and when one must [make an effort] and is anxious to [be successful in] being heard.[33]

In completing our references to Italian sources it is only necessary to add the unquestioned authority of the greatest Italian opera librettist of the eighteenth century, and the most prolific of all time, Metastasio. Throughout his letters, when a singer is mentioned, there is usually an opinion expressed, favorable or unfavorable, as to his appearance or personality.[34] One is forced to the conclusion that this well-educated man, of the broadest experience in the theatre, placed great emphasis on these attributes of successful public performance.

German Sources

Our first German source is none other than Heinrich Schütz (1585–1672), nor could we wish for one who commands greater respect. He discusses the question as to whether a singer should use the face and general demeanor to aid in accomplishing desired emotional effects. It is his opinion that the singer should rely on the voice and vocal ornamentation to gain the proper expression, this being spoiled by undesirable facial contortions. This sort of singer should perform behind a curtain or, still better, in comedies, as here he would have more opportunities to make use of such talent.[35] After further direct and positive suggestions on the art of singing, Schütz sums up his argument:

> In short, a singer should not sing through the nose. He should not stammer, otherwise he is unintelligible. He should not have a speech impediment or lisp, else he is scarcely half understood. Also he should not close the teeth together, nor open the mouth too widely, nor stick out the tongue over the lips, nor pout the lips, nor twist the mouth, nor move around the cheeks and nose like long-tailed monkeys, nor knit the eyebrows, nor wrinkle the brow, nor roll the head and eyes, nor wink with the latter, nor let the lips tremble, etc.[36]

These are a set of rather strict regulations for any singer.

There is no other important German source until Johann Mattheson (1681–1764). He is likewise precise in his rules for posture in singing. According to his advice a singer never succeeds as well sitting as standing, moreover he should stand straight, not leaning forward nor backward, for the carriage of the body, the turning of the face, the movement of the hands, the manner of holding the music (if singing from the notes) all contribute to the advantage and good effect of the singer. If singing while sitting one must sit "like a coachman on a box." [37] Speaking more directly on appearance Mattheson says,

> Many turn their faces, while singing, so far to the right that the audience on the left cannot hear them at all. Another does the opposite. . . . Some throw the head upward, which throws the tone up where there is no audience,

others bend it down on the chest, singing into their beards, as a common expression says, thus losing the proper effect, be they otherwise capable as they may. Many cannot keep their hands quiet, which would be best when they do not know the proper gestures, believing that they must, if not making useless gestures, give the unrequested beat in one way or another, which is a matter that will never lead to the hearts of the audience. Many hold the music, either due to nearsightedness which is to be excused, or habit, which is to be condemned, so close to the mouth and eyes, that the voice is stopped there and heard clearly by nobody but the singer himself, especially in large churches.[38]

Another authority is F. W. Marpurg (1718–1795), who advises us regarding posture in words similar to Schütz and Mattheson. He says that since one does not sit while singing in concert, so must the student, if at all possible, stand during the lesson, since sitting interferes with proper breathing. Moreover, "He must stand up correctly and not hang his head to the ground and thus constrict the throat." [39] Even though they may be beautiful, a singer should not show his teeth, nor should he keep them too close together. The mouth should be held still,

and one should not chew and the neck should not be bent outward or inward. In addition to these the singer should, because of his own appearance, beware of unusual grimaces . . . for the correction of which one should use a mirror and take the advice of a good friend. Hereto belongs particularly the twisting of one's head, the rolling of one's eyes, the nodding of one's head at each note, the shaking of one's head, the shifting and making noise with the feet, the placing of one's hand behind one's ear, the touching of one's mouth with the hand, the distortion of the same, the shaking of the same when executing a trill, and so on. Who can count all the grimaces? A decent posture; neither too sweet nor too sour a face, neither too prankish an attitude nor too stern an air, and neither too timid nor too free a behavior should be most earnestly recommended to every singer, just as to every speaker.[40]

Hiller (1728–1804) suggests that the singer's face should bear the expression of a gentle smile with the mouth drawn slightly to the sides and the lips held so as not to show the upper teeth and only partly showing the lower row with the teeth apart about the width of the small finger.[41] After quoting Mattheson on the reasons for standing rather than sitting while singing, Hiller cautions the singer about his appearance:

Careful attention must be paid to all improper motions of the body, such as swaying to and fro, shuffling with one's feet, shaking one's head, etc., to all grimaces of one's face, such as distortion of one's mouth, blinking with one's eyes, and the like, because such things can otherwise become a habit. I knew an Italian *cantatrice* who, while having a manner of singing not to be despised, yet she had the unpleasantness of throwing her head back, of constantly turning her eyes toward the ceiling, and of distorting her face to such a degree that one could have believed she was having convulsions. In order to safeguard oneself against such improprieties it is advisable to sing at times in front of a mirror, and certainly to anyone who is anxious to appear always with the most advantageous mien, no better advice can be given.[42]

The directions given by Petri (1738–1808) are shorter but to the same end as the foregoing German authorities. The singer must stand properly and with a cheerful face. The mouth should not be too wide nor too closed since this latter would interfere with good diction. Neither the head nor the body should shake and all or any uncomely behavior should be avoided.[43]

The last of the German sources is Kuerzinger and he has the least to say about appearance. Among the principal faults in singing he includes, "When one sings through the nose, with set teeth or the contrary like a 'miller's lion' with a mouth opened too much and with similar bad habits, from which there originate not only a visible disgust but also an inability to understand on the part of the listeners." [44]

French Sources

Only one of the French manuals offering suggestions concerning the appearance and personality of the singer dates from the seventeenth century. Jumilhac (1611–1682) was concerned first of all with plain song but in contrast to the majority of his contemporaries his approach was also practical. According to this writer the head and chin should not be lowered too much for this will interfere with the articulation of the syllables and the clear pronunciation of the words. Nor should the head and the neck be elevated too much for this causes the voice to be hard and dry with "too much strain on the nerves and arteries" ("trop grande tension des nerfs et des arteres"). The neck and the mouth should not be twisted and there must be given careful advice as to how all these defects may be corrected in order that the voice will become as smooth, clear, distinct, and just as possible at the same time keeping all other movements of the body within the bounds of good taste and propriety.[45]

Blanchet (1724–1778), though not a musician, had done considerable research on the mechanism of the voice and published his treatise on singing in 1756.[46] Although his advice is offered more from the standpoint of stage deportment only, it is nevertheless entirely pertinent. Movements of the arms and eyes, and facial expressions, are most important. He suggests that these may be slow or rapid, sustained or abrupt, varied or monotonous, and their careful use are a necessity for good expression and characterization, and render the greatest joy to the spectators. The correct countenance together with eloquence in bodily carriage all combine to give a great variety of the most subtle qualities of action and style.[47]

Antoine Bailleux (?–1791) is mostly concerned with rudiments and explanation of the various ornamentations. His hints are brief and pointed.

> One should, standing or seated, maintain a graceful posture, with the body erect and head lifted without affectation. It is not necessary to gesticulate while singing nor to make grimaces with the mouth, the eyes, and forehead. It is not necessary to beat time with the head or the body. . . . The trouble of beating the rhythm may be spared if one has the value of the notes and the rhythm well implanted in the head.[48]

In 1760, the great French composer and theorist, Jean Philippe Rameau (1683–1764), brought out his *Code de musique pratique*. Among many practical suggestions he includes the following: the singer should stand during vocal exercises, keeping the body at ease and without discomfort, making certain that all parts of the body are without tension, for in no other way can the voice be kept flexible and produce its most beautiful sounds and sentiments necessary for perfect and natural performance.[49] Rameau condemns the common practice of shaking the head or the hands or even the whole body while executing a trill and then sums up his discussion by saying that if a singer possesses complete freedom of action, then nature can work through him and perfection of performance is the result.[50]

Raparlier's comments on pose and personality are almost

word for word the same as those of Bailleux and need no further comment.[51]

Our next source, Martini (1741–1816), is not only brief but repeats what others have said before him. The mouth should be in a natural smiling position for if it is too nearly closed it will interfere with pronunciation and hold back the voice. A mouth that is, on the other hand, too widely open looks hideous and strains the throat thus preventing facile voice production. If the teacher cannot correct these faults the pupil should discontinue his lessons.[52]

Tomeoni (1757–1820) was one of the most influential voice teachers in Paris toward the end of the *bel canto* period. Son of an Italian voice teacher and singer, he came with his father in 1783 to Paris where he became famous as a teacher after the Italian methods. He cautions the singer against abandoning himself to making faces or contorting the head, arms, and body in interpreting his music.[53] The careful teacher will not allow the pupils to beat time with the feet. "Several physical reasons prevent the foot from beating the exact rhythm. The first is that repose and correct poise of the body are necessary for the performance of the music. Movement of the foot can only be contrary to this." [54]

Tomeoni advises the singer to beat rhythm with the hand until the song is learned and then the indication of rhythm with the head or the body should cease.[55]

Another Italian singer transplanted in Paris had a very substantial influence on the art of singing in all of France. Mengozzi (1758–1800), also a composer of operas, came to Paris in 1787 and at the time of the organization of the *Conservatoire de Musique* was called as professor of voice. Before his death he had prepared the material for the *Méthode de Chant* used by that institution.[56] Asserting that the scale is the most difficult and the most necessary of all the vocal exercises Mengozzi gives six rules for the proper pose.

In preparation for singing a good scale the pupil should, first, stand in a naturally correct position and without making the slightest effort; second, hold up the head without bending too far backward, for if the muscles of the throat should be too tense they cannot move freely; third, the mouth should be somewhat smiling and comfortably open to the extent that the conformation of the pupil will allow, resulting in the pronunciation without alteration of the vowel which he should use to sing the scale; fourth, it is necessary that the pupil take heed, that in opening the mouth his features should not borrow an unpleasant expression; he should avoid also making any grimaces with the mobile part of his face; fifth, he should rest lightly the tongue behind the lower teeth; sixth, the upper jaw should be perpendicular and moderately apart from the lower jaw.[57]

The author adds that the singer should remain immovable all the while he is singing the scale.

English Sources

The sources on appearance and pose in English are sparse, being scattered general comments. Burney (1726–1814) offers a number of particular observations which indicate that he held these qualities important in a singer. He heard Signora Lodi sing at Munich in August, 1772: "The Lodi sung charmingly; her voice and figure would make her a capital singer in a serious opera . . . she is admirable; having a pretty figure, a good expression, and an exquisite manner of taking appoggiature." [58] Earlier he had praised her singing but added, "One would wish that she had as to person, a little less *embonpoint.*" [59] Of Signora Francesca Danzi, a German girl, Burney says that her "voice and execution are brilliant: she has likewise a pretty figure." [60] His comments on Signora Manservisi are: "Her figure is agreeable, her voice, though not strong, is well-toned, and she has nothing vulgar in her manner, sings in tune, and never gives offence." [61]

While in Vienna in September, 1772, he heard Costanza and wrote, "This singer is young, has good features, the *embonpoint charmant,* and is upon the whole a fine figure." [62] These few examples of Burney's observations indicate, in fact, that it was usual with him to comment on the appearance and attitude of those he saw perform.

There remain two English publications from which we may quote. The first was written by Domenico Corri (1746–1825), an Italian and former student of Porpora who came to England in 1771 where he was active as a composer, publisher, and singing-master. In his opinion the physical requisites of a good singer consist of "spacious lungs, muscular larynx, wide mouth, with regular teeth; and, if added to these, an expressive countenance, it will greatly contribute to the perfection of a singer." Also, good expression is derived "from great sensibility, which portrays in the countenance every passion and feeling that affects and stimulates the heart." [63] Gesualdo Lanza (1779–1859) was also born in Italy, his father having been a singing teacher who went to London where the son also established a material reputation as a singing master. Lanza says, "The pupil should never close his eyes when singing; the body must be kept perfectly steady while singing; when shaking [i.e., trilling] on any note the outside of the throat should not be perceived to move, for by such movement a guzzling sound is produced." [64] Under the heading "The Countenance," he says,

> It has been advised by masters generally, that a singer should try and preserve a smiling expression in the countenance when singing; but when this is considered, it will appear to be wrong, and productive of bad effects; for if the mouth is always kept in such a position as to have the appearance of smiling, many of the tones will be impaired, the real expression of the sentiment will be lost, and the style will suffer equally: Singers who possess a fine set of teeth are anxious to show off this gift of nature to the best advantage, but how often do they sacrifice the tone sound and character of words, to this vanity of the "bocca ridente." [65]

Comparisons and Summations

With respect to appearance and pose the Italian authorities in the seventeenth century are concerned only with the salient external factors of correct singing such as posture, facial expression, movements of the body and its various members, etc. As we move into the eighteenth century, the advice to singers becomes more insistent, more personalized, more inclusive and more detailed. Tosi and Mancini, especially, are quite incisive in their directions both for the student and the public performer. They not only tell us what should be done but they also reveal how they accomplished these matters in the studio and outside. Certain psychological factors are emphasized such as the mental attitude of the student both in study and performance along with its effect upon his outward appearance and thus upon the auditors.

The remarkable feature about the advice in the German manuals on singing is that it is almost wholly concerned with what the singer must not do. Very few positive suggestions are offered and the distinct feeling is obtained that the singer must have felt himself in more or less of a strait jacket, those actions that are allowed being so limited and so carefully prescribed that there is little opportunity for self-expression. All the "verbotens" of the Italians are here but only a few helpful directions are in evidence. All the instructions deal with the external mechanics of appearance and posture.

While the French may also advise the singer what not to do, they give their reasons at the same time as to why certain actions are improper. Also, the attitude is far more positive and, true to the French philosophy of the eighteenth century, much emphasis is placed on keeping out artificiality so that nature can function in its own unhampered manner. Toward the end of the eighteenth century two Italians, Tomeoni and Mengozzi, were influential in directly transplanting the Italian method in Paris. All the French writers, however, emphasize the importance of an agreeable appearance for a successful singing career.

There is little or nothing indigenous to be found in England that can contribute to an understanding of *bel canto,* except to show the extent of Italian influence. Burney's comments deal mostly with Italian singers and their manner of performing while both Corri and Lanza were purveyors of precepts learned in Italy. Attention should be called to Lanza's criticism of the "bocca ridente" or smiling position of the mouth so frequently recommended by others. We noted that Tosi had already questioned its efficacy for the expression of all sentiments. (See above, page 61.)

VIII. BREATHING

He who knows how to breathe and pronounce correctly knows how to sing well.[1]

Italian Sources

We have already noted [2] that before 1600 breathing was thought of in rather simple relationships to singing. Singers should not breathe audibly, should take sufficient breath not to breathe in the middle of a word, should breathe easily and be able to expend it at will. This is all well and good, but Caccini (*ca.* 1546–1618) in the preface to his famed *Nuove Musiche* tells us why control of the breath is so necessary for his "noble manner" (nobile maniera) of singing which he calls "canto in sprezzatura." [3] Since there are so many effects employed, good breathing is just as important as a good voice in order that the singer may have the necessary freedom.

A man must have a command of breath to give the greater spirit to the increasing and diminishing of the voice, to exclamations and other passions as is related. Therefore let him take heed that [because of] spending much breath upon such notes, it [the breath] do not afterward fail him in such places as it is most needful . . . employing his breath in such a fashion so that he commands all the best passionate graces used in this most worthy manner of singing.[4]

In his *Arie Devote,* Durante (1608) says that the singer must breathe at such a time that the passages (passaggi) will be perfect, whether or not there are rests.[5] Cerone (1613) complains of those singers who, not having enough breath, breathe before the last note. In his opinion it is just as bad for a singer to continue without breathing in the proper places so that he must continually gasp at the wrong time.[6] Donati (1636) is obviously thinking of breath control when he speaks of singing from the first note to the last with "fiato equale," i.e. equal breath.[7] For florid passages he advises that they be sung slowly at first, repeating them always a little faster until the singer can be made to establish the habit of singing them all on one breath.[8] But Doni (*ca.* 1594–1647) tells us that "modern singers" put so many notes on a syllable that they cannot possibly sing it in one breath but have to break it up.[9]

Tosi offers the singing teacher lucid suggestions and explanations in regard to breathing.

Let him [the master] forbid the scholar to take breath in the middle of a word, because the dividing it in two is an error against Nature; which must not be followed if we would avoid being laughed at . . . in long *Divisions* it is not so rigorously required when it cannot be sung in one breath. . . . The master may correct this fault in teaching the scholar to manage his respiration, that he may always be provided with more breath than is needful; and may avoid undertaking what, for want of it, he cannot go through with. Let him show, in all sorts of compositions, the proper place where to take breath, and without fatigue; because there are singers who give pain to the hearer, as if they had an asthma taking breath every moment with difficulty, as if they were breathing their last.[10]

The comments of Vallara (1724) are barely worth mentioning. He says in rule 7 that the singer should not breathe after every note, but sing three or four notes at least and then breathe.[11]

Mancini is our most important Italian source on the use of the breath in singing. He even goes so far as to show interest in the physiological production of tone but his statements in this respect are superficial generalizations of contemporary physiological knowledge. The general belief, says Mancini, is that an elevated chest and a well developed thorax with the capacity for lots of noise are the essentials for becoming a good singer. He agrees with those who say that the strength of the voice depends on chest capacity and the force and velocity with which the air can be expelled from the lungs; also, if the chest is larger, then the windpipe and larynx are also larger, all of which qualities combine to create greater strength of voice. But he warns that it takes more than this to make a singer.

In the opinion of physiologists the lungs are the instruments which aid in speaking and in singing with more or less force, according to the degree of expansion of the lungs and chest and their ability to expel the exhaled air. But then it is also their opinion that the lungs are not the real organs which form the voice in the throat. . . . The air from the lungs acts upon the larynx in singing, just as it acts upon the head of a flute that is leaned to the lips for playing. The lungs are not the actual organs of the voice; they merely furnish the material, the air. . . . I conclude by saying that it is not enough for one to have merely an elevated chest and a capacity for big noise to become a successful singer.[12]

In order to acquire the proper control and management of the breath Mancini suggests very careful and simple singing exercises for the strengthening and development of the chest.

For those who cannot hold the breath so long and for those whose chests are not so strong, the solfeggio should be written of only two notes in each measure, and they must be two half notes (*minime*) giving to it a slow movement, so that the voice may have time to expand; the student must not take breath between the first and second note. If the student can sustain these two notes without too much effort, he may be permitted to sustain three notes, but no more, so as to avoid weakening his chest. I conclude, that even if a student were found with a very strong chest, he must nevertheless be treated with the same precaution, and in order to favor the further development of the chest, he may be allowed to sustain the notes longer only when maturity has strengthened his vocal organs. . . . In order to obtain a perfect control he will conserve his breath with good economy, and will accustom the bellows of the voice in this way to support it, graduate it and take it back at will, to attack and abandon a tone, and to breathe, all with insensible effort or fatigue. I admit that this exercise will prove very painful and fatiguing at first, but it will enable the singer to sing with easiness and delight in any style of music. In this way he will acquire strength of the chest and ease in passing from one tone to another. The voice will become established and he will be able to sing to the heart of his audience.[13]

If this author seems to be overly cautious and vigilant we must remember that he had in mind the young castrato who often began his voice training as early as the age of seven.[14]

The *messa di voce* or "swell tone," considered the most important of all the ornamentations of the *bel canto* period, is only acquired by proper use of the breath according to Mancini. The student may not presume to execute this vocal ornament before

he has acquired the art to hold, reinforce, and take the breath back, because, upon this depends whether he is able to give the start, and to graduate the voice proportionately in value, and to retire it without apparent effort. I then will say, that if the student wishes to conceive the *messa di voce* without defects, it will be necessary for him to not push his breath violently, but to start it very quietly.[15]

He urges the singer to economize the breath, using a very little of it so that the first tone may be started with a soft voice and very slowly graduated to its "full strength of loudness" from where it should be gradually decreased by the same degrees to the soft tone with which it began. From such an exercise he insists that it will be found easy to sustain tones from the beginning to the end and "will avoid that inconvenience which usually happens to singers, of finding themselves exhausted at the end of the tone." Mancini observes that to start the tone with too much breath pressure causes it to go sharp at the beginning and flat at the end "producing the most disagreeable effect upon the listener." And as a final warning he advises the student only to undertake the study of the *messa di voce* with the greatest care, "otherwise he will run the risk of tiring his chest. This study should be practiced daily, and many intervals of rest should be allowed in the practice." [16]

Mancini advises that the study of cadenzas should likewise be approached very carefully and are not to be attempted until the student has his voice well under control. At first the cadenza should be quite short and the number of notes should be increased only as the voice gains strength. "Continue in this way until the cadenza reaches perfection." He also tells us that some schools will not allow the student to attempt cadenzas until they have reached a certain age, "fearing to harm their chests. This retards them and has great disadvantage." [17]

It is of no little interest to note the importance that Mancini attached to chest strength, or "la forza del petto." The singer must possess chest strength in order to sing runs (*volatina*) properly,[18] and arpeggios (*arpeggiati*) must at first be sung slowly in order that the chest will not be overtaxed. Caution must be observed "so that the student will be able to stand the effort it costs the chest and throat." [19] The same care is solicited in studying the *cantar di sbalzo* (literally, singing by leaps). While this sort of vocal exercise calls for rapid execution, he prescribes that it must be begun at a slow pace, quietly, and with careful precision "in order that each tone be perfectly pitched and pure." This exercise should be adjusted to the "age and strength of the pupil" and not until he has become strong and robust "must he be allowed to sing this exercise with increased velocity. Thus he will finally be able to unfold and loosen his voice, and perform the exercise in its required quick tempo." [20]

We have seen that Tosi would allow breathing in the course of long passages. Mancini, however, was adamant against such practices saying that the *volatina* "must never be interrupted, but carried through to the final tone in one breath." [21] He was equally insistent about performing the *arpeggiato*. "One must not break the melody by taking breath, for it can be rendered perfectly only by the insuring of the breath." [22]

Mancini sums up his opinions concerning the importance of the proper use of the breath in this statement. "One must acquire through study the art to conserve, hold, save, and retake the breath with perfect ease. Without such an acquisition, no agility of any kind can be performed." [23]

The last of the eighteenth century Italians to discuss breathing was Manfredini. According to this author, taking the breath at the proper time and place is essential to correct and perfect intonation.[24] The voice will deteriorate and may even be lost if the singer does not know how to breathe, "that is, to take breath in the requisite manner and at the proper time." [25] Ignorance of how and when to breathe prevents many a singer from realizing his possibilities, therefore he should not neglect this rule "which consists principally in the precept of taking breath with great promptness and in such a manner that nobody can notice it." [26] He advises that if necessary, the notes need not be held out their full value if breath has to be taken in order to start the next note in time, a most important rule in the author's opinion. Manfredini allows more freedom in taking breath than either Tosi or Mancini. "If, however, by the weakness of one's voice or the nature of the song, one is sometimes obliged to take breath in the middle of a word, then one takes breath at that point but with great care so that the splitting of the word would be the least perceptible as possible." [27]

He continues to say that breath should be taken somewhat frequently so that enough will always be on hand for all the requirements of expression and ornamentation. In the next sentence this author also advises against breathing in the middle of a word, a cadenza or before a trill. "One should, however, carefully see to it that one avoids not only taking breath in the middle of a word, which, as has been said, should be done only in some special cases, but not even after a trill; nor should breath be taken before having finished the sentiment of the phrase or before having finished a cadence." [28] The very interesting observation is added that there are other rules which vary with the student; however, these are better taught by example rather than by the written word. He adds that it is better for the student to hear the master or other good singers in performance.

German Sources

The directions given by Calvisius (1612) for breathing are brief. In rule 5 he says that the rhythm must not be broken because of taking a breath, and in rule 8 we are told that singers must not breathe together except at rests.[29] Praetorius (1571–1621) is even more terse. Among vocal vices he includes that of breathing too often,[30] and later we read the simple comment that some can hold a very long breath.[31] It is nearly a century later before we find further advice and it also is concise. Printz (1641–1717) suggests that, among other means, the singer will avoid mistakes "if he takes breath before starting the figure and knows the advantage of having a long breath." [32]

With Mattheson we meet the first substantial German appraisal of the importance of the breath in singing. When it comes time to begin the cultivation of the voice the student must be careful "to sing with restrained voice as long in one breath as can be done without hardship." [33] More depends on the natural size and condition of the lungs than on will, but even so,

> diligent practice will produce the advantage that the breath will hold out longer than usual, when the inhaled air is let out not at once nor too liberally, but sparingly, little by little, being careful to hold it back and save it. This is the art by which one singer can surpass another and which the Italian artists know to perfection, while other peoples pay little or no attention to it.[34]

In the next paragraph Mattheson explains how the voice can be made strong by first singing softly, then medium followed by loud and very loud tones, adding the very significant comment that he has never known a German teacher to do these things, either because of lack of interest or knowledge. Sufficient and full breath should be taken into the lungs, "then with carefully controlled distribution of the same, through the glottis and its delicate cleft, the tone should be given its proper volume." [35]

Later, this author tells us that in his opinion probably the first and foremost impropriety in singing is the separation of words and thoughts of a song through frequent and untimely breathing which also interrupts the "figures." [36]

Johann Friedrich Agricola (1720–1774) was the German translator of Tosi's *Observations* which he published in Berlin in 1757.[37] Highly regarded in Germany and especially in Berlin both as organist and singing teacher,[38] Agricola's work opens with a rather lengthy preface in which is discussed the prevailing physiological opinions on phonation. Our attention will be confined to this preface since Tosi's text is considered along with the Italian sources. In contrast to his discussion of other physiological factors in singing Agricola has very little to say about the breath. He says that because of the structure of the lungs and the cartilaginous nature of the larynx the breath is always at our command and it may be used with varying degrees of strength.[39]

Marpurg tells us that the singer should not breathe too often nor should he breathe in the middle of a phrase, i.e., a passage expressing one idea. He also considers it incorrect to breathe after a short note, in the middle of a word or between short groupings of words that are grammatically connected.

In this connection it would be well if the master acquaints his pupils slightly with the breaks of the melody as it is after these that one can draw in fresh air most conveniently, although it is by no means necessary to draw breath at every break, viz., when there is a succession of many short breaks which amount to say, but half a bar. One should note, in general, that the best point of time for drawing a breath is at any interruption of the progress of the song. . . . If it is necessary to take a breath in the course of a long passage, then one should weigh or consider all the foregoing circumstances in order to hit or find the proper place. The prohibition of drawing a breath between a trill and the following note is already of long standing.[40]

Marpurg believes it a very good practice for the pupil, when at home, to sing from time to time long passages with a single breath "and this he should do now with a weak voice, now with a moderate voice, and then with a loud voice." [41] He warns that this should be accomplished not by blasting out the air but rather by careful control so as to avoid all forcing. When practising this exercise care should be taken to start with shorter passages gradually increasing their length "in order to gradually procure a long breath without causing injury to the lungs." [42]

According to Hiller a singer should have command over varying degrees of loudness and softness of the voice and this may be obtained by singing first with a forte tone, then with a half-voice, then with soft tones. He observes that some people have weak voices because of weak lungs and this may be improved not only by exercise but also by encouragement.[43] He adds that singing would be a very simple thing if there were but one tone to each breath and anyone who cannot sing more "should certainly be advised against occupying himself with singing." And since every beginner always wastes more breath than necessary, "one of the main tasks of the singing master consists in accustoming his pupils to economize with their breath right from the outset." [44]

The approach to the problems of breathing recommended by Petri is almost wholly concerned with the time and place to breathe. After stern warnings against singing florid passages with an aspirate "h" on each note the singer is advised to take advantage of rests and ends of phrases for taking breath. In long passages without rests it is necessary sometimes not to hold the final note for its complete written value, and as for both singers and players of wind instruments who do not wish to offend the audience by gasping for breath or making gaps in the melody Petri offers the following rules.

1. One should not delay the breath-taking to the last moment, for otherwise there will result a gasping or panting for breath; on seeing or hearing this, the audience will become apprehensive that the singer is choking and will think less about his song than about his health.

2. One should, therefore, take a fresh breath betimes and specifically on the last part of the unimportant notes in order

that the subsequent important ones may be performed stronger and better.

3. In important measures, too, breath may be taken if one cuts off a little of the end for breath-taking. For, in fact, their last portion represents the weak part anyhow. If there is a syllable of text for every note then a breath may be taken between words unnoticed by the audience.

4. But if there is a long note before a rapid passage, then during the course of the long note the tone may be made to die out, a breath may be taken, and the voice enter softly so that the audience will not realize that a fresh breath was taken.

5. When in rapid and running passages the short notes proceed uninterruptedly for so long a time that it would be impossible to execute them all with a single breath, then one can at times leave out one or two short notes and feign short rests. Also if one short note is repeated it is possible to omit one and make use of that time for taking breath. "However, skilled instructors, if they personally have full command of true singing, will best be able to show the pupils these advantages in practice, i.e., in the arias during the singing lessons." [45]

Kuerzinger, on the other hand, is very brief. Among the principal faults to be avoided in singing, the first is "when one, through much too frequent, ill-timed breath-taking splits the words and the ideas of the recital, and breaks or rends the running passages." [46]

The last German source is the "Singing Method" by Johann Baptist Lasser (1751–1805). Himself a singer, composer, and director, he was married to a singer and spent all of his life in and about Vienna. He is quite direct in his advice on breathing. Diligent and frequent practice according to precept in singing the scale will make it possible to sing more and longer on one breath than before "because also in this matter much depends on exercise and habit." [47] Air should not be inhaled rapidly nor with noise and the singer should then be very economical with the same, exhaling only so much as is necessary for the loudness or softness of the tone. By means of this the lungs will gradually become able to hold and retain more air than before, and the singer will subsequently be able to sing longer and more with one breath. Lasser insists that anyone can observe on himself that a breath which is drawn rapidly and violently will not last long, for ordinarily in this case, too much air will want to get out again with the first note, "and besides even the listeners will become uneasy or nervous when they hear the singer taking his breath with so much difficulty and noise." [48]

Fear is a very important factor in breath control according to Lasser for the voice in this emotional state is no longer normal, since fear "affects the lungs and the vocal organs with equal intensity." [49] He adds that the teacher should take great pains to guard his pupils from fear for great talent may be offset by timidity and a pupil that gets upset because of a wrong move is already half-lost. "A moderate amount of audacity, which, however, should not degenerate into a reprehensible complacency with one's own errors or defects, is most useful in this respect." [50] Breathing at rests and ends of phrases is recommended and this author offers musical examples, after which the rather significant statement is made that there can be no general rule as to just where a breath can be taken, but a singer will soon find out from experience where he can take a little from the value of notes in order to breathe without interfering with the text.[51]

French Sources

Bacilly (*ca.* 1625–*ca.* 1690) is the first of our French sources on singing. He observes that breath is one of the natural gifts necessary for singing and just as this seems to depend entirely on the good constitution of the lungs, "it is certain that this can be acquired and developed through exercise, just as the other elements of the art of song." [52] These comments are brief but to the point.

Lack of sufficient breath can be responsible for defects in voice quality, according to Jumilhac.[53] He adds that it is necessary for some singers to breathe more often than at the rests or pauses. This is permissible and should be done so that the singing will always be easy, for the breath should be managed in such a way that the singer is always free to use his voice flexibly in order to sing all the intervals, rhythms, cadences, etc., that are to be found in the course of singing. We must keep in mind that Jumilhac is only considered with plain-chant rather than a soloistic art.[54]

With Blanchet, however, we meet with considerable detail. First he presents a simple description of the action of the chest, lungs, and diaphragm in breathing and since the compression of the air from the lungs is necessary to phonation, it is therefore fundamental to singing.[55] He considers the voice to be far superior to all other instruments in expressing human emotions but before this can be done it is necessary to learn to manage the breath well.

> In order to inhale properly it is necessary to raise and expand the chest in the manner of a swollen body: by this means one will fill all the cavities of the lungs with air. In order to exhale properly it is necessary to let out this inhaled air with more or less force, with more or less volume according to the nature of the singing.[56]

In subsequent pages Blanchet describes various graces and vocal effects and explains how the singer should breathe to achieve each of these. Moreover there are many nuances and passions that one learns to express "with precision and truth" (*avec précision et verité*). Many singers are named whose success he claims to be due to his method. Although the Italian singers have sung with softer and higher voices than the French, the latter who follow his precepts can sing just as well as the Italians who have known for a long time the value of his method.[57]

In the opinion of Rameau perfect singing consists "in the manner of letting out the air from the lungs easy and unrestrained." [58] Everything hinges on the breath. "Yes, all the perfections of singing, all its difficulties, depend only on the air which leaves the lungs." [59] We cannot control all the various changes that take place in the different vocal organs as they follow their free and natural movements. But we know only that we are "masters of the breath and consequently it is for us to know how to control it so well that nothing can then mar the result." [60]

Rameau warns against forcing the voice for when more breath is forced out than is necessary for the tone the glottis is tightened. If this is repeated often the edges of the glottis are toughened and all flexibility is lost and a constraint or lack of freedom enters which is the real obstacle to beautiful tone as well as to vocal flexibility. Then the tone becomes throaty, false, and the voice trembles and can no longer perform any of the ornaments.[61]

The beautiful sound of the *messa di voce* (*le son filé*) is attributed by this author to the fact that the breath is controlled and increased so gradually that the action of the glottis is so easy as not to toughen it.[62] The force of the breath should be in proportion to the loudness of the sound and this can only be acquired "through frequent exercise" and never by a happy coincidence. This very precise control of the breath must become so habitual that the singer need never think of it and therefore may give his entire attention to the sentiments he wishes to express.[63] He advises the student that all the various vocal ornaments, i.e. trills, roulades, portamentos, etc. must be practised on all degrees of loudness with more or less breath several times a day, also with augmented and diminished breath on each so that they may be performed with ease; and always on one breath. Such practice will make the performance easier and increase the length of the breath.[64]

The brief manual of Raparlier, including musical examples as it does, prevents discussion in detail. In essence he repeats what we have already read from others. Proper breathing is essential to correct phrasing. Breath should be taken at rests and when allowed by the meaning of the words. Breath should never be taken between a noun and its adjective nor between the verb and its object. Words should not be broken and, most important of all, proper inhalation and exhalation are necessary for the natural and correct performance of the ornaments of singing.[65]

Besides its contribution to the maintenance of good health, proper breathing strengthens the voice and makes the singing clear, in the opinion of Martini. This, he says, calls for special exercise and continual attention. First of all the chest must be raised in order to hold as much air as possible. The habit must be acquired of breathing promptly without making any disagreeable sounds in the throat.

When, through taking of breath, the lungs are well filled with air, it is necessary to exercise the most careful control in allowing just enough breath to flow out to give vibration to the voice. This manner of breathing permits the swelling or diminishing of the tone at will; it increases the volume of the voice in both the low and high ranges; it gives facility and smoothness in difficult passages, as well as the ability to sing to the end long phrases; and even more it gives to the singers an unshakable self-confidence.[66]

In a rather short chapter on breathing, Tomeoni also gives us the same fundamental rules on breathing that we have met in almost every one of our sources. Breathing is not permitted in the middle of a word and should be done, if it is at all possible, only at the end of a phrase. "If by chance one is obliged to interrupt the phrase by breathing, it should then be done with enough ingenuity and in such a manner as to be unnoticed by the audience." [67] The tendency, notable among the Italian singers, to put the vowel sound "eh!" before words beginning with a consonant, or, the consonants "n" and "h" before words beginning with a vowel, is objected to most strongly.[68]

Mengozzi offers an elementary yet succinct analysis of the breathing process. After defining the terms "respiration," "inhalation," and "exhalation" he notes the differences in breathing for singing and for speaking as follows:

It should be noted that the action of breathing for singing differs in several respects from breathing for speaking. When one breathes in order to speak or to simply renew the air in the lungs, the first action is that of inhalation when the body swells and the upper part moves forward a little; when it sinks, it is the second action called exhalation. These two movements work slowly when the body is in its normal state. On the contrary, in the action of breathing for the purpose of singing, in inhaling, it is necessary to flatten the body and make it rise again quickly, while swelling and lifting the chest. In exhaling, the body should return very slowly to its normal position and the chest should fall gradually in order to conserve and control, just as long as possible, the air which one has inhaled; it should only be allowed to escape slowly and without agitation of the chest. It should, so to speak, slip away.[69]

In an extended footnote to this statement, Mengozzi says that the student cannot give too much attention to breathing for it is all-important to singing. He suggests daily breathing exercises, without singing, in taking breath and holding it as long as possible, following exactly the directions he has indicated as proper for singing. In the beginning one should use moderation, but a singer who does not practice breathing exercises will have to breathe often, his breath will become exhausted and his tone feeble and wavering. Without plenty of well controlled air the voice has neither power nor timbre and correct phrasing is impossible.

Later in discussing the *mise de voix,* i.e., the *messa di voce* or swell-tone, the necessity for the most careful control of the breath is again stressed. Indeed, in his opinion those singers who lack this skill will never advance beyond the stage of mediocrity. A great amount of exercise is required but always, at first, in moderation and never to the point of tiring the voice.[70]

English Sources

The essential part of the breath and the chest in singing was noted at an early date in English literature, in fact the word "breast" or "chest" was often used interchangeably with "voice." [71] The English singing manuals have little enough to say and even this little bit was almost wholly due to Italian influences. In his *Treatise* on singing, Anselm Bayly (1718 [19]–1794) admits that he made "considerable" use of Tosi's *Observations* and indeed this is quite evident. Six steps are listed as important to the teaching of singing, the sixth being: "Taking breath and supporting the voice."

> Observe there can be no command of the voice without a perfect command of the breath. This therefore should be gained by learning to draw up the breath quick and without the least noise, fully into the chest or lungs after the manner of holding the breath, and letting as little expire at a time as possible.[72]

This author then suggests ways of acquiring a long breath, such as running up a slope. Temperance in eating and drinking malt beverages is also strongly urged as of benefit.

Sir John Hawkins (1719–1789), an excellent musical scholar for his time, has these words to say about breathing: "In singing, the sound is originally produced by the action of the lungs, which are so essential an organ in this respect, that to have a good breast was formerly a common periphrase to denote a good singer." [73]

Tenducci (*ca.* 1736–180–?), another transplanted Italian singing-master in England only offers one page of text, with twenty-one rules, in his instruction book for singers, two of which are concerned with breathing:

XIII. To rest or take breath between the Passages, and in proper Time; that is to say, to take it only when the Periods, or members of the Melody, are ended; which Periods, or Portions of the Air, generally terminate on the accented Parts of a Bar. And this Rule is the more necessary, as by dwelling too long upon the last note of a musical Period, the Singer loses the Oppertunity [*sic*] it affords of taking Breath, without breaking the Passages or even being perceived by the Audience. XIV. That without the most urgent necessity, of either a long Passage, or of an affecting Expression, Words must never be broken, or divided.[74]

Lanza is primarily concerned with the place to breathe rather than how to breathe. After the comment that the breaking of words is a common fault, he recommends that those who are habitually short of breath may breathe between two words, the first ending and the second beginning with a vowel. Breath should be taken, whether the singer needs it or not, where the sense of the words demands it in order that the significance of the text will be evident to the audience.[75] His advice on how to take breath is both elementary and brief.

It is a great fault that you should take breath so as to be heard audibly (except where there is much passion to be expressed) as it excites the feeling that you are in pain, and everything of this kind must be avoided, and to prevent this it may be observed that the body should be kept erect, the head rather elevated, and the throat on a line with the body, that there may be no angle or curve in the windpipe to prevent the free entrance and exit of the air. All occupations which require the body to lean forward, must be avoided by singers.[76]

Comparisons and Summations

All of the evidence gathered together in this chapter points to the empirical nature of the breathing methods. All exercises were considered from the standpoint of the skills that resulted. To say that proper breathing and breath control were held to be essential to the art of singing is indeed obvious. In fact, there is remarkable unanimity of opinion in all the sources considered above, regardless of the nationality of the authors, certain words and phrases being repeated in essence if not word for word. While it is true that many of these earlier writers on singing were only concerned with the proper place and time to breathe, already with Caccini we meet one who is very much interested in the proper management of the breath while both Tosi and Mancini tell how it can be accomplished. While Tosi merely says that the singing master must show the pupil how, the latter suggests a series of progressive singing exercises that will gradually strengthen the chest and afford the control necessary for any demands that may face the singer. The *messa di voce* was the great test for breath control and its practice was highly recommended.

The earlier German writers, also, merely tell the singer where and when to breathe and these directions are quite concise. With Mattheson there is evident appreciation of breath control. What is most significant is his contention that only the Italian singers understand it and practice it to perfection, while all other singers ignore it. This remark plus the fact that Agricola translated Tosi's book into German shows to what extent the Germans depended on the Italians not only for singers but also for guidance in the art of singing. Hiller says in his preface that Tosi's book is the best for the student of singing.[77]

From the available references the French appear to be the most scientifically analytical about the singing process. They mention the primary organs involved and give superficial descriptions of their actions. All of this is largely concerned with the control of the breath and how it can be acquired although the statements made are often inaccurate as to the precise physiological actions taking place. Much advice is offered, very much as we have found among the Germans and Italians, about the long and careful exercises necessary for the managements of the breath before the singer can expect to cope with the demands of his art. Blanchet's comparisons between the Italian and French singers are of interest and the Italian background of both Tomeoni and Mengozzi have already been noted.

Almost all the English ideas on breathing were borrowed from Italy. Bayly frankly gives Tosi credit for his ideas while Tenducci and Lanza were direct transmitters of Italian methods.

IX. EAR TRAINING

When the ear heard me, then it blessed me.[1]

The ears are two music-rooms.[2]

Italian Sources

A PROPERLY trained ear was given a place of importance, hardly subordinate to the voice itself, by the singing teachers of the seventeenth and eighteenth centuries. This "supreme umpire," [3] if attuned in correct fashion, was held to be an absolutely necessary adjutant to vocal artistry, without which the singer was lost. Of an insidious nature was the fact that the ear could so easily lead the singer astray in the event of its defectiveness or lack of use. Artusi (d. 1613) would seem to give the ear preeminence when he advises that those who have to recite [4] should perform "more with the ear than with the voice." [5] When singing in concert or ensemble the performer must listen to be sure he is not more prominent than the others.[6] For Guidotti a well intoned voice is equally as important as a beautiful voice if the singer wishes to excel.[7] Here are the opinions of Caccini: "To proceed in order thus will I say; that the primary and most important foundations of this art are the tuning of the voice in all the keys not only that it be neither too low nor too high but that a proper manner of sounding it should be used." [8]

The next few lines explain what he means by "a proper manner of sounding." Some singers sound the pitches by starting as much as a third under, somewhat in the manner of a grace note while others "tune the said first note in its proper pitch." The latter practice is recommended because in starting below the note, some stay on it too long which is unpleasant to the listener. Caccini is merely asking the singer to attack cleanly, without "scooping," and to sing on pitch, which can only be accomplished by having a good ear.[9] Diruta says that the ear is a necessity in learning to sing [10] while Cerone considers the ear to be the rein of the mouth and adds, "The finished singer sings more with his ear than with his mouth." [11] The ability to sing the intervals correctly, whether easy or difficult, was held to be the first of the four vocal skills to be required, the others being ornamentation, elegance or charm and decorousness, and sweetness of voice, in that order.[12] Avella states simply that the end of all the rules of singing is to intone every song well.[13] Tosi is brief but positive:

> Let the master do his utmost to make the scholar hit and sound the notes perfectly in tune in Sol-fa-ing. One who has not a good Ear, should not undertake either to instruct, or to sing; it being intolerable to hear a Voice perpetually rise and fall discordantly. Let the instructor reflect on it; for one that sings out of tune loses all his other perfections. I can truly say, that, except in some few professors, modern intonation is very bad.[14]

As usual Mancini proves to be a fertile source of information and opinion on ear training for here we get not only an evaluation, but causes and remedies as well. "There is nothing worse than to hear one singing out of pitch, and a throaty or nasal voice is to be preferred to singing out of tune." [15] In his opinion, if the voice is out of pitch it spoils the instrumental harmony and singing out of pitch cannot be disguised or covered up. If Nature has not endowed us with an ear, correction is impossible because there is no way of modifying the imperfect organs of the ear as one can modify the strings or air vibrations in instruments.

> It is the stern duty of the teacher to examine and find out what causes the dissonance. This is not difficult to do, but it requires wide experience. One must go very slowly and observe every detail in order to discern causes. The student should be tried at singing early in the morning before eating; and during the day, when the sky is cloudy and also when it is serene; when the air is placid and tranquil, on windy and stormy days; also soon after a full meal. If on all these occasions he sings out of pitch without noticing it and every possible correction is of no avail, then one can state with surety that the fault comes from Nature herself, or from imperfect hearing. This defect is impossible to correct and the student should be discharged at once.[16]

Mancini says that there are a number of things that may cause one to sing off pitch temporarily. Among them are weakness of chest resulting from disease or a passing illness, or even digestive disorders due to eating too much or at irregular times, or from other like indispositions.

Another cause for singing out of pitch is lack of concentration upon what one is doing, failing to realize why he's taking his lesson. Also, it happens when the student attacks a tone without the help of the teacher's voice, or of the piano, or both before feeling perfectly sure of the pitch of the tone he is to attack.[17]

In his opinion muted instruments are a cause of singing off pitch. Moreover, until a student is certain of his intonation he must not be allowed to sing alone but rather should be given every aid by striking the tone very loudly several times on the cembalo and with the aid of the teacher's voice at the same time. Mancini insists that every one knows that the help of the teacher's voice is indispensable to insure success. "We conclude, then, that the teacher's voice is of great help to the student who is not sure of intonation and who with the aid of the accompaniment only would never be sure of his tone."

This attention to the training of the ear is fundamental and the teaching of skill in ornamentation should not be attempted until this is established.[18] He suggests that a good and practical way to insure correct intonation is to make the student understand the exact distance between the notes of the scale as well as in all wider intervals by showing him these differences in pitch.

The experienced teacher knows perfectly well which way is the easiest and most natural to insure intonation. This demands time and persistent effort. After the student has been tested as to his ability in intonation, and after having found him to have a good ear, then, in order to insure him, he must be kept Sol-fa-ing on graded tones; first on the ascending and then on the descending scales. All this work must be executed with scrupulous attention, seeing that every tone is perfectly in pitch. Then, a solfeggio must follow with notes forming the normal intervals. After these obstacles are overcome the teacher must enforce the following rule: If the student sings soprano, the teacher must help him to gain the high tones little by little (as the age permits), for an extensive head register is essential for a soprano voice.[19]

Two other difficulties are mentioned which present pitch problems to singers. One is the fact that string players like to tune their instruments high because they sound better, which, of course, presents a problem for singers. The other is the practice of tuning keyboard instruments to the equal-tempered scale which of course are not the pitches the singer would naturally sing.[20]

Throughout the entire chapter on agility, i.e., chapter 12, the importance of correct pitch and intonation is stressed. A voice only moderately endowed with agility but with correct intonation can, with careful study, master the ascending and descending chromatic scales. He also emphasizes that when the pupil has reached a certain stage the teacher must not delay having him sing sustained solfeggios so that he will learn to pitch his voice perfectly on every syllable. To accomplish this much patience is necessary on the part of the teacher and assiduous study on the part of the student to the end that the many obstacles that arise will be overcome. The slow solfeggio must never be sung languidly and if such a passage be executed with precise intonation it will bring credit both to the teacher and pupil.[21] In executing the *Martellato* [22] "the intonation must be perfect, so that every hammered note will be distinct and perfectly pitched." [23] In studying to perform the *Arpeggiato,* the teacher must "be very particular that the student attacks each note at its right pitch." [24] As to *Cantar di sbalzo* (i.e., singing by leaps),

> The intonation may be perfect in the other styles, but it must be studied again in order to accustom the voice to leap from the low tone to the high and vice versa with perfect intonation. . . . The first note must be perfectly pitched in order to be able to leap over a number of tones without taking breath. . . . The establishment of perfect intonation . . . will allow the student to enter with more certainty into the narrow path of this difficult style.[25]

Mancini says in conclusion, "Each student, then, should recognize without any doubt, that the beauty of every passage consists in the perfect intonation of each tone." [26]

Manfredini warns the singer possessing a good ear against depending upon it wholly and thus neglecting to study and develop basic musicianship with the result that time is not taken to perfect oneself. A singer may learn an aria just from hearing it and be totally ignorant of music theory. This is one reason why there are only a few great singers. On the other hand, unless a singer possesses at least "a favorable ear," the teacher should without delay advise him against undertaking the study of singing, "because he certainly never would succeed in being a perfect singer." [27] Intonation is defined as the adjusting of the voice correctly and precisely to each tone and each interval. It is a most essential part of singing "because there is nothing in music so displeasing as false intonation." [28] If a singer does not try to sing too high nor too low and has had the requisite practice in singing intervals, then he cannot fail to intone correctly, "provided, however, that there is always the absolute authority of an ear capable and predisposed to music; this being the principle requisite for the execution of a just and perfect intonation." [29] Manfredini closes his chapter on singing by saying that it is most difficult to succeed as a singer without being endowed with natural gifts of a beautiful and flexible voice together with a "good ear" (*buon' orrechio*).[30]

German Sources

Sliding up to a tone or "scooping" was more prevalent in the early years of the *bel canto* period than later. We have already noted Caccini's comment on the practice of attacking a tone as much as a third below but that in his opinion it was best to sing the tone on its true pitch.[31] Praetorius does not indicate his preference. Intonation to him is the beginning of a song and while some say it is beginning with the right tone, others say it is "beginning a second under the right tone and ascending to it; some say a third or a fourth under." [32] Nearly a century elapses before we find another German reference to intonation. Printz is brief and his remarks seem to imply that he does not favor ascending to a tone from lower pitches. "At the beginning of each song, each singer should learn his tone either from the preamble by the organist or from the intonation of the director, in order that he begin correctly and not make a mistake right at the beginning." [33]

Again we are forced to skip a considerable period, this time a half century, before further evidence comes to light, but by this time the problem of correct intonation was greatly clarified. According to Marpurg a tone must be pure and firm (*rein und sicher seyn*). It is pure when it is attacked neither too high nor too low. It is firm when it is begun without an aspiration and when it does not slide up from other notes. This sliding up to a note is called "tone-seeking" (*Tonsuchen*).

When one reads in the writing of some old singing-masters that the musicians do not agree among themselves as to whether one should attack with the right or just tone, or with a second, a third or a fourth, etc., lower or higher, then one perceives from this that the defect of tone-searching or tone-groping must have been considered a musical virtue in olden times. But in these days of ours no other persons but little old women or grannies, children's nurses, etc., are permitted to make easy for themselves the leap of a note in their ditties. The singer must, with regard to intonation, take as a model the instruments which in turn must follow [copy] the vocal line.[34]

Petri says that the study of an instrument is most helpful to singers, especially if they are already familiar with it before they have begun the study of voice. In this way their ears will have become accustomed to pure tones (an reine Töne gewöhnt sind). The piano or flute is best for this purpose and to a lesser degree the violin. Beginners on the latter seldom play in perfect tune, therefore the ear is not helped as with the piano.[35] The singer is advised to practise scales, ascending and descending, frequently with a perfectly tuned piano or, if no piano is available, with a very purely played violin, "in order that the pupil might be lead to a pure intonation right from the start." [36] Petri is of the opinion that a good ear is to a great extent a gift of Nature. While diligence and training can assist and improve upon Nature, there are some who have no ear at all, nor will they ever acquire one.

These persons can be recognized in this way: if one sings to them some tone which they are to sound or sing thereafter, one will, generally, notice that those who after several lessons still remain in the [stage of] tone-seeking, and are barely able to hit one out of ten best-tones, are for the most part completely unfit for singing and have no musical ear at all.[37]

The ear is the natural means of learning music in the opinion of Kuerzinger, "as with the herdsmen and shepherds of old." It is important to test the ear of the beginner as to "whether he can catch at once and repeat exactly a few notes sung to him, otherwise his ability may be not the best and all pains may be in vain." [38] In contrast to Petri, this author considers the violin to be the best instrument to train the ear of the beginner. When practising alone the beginner will learn to sing falsely "inasmuch as the human voice is always apt to drop when not accompanied with an instrument." [39]

Lasser is the last of our German sources on ear-training. The first quality of a good teacher is that he must have a good ear. "A singing-master must have a fine ear; if he is wanting in this or if he himself sings off pitch, how is he going to make others sing truly?" [40] The first duty of the teacher is to test the ear of his pupil.[41] No particular instrument is mentioned but it should always be in perfect tune when used as an accompaniment. Moreover the slightest errors in pitch should be corrected at once. Since there was no accepted standard of tuning, Lasser advises the teachers to sing in a higher key.

> In view of the fact that the pitch of the pianofortes, organs, and other instruments in the musical world is so variable, I would advise the master to instruct his pupils much sooner according to a higher pitch, because to any singer used to a lower pitch, it will then be difficult to sing at a higher pitch.[42]

French Sources

Hearing and intelligence are combined, writes Bacilly, or rather the correct interpretation of, and reaction to, what we hear denotes a good ear. His chapter on ear training is entitled "De l'oreille, ou Intelligence, à l'égard du Chant," [43] in which the ear is said to be the third gift of nature for good singing and is as rare as the second, i.e., the healthiness of the throat.[44] The ear is always our guide and without it the natural disposition of the throat and the voice itself means nothing.

> By means of it the voice corrects itself when it is off pitch; sweetens itself when it is hard; modulates itself when it is too loud; sustains itself when it trembles. By means of it the throat is accustomed to note that which is wrong and to pass over that which should be noted only slightly. That is to say by means of it [the ear] one can well understand all that is practical in the Art of correct singing; even one may say that with a good ear one can acquire a voice and make it come out of almost nothing, by study and in every instance with the help of a good teacher as I shall say in the following chapter.[45]

With intelligence, or comprehension through the ear, one may achieve that finesse of execution which singing requires. Bacilly goes on to apply this "intelligence" to "chanter juste," i.e., singing on pitch, which some call singing the notes just as the composer wrote them and in correct rhythm and on correct pitches. If the singer lacks the ear to do these things, then a teacher who possesses such "intelligence" is absolutely necessary, for without him errors and faults will be augmented and made uncorrectable by wrong habits which then become second nature.[46]

It is necessary to give constant attention by means of the ear to the sound, interval, rhythm, key, voice quality, cadences, etc., says Jumilhac. By means of the ear we can bring reason to judge that which is good. After repeating "the common proverb which says that one should sing more with the ear than with the mouth," [47] we are told that the ear is just as necessary to the singer as the eye is to one who studies the stars or paints pictures. Just as the eye discerns the colors of the painting, its composition, the perspective, the placing of the figures and their postures, the lights, the shadows, and all combine with reason to guide completely the hand and the brush,

> in like manner it is the ear which recognizes and understands all the sounds and all their intervals, their good or bad results, their consonances or dissonances, their duration and rhythm, their cadences and their rests, their softness or loudness, the harmony or discord of the different parts, and universally all the other factors which concern the sounds and voices which are the subject of this study.[48]

Jumilhac adds that hearing and reason join to accept that which is suitable and to reject that which is not, thus leading the voice to perform that which has been ordained.

A singing manual by an anonymous French author has the following to say: "Finally there is nothing on which one should depend so much in all this matter [i.e., singing] as the ear which is over the rules of the art itself since it is it which must judge." [49]

A singular approach to intonation in which the factor of hearing is dispensed with is presented by Blanchet. Since the larynx rises and falls as a singer sings high or low, one may learn to sing with correct intonation, even though having a bad ear, by learning to control this rising or falling action of the larynx.[50] In his opinion hearing has no part in giving pitch to the sounds of the voice, this being the result of the varying tension of the vocal bands. If one can learn to establish control over this tension, then correct pitches may be sung without depending on a poorly disposed ear and one will have "an infallible guide" (*une regle infaillible*) for singing correct pitches. Blanchet continues to explain precisely how this could be achieved, the end being that one could sing exactly on pitch without accompaniment or the aid of other voices. He continues:

> The method which I have come to teach will contribute not a little in extending the realm of song and in increasing the talents of many people. Ladies who have voices without an ear, are able by means of my rules to add to their charms, assuring themselves against the afflictions of age and trusting to be again charming when they have ceased to be so.[51]

Rameau says that the ear must be somewhat accustomed to harmony if the voice is to have freedom necessary to perform the many graces, a fact easily confirmed "in all the able singers, of which the number is infinitely greater in Italy than in France." [52] A keyboard instrument, either the harpsichord or organ, is recommended which may be sounded as the pupil executes the swell tone or *messa di voce*. The accompaniment should be easy, and as the singer swells and diminishes the tone the arpeggio based on the tone being sung is to be played several times.[53] Rameau suggests that this may be accomplished by starting on the lowest notes of the voice and rising by half tones. In this way the ear of the singer will be trained and according to this author it "is a primary means of training the ear." [54]

The importance of the ear cannot be overemphasized from the beginning of voice study according to Lecuyer.

> When one begins to sing, too much attention cannot be given to understanding and making understood the interval and the differences that exist between one sound and another. I cannot recommend too much singing with an instrument for I am quite certain that if one sings falsely often and obstinately, this comes from too little practice in hearing the accompaniment.[55]

There are two ways to teach singing, declares Martini, one with the violin, the other with the piano. The former is the better, especially at the beginning of study since "a scholar taught with a violin will sing his part with accuracy and precision." [56] After the music is well learned then he should sing it without the violin but with the piano accompaniment in order to hear the harmonic background of his song.

> Correct intonation is the first thing to be considered by the pupil and teacher. One cannot bear to listen to false singing. This will happen sometimes because of a weak stomach but a scholar who at the end of a month does not learn to recognize with certainty the sounds of an instrument or to sing in unison with a voice of his range should be advised that his deficiency of hearing is an obstacle because of which he can never sing nor consequently make progress.[57]

Mengozzi's comments on ear training are confined to proper intonation or attack. The ear or the sense of hearing is not directly mentioned, their part in the process only being implied. "One should attack the tone cleanly and exactly, without preparation and without reaching the sound by means of sliding." [58] Each note of the scale should be executed in such a way that there will be no sign of any breath heard before or after.

English Sources

The English sources on ear training are so insignificant as hardly to deserve consideration. The importance of a teacher or "living tutor" is stressed in a small rudimentary manual by Turner.

> I would not have you imagine that I propose anything I can say here, in *Dead Letters* to be sufficient to instruct you in the Art of Singing, without the assistance of a Living Tutor . . . for the meaning of *Sound* which we are unacquainted with, cannot be communicated to us without our hearing them.[59]

Bayly emphasizes the importance of attacking each note "plain and firm like one who walks and marches well, with his foot set on the ground and lifted up without any shuffling and stamping." This should be practised on both low and high tones, both soft and loud, "after having collected the breath by inflating the breast like a pair of bellows, and letting it out again gradually in respiration." [60] Tenducci is indeed terse. It is necessary "to be exactly in Tune; as without a perfect Intonation, it is needless to attempt singing." [61] Corri gives considerably more attention to the training of the ear. Among the requisites for a good singer are, "First, —a singer ought to have a good ear, which is a most important and indispensable requisite; a gift without which no perfection can be obtained." In his opinion a good ear is due to two things, first, the natural acuteness of the ear because of the construction of the auricular nerves, and second, the opportunity to hear good music from childhood where the sounds become habitual and, like the spoken language, are learned without study. Corri is much concerned about the teaching of correct intonation and offers a substantial number of exercises to bring this about.[62]

Comparisons and Summations

A good ear along with its correct use to insure exact intonation was almost unanimously held to be the prime requisite for a singer among all the writers in whatever country we have under survey. This is understandable since a certain measure of artistry is possible even in a voice of mediocre abilities as long as the intonation is good, while without it any attempts at singing are worse than no attempts. All of the earlier Italian sources reiterate that a singer must have a good ear which will serve as an ever present guide, but not until we meet Tosi, Mancini, and Manfredini are we given any suggestions as to how it is to be obtained. It is assumed that anyone who presumes to teach must have a good ear and it is the ear of the teacher which listens to the pupil and assures him which tones are sung correctly. The pupil in turn becomes accustomed to that which is correct and sings accordingly. Long years of study with assiduous practice are absolute requisites.

The earlier German manuals speak of the necessity of good intonation but the practice here seems to have been rather lenient toward the attack, allowing for considerable scooping or sliding up to the pitch. However by the time of Marpurg (1763) all "Tonsuchen" was ruled out as it had been in Italy since the beginning of the *bel canto* period. The use of a keyboard instrument or a violin was regarded as a most important aid in developing the ear and the teacher's advice was considered essential.

The French writers emphasize in general the same things noted already by the Italians and Germans with a little more emphasis placed on the part played by reason and judgment together with consideration of a good ear as being a gift of Nature. The use of an instrument and the part of the teacher are discussed very much as we have noted above. Blanchet is the one exception but his approach was wholly scientific and need not be given too much weight. As for the English manuals, everything seems to have been Italian in origin or inspiration.

X. RESONATORS

Ful wel she song the service divyne,
Entuned in hir nose ful semely.[1]

Italian Sources

THERE may have been an appreciation of the part played by the cavities of the throat, mouth and head in reinforcing the sounds produced by the vocal bands but the singing manuals do not have much to say about it. The directions are mostly concerned with the manner of opening the mouth so that a natural tone would result, without the strain of its being too wide open or the nasal quality which comes from the mouth being too closed. Durante merely says to open the mouth when singing broad vowels and narrow it on the closed ones,[2] while Donati recommends that the singer hold the head high with the mouth half open.[3] Tosi is likewise brief. "If the Scholar should have any Defects, of the nose, the Throat, or of the Ear, let him never sing but when the Master is by, or somebody that understands the profession, in order to correct him, otherwise he will get an ill Habit, past all Remedy.[4]

Mancini on the other hand is quite explicit. According to him the prospective singer must know how to open the mouth because upon this depends the clearness of the voice. He proposes to dwell upon this topic and discuss the common defects because when these are recognized, ways can be found to correct them. "The first fault comes when one draws out the voice, without paying any attention to the mouth, and thus opens it badly. Therefore the voice does not come out clearly, sonorously and pretty." [5] Although this is the most common fault and would seem to be a very easy one to remedy, Mancini insists this is not the case. Many teachers consider their duties at an end when they have told the pupil: "Aprite la bocca" (open your mouth), but this is just the beginning since it is not only necessary to tell them many times, but also they must be told patiently and pleasantly.

It is necessary for a pupil to know from the beginning how to open the mouth correctly and to open it by the rules of art, and not merely to his fancy. Be it known that the rules for the opening of the mouth cannot be general, nor can they be made universally the same for every individual. For every one knows that each individual does not open his mouth in the same way. Some have wide openings, some narrow, and others medium. Add to this the irregularity of the teeth. . . . All these and other differences concerning the organs of the voice compel the teacher to observe diligently in what size of the opening of the mouth the voice comes out clearest, purest, and fullest. Thus he determines the size of the opening for the correct position of the mouth. Experience teaches that a mouth too widely open, or too closed besides looking awkward and distorted, renders the voice rough and unpleasant. I am of the opinion that to know well how to shape it can reasonably be kept as one of the essentials most important to a singer. Without this knowledge, although he may possess all the other abilities of the profession, he will never be able to please, and will often render himself ridiculous and disgusting.[6]

He continues that while there are many wrong positions of the mouth the most common are when it is opened too widely and when it is too closed. In the first case the strain in the fauces is such as to cause throatiness and loss of that flexibility so necessary to clear and facile singing. If not corrected the tone will have a "suffocated, crude, and heavy quality." In the latter, three grave consequences are the result. First the quality becomes doleful and dead, second, the tone is forced into the nose, and third, the enunciation is not clear. When the mouth is opened too widely the tone does not come forward clearly and sonorously but remains in the throat. When not open enough the tongue cannot function and the enunciation "will sound mumbling and blubbering." Singing with the teeth close and tight "is the greatest of all defects." It is a traitor to the voice because it robs the singer of his tone and enunciation.[7]

According to this author experience proves that the opening of the mouth is what directs and regulates the voice.

In fact, the resounding quality of the voice always depends upon the shaping of the position of the mouth, when there is the natural strength of the chest and a harmonious disposition of the vocal organs. Therefore, it will be useless for a teacher to correct the pupil by merely saying, "You open your mouth too much," or "too little," or "you sing with your teeth closed." The general precepts are usually of little value just as the practical applications are good. In giving the precise rules to a student, let the teacher not only tell him and explain to him, but let him illustrate his meaning by making himself an example, by assuming the different positions of the mouth, the wrong as well as the right. The student will then be able to know and choose which is the correct one and why, through both seeing and hearing. Let the experienced teacher follow this method and he will soon be convinced how much more preferable are practical demonstrations to general rules.[8]

Mancini adds that when his pupils opened their mouths incorrectly he would show them how to do it correctly.

The weight of evidence from a great number and variety of pupils causes this teacher to arrive at a general rule: "Every singer should shape his mouth, just as he shapes it when he smiles, in such a manner that the upper teeth are perpendicularly and moderately separated from the lower ones." [9]

By following this rule Mancini claims always to have gotten results; moreover, he adds that it conforms to the methods taught in the best schools. With this smiling position of the mouth he maintains that the vowels *a, e,* and *i* can be sung while very slight changes are necessary for *o* and *u*. For clear enunciation other slight alterations have to be made. "But it is necessary that the teacher observe carefully in which position [of the mouth] the voice of the pupil comes out best and have him practice in that position, in order that he may take advantage of his natural disposition and talents." [10]

Singers are warned against the habit, often noticed, of singing low tones with lips almost closed and abnormally opened on the high ones. This gives a very different character and quality to each which is essentially wrong and also unwelcome to an audience.[11]

The throat must also act in harmony with this natural position of the mouth. It must "unfold the voice with ease and also clarify each vowel." The rough and suffocated voice results when the singer does not open up and "does not sustain the voice by the natural strength of the chest but thinks he will obtain a good result by tightening the fauces." This, says Mancini, is all wrong and absolutely harmful to the voice.

The voice cannot come out natural and spontaneous, if it finds the throat in a strained position which impedes natural action. Therefore the student must take the trouble to accustom his chest to give the voice with naturalness and to use the throat smoothly and easily. If the union of these two parts [chest and throat] reaches the point of perfection, then the voice will be clear and agreeable. But if these organs act discordantly, the voice will be defective and the singing will be spoiled.[12]

Manfredini gives almost word for word the same advice as Mancini but without elaboration or discussion.

The rule governing the manner of opening one's mouth is most essential because on it depends the formation of a clear voice as well as a pure and clear pronunciation of the words. Yet, this most important rule is observed by but few singers with exactitude, certainly because of carelessness of their first teachers. . . . Now the mouth should, in singing, be opened neither too much nor too little, and the correct way is to keep it open as in the act of smiling; neither should one put out the tongue onto the lips, which causes one to sing through the nose and to enunciate lisping.[13]

And later he says that a great many singers have the pernicious faults of opening the mouth too little, of pronouncing badly, and of failing to bring out the voice as required. But here instead of blaming it on the carelessness of the early masters, he says it is often due to having practiced solfeggii too much.[14] It is most interesting to read here also that the singer is advised to use solfeggii not longer than a year and then follow with nothing but vocalises. After a year of these, the singer should sing with words, but only the very best compositions such as those of Pergolesi, A. Scarlatti, Porpora, Sassone (Hasse), Marcello, etc. In another year, making three years in all, the singer should be able to sing impromptu, that is, at sight.

German Sources

Praetorius is the only seventeenth century writer of German origin to comment on the vocal resonators and he is superficial and brief. Among the vices of singers, some sing "through the nose suppressing the voice in the throat." [15] Also some sing with their teeth together. Almost a hundred years later (1714) Printz, in discussing diction says the following:

In pronouncing vowels, the mouth must have the correct opening relative to their sounds, which should not be changed to others. It would be awful if one sang "Dius" instead of "Deus," "nuster" instead of "noster," "gretia" instead of "gratia," etc. . . . The voice must not be formed between the lips or in hollow cheeks, but in the throat.[16]

Mattheson, as usual, takes a disparaging attitude toward the German singers, comparing them unfavorably with the Italians and French. According to him no one in the German singing schools seems to care if the voice comes gratingly from the throat, hindered by the tongue, or is formed between the cheeks and the lips, all of which the French call "chanter de la gorge" which they despise. After the tone is produced in the larynx then the proper opening of the mouth and fauces will permit advantageous passage.[17] Further discussing the production of the voice he says that the soft palate, lips and teeth must make room and in no way hinder the tone, "because they have no other duty than to stand aside modestly." [18]

Agricola, in his translation of Tosi's *Observations,* offers extended notes on the anatomical and physiological nature of the process of phonation. As to the resonators he says that when the sound is produced in the throat it goes out partly through the mouth and partly through the nose, wherein it is reflected and from which reflection arises the most important and pleasant quality of the voice. He calls the nose a speech-arch or vault (*Sprachgewolbe*) and stresses its importance but says nothing about the function of the sinuses to the same end.[19] In his opinion anything that interferes with the free passage of the air through the larynx or with its resounding in the mouth or nose will cause the tone to deteriorate. Such obstruction may be due to natural defects such as when the inner cavity of the nose is not large enough, or if its interior is not perfectly constructed, or if it is closed up because of a cold or through excessive use of snuff, or if its function is impaired through any other sickness.

But they [the obstructions] may also be caused by arbitrarily accepted incorrect habits, e.g., if one retracts the tongue when it is not necessary, or bends it, when it should really be in the mouth flat and straight, also when one neglects to open the mouth wide enough, or clenches the teeth. The first and second cases produce the so-called singing through the nose, and in the third originates the singing in the throat [il cantar di gola], and there may be many other such defects. If they are casual or acquired habits, the causes must be eliminated or one must try to give the correct position to the parts of the mouth, which will correct the mistakes.[20]

The advice offered by Marpurg is quite similar to that which we have already found. The singer should not open his mouth so widely that the listeners are able to look down his throat but it should be opened widely enough that the tone is not suffocated in the throat or forced out through the nose. The cheeks should not be made hollow, the teeth should not be set, and the tongue should lie flat and straight in the mouth "in order not to be obstructive to the free passage of the tone." [21] Later he cautions the performer against changing the shape of the mouth while singing fermatas or figures and insists that as long as the figure lasts the mouth should be kept in the position naturally required by the vowel being sung.[22]

"Clear is the voice when it comes out through the open mouth, freely from the chest, without forcing and squeezing of the throat." [23] So says Hiller and then goes on to enjoin the teacher to see that the pupil does not set his teeth, which should be kept apart so that the finger may conveniently be put between them. In general the look or expression of a gentle smile during which the mouth is drawn slightly to both sides is "the most proper in singing and the most convenient for the production of a good tone of one's voice." [24] Here is also repeated the warning that if the tone is held back in the throat it will result in the bad habit of singing through the nose.

Among his many and varied works, Abbe Vogler wrote a very short treatise on singing. In it he sees fit to repeat that the singer must not sing through the nose, in the throat or with the mouth opened too widely or too narrowly.[25] Petri merely says that the singer should keep his mouth neither too open nor too closed, the latter causing him to sing through the teeth, thus interfering with pronunciation.[26] The same warning is given by Kuerzinger. Among the chief faults in singing is to keep the mouth and teeth too closed which causes poor enunciation and singing through the nose. He seems to object to the mouth too widely opened only because of its ugliness.[27]

Aubigny offers slight elaborations on the proper use of the resonators in singing. He says that good tone is achieved if the mouth, on which success rests, is in the form of an ellipse, rather than oval, and if the tongue is flat in back of the teeth so that the tone may not be hindered by the throat, tongue, or teeth. The natural relationship of the throat, mouth, and nose should not be spoiled.[28] The position of the mouth is described as very important and the worst mistake is to sing with a throaty tone (*Halsstimme, chanter gros,* or *cantar di gola*) produced by a curved tongue in which the tone hits the upper gum and has a repercussion which becomes very unpleasant.[29] The use of nasal resonance is stressed and if the nasal passages are narrow it is advisable to draw in fresh water morning and evening, this especially with young singers.[30]

Lasser, our last German source, repeats that the teacher should see that the pupil does not open his mouth too wide, but also that it should not be closed so much as to make him sing through his teeth. Putting wooden wedges into the mouth in order to keep it open is not good "for the fact is that the opening of the mouth is not quite the same with every vowel." [31]

French Sources

Both throaty and nasal tone qualities are objectionable to Jumilhac, and he blames these faults, along with many others, on twisting the mouth or neck, holding the head too high or too low, and on rigidity of all those parts of the body directly allied with the singing process.[32] No remedy is suggested except to sing with a natural pose that avoids all constraints, thus making it possible for the voice to be free, clear, and accurate in pitch. Bailleux warns against changing the shape of the mouth while singing a tone and especially on the *portamento*. Moreover the voice should not master those who sing but on the contrary the voice should obey the singer right from the beginning. It should come out full and natural, directly from the chest, "lest in passing into the head or into the nose it degenerate into falsetto by its muffledness." [33]

In his advice to the teacher Martini says that he should note the position of the mouth and teeth of the pupil. A circular mouth or a mouth too closed can only suffocate and stifle the tone while serrated teeth hinder articulation by the tongue and hold back the voice. On the other hand when the mouth is too widely opened the fauces and throat are constricted which in turn prevents the tones from coming out easily. "The position of the mouth should be natural and slightly smiling." [34] This author then adds, "The Master should also correct the pupils who have the defect of singing in the nose or in the throat. If he cannot succeed in doing this he should dismiss them." [35] There are no suggestions as to how nasal or throaty tones may be eliminated.

The wrong position of the various parts that make up the mouth is among the most vicious defects of singing in the opinion of Mengozzi. Although the tone is not formed in the mouth, it serves to modify the tone in such a way that the teacher is advised first of all to devote his particular attention to this matter. Since Nature does not treat all alike, many pupils have malformations of nose, mouth, jaws, lips, teeth, etc., all of which call for special care if there is to be compensation for these "natural defects." He also advises the smiling position of the mouth with the teeth comfortably apart in natural conformity with the general physiognomy so that the vowel on which the exercise is being sung will be pure and remain unchanged.[36] Later Mengozzi sees fit to emphasize this same thing. "In vocalizing the pupil should always be certain to hold the mouth equally open and above all never to move the chin nor the tongue." [37]

English Sources

The English sources are rather meager and in general repeat the same advice already found in Italy, Germany, and France. This is to be expected from Bayly who as we have already seen, freely admitted the influence of Tosi. "Let the master carefully instruct the scholar how to open his mouth that the tones may come forth freely without any interruption of the throat, tongue or lips." [38] And again he warns the "master" to see that both the chest and head voice "come forth neat and clear, neither passing through the nose from the fault of heaving back the tongue towards the passage, nor choaked [*sic*] in the throat from the fault of contracting the windpipe, which are two most insufferable defects in a speaker and singer." [39] As to vowels, diphthongs, consonants, and words, the pupil must be taught to sing and pronounce them with "the throat and mouth properly open, and the lips shaped according to the nature of the vowels, that the tones may proceed freely, and the vowels be heard distinctly as in speaking." [40]

Burney's comment concerning the Italian soprano, Costanza, from Bologna, who was heard by him at Vienna on September 1, 1772, is testimony to his approval of this free and unconstrained manner of singing. He describes her voice as being "admirably free from the nose, mouth or throat. There was such a roundness and dignity in all tones, that everything she did became interesting; a few plain slow notes from her were more acceptable to the audience than a whole elaborate air from anyone else." [41]

Among his "necessary rules" for singers, Tenducci advises the singer "to give as open and clear a Sound to the Vowels, as the Nature of the Language in which the Student sings, will admit." [42] A stern warning is given never to incur "the disagreeable Habit of singing in the Throat or through the Nose;—unpardonable Faults in a Singer." [43]

Only one English source remains to be considered. Lanza says that the forming of the human voice is best done by sol-fa-ing. "My manner of Sol-fa-ing is in the old style which Sig. Aprile used." [44] There follows a description of the shape of the mouth for each vowel with accompanying plates showing a young female singer with her mouth in the desirable positions. The expression is easy and natural with evidence of a smile and the mouth comfortably opened.[45]

Comparisons and Summations

The exponents of singing methods during the *bel canto* period either ignored or took for granted the resonators in singing. They were far more concerned with the free emission of the voice as Nature intended. Great interest was shown in keeping the tongue, teeth, and lips out of the way in order that the voice could come forth free from all constraint and without being forced through the nose. Mancini especially gives many details, both as to the common errors and ways of correcting and avoiding them. Only Aubigny, a German writer, places direct emphasis on resonance in singing and his book comes at the extreme end of the period under survey. Here again we find only the external mechanics of singing emphasized, that is, the position of the mouth, tongue, teeth, lips, etc., that is most conducive to ease in singing.

The remarkable thing is the almost unanimous agreement upon the desirability and means of producing a free and natural singing tone as well as faults to be eschewed. The same admonitions and advice, sometimes almost word for word, are found in these sources, regardless of their national origin or language. It is stout evidence that there were generally accepted standards during this era of the history of singing.

XI. VOICE REGISTERS

His voice no touch of harmony admits
Irregularly deep, and shrill by fits.
The two extremes appear like man and wife,
Coupled together for the sake of strife.[1]

Italian Sources

We have already found that the recognition of voice registers long preceded the *bel canto* period.[2] Our survey reveals continued and increasing attention given to them as the seventeenth and eighteenth centuries pass. Caccini was offended by the falsetto voice and urged the singer to select a pitch "in which he could sing in a full and natural voice in order to avoid falsetto. . . . For from falsetto, this noble manner of singing [3] cannot arise. This comes from a natural voice suitable to all the chords." [4] Cerone not only prefers the chest voice over the head voice but implies that this was the general preference. He says, "I find that between head voices and chest voices, according to common opinion, chest voices are better." [5] A statement by Rognoni is difficult to interpret but shows his preference for the chest tones. He says that the "gorga" must come from the chest and not from the throat.[6] Della Valle, on the other hand, describes Giovanni Luca as a falsettist and a great singer of "gorge" and "passaggi," who sang as high as the stars.[7]

In his directions to choir masters, Andrea di Modena says that the song must be suited to the voices of the singers. If they have head voices, high and piercing, the choir master must begin with a very spirited voice (*voce amai spiritosa*). If they have chest voices, throaty (*gutturali*) and low (*basse*), in order to avoid shrillness the song should be begun at a lower pitch. If the voices are mixed, it is advisable to begin with medium tone suited to all.[8] In speaking of the range of voices, Santoro says that if the compass exceeds fifteen notes (he apparently means two octaves), it will be falsetto,[9] while both Nassarre and Vallara advise the singers not to sing in registers too high or too low.[10]

Tosi considers the use of the falsetto as a necessity for successful singing.

A diligent master, knowing that a Soprano without the Falsetto, is constrained to sing within the narrow Compass of a few Notes, ought not only to endeavour to help him to it, but also to leave no Means untried, so to unite the feigned and the natural Voice, that they may not be distinguished; for if they do not perfectly unite, the Voice will be of divers Registers, and must consequently lose its Beauty.[11]

According to this author the full or natural voice terminates generally on C of the treble staff or sometimes D and above this the feigned voice, or falsetto, "becomes of Use, as well in going up to the high Notes, as returning to the natural Voice; the Difficulty consists in uniting them." If this is not solved the singer is ruined. Again it is obvious here that Tosi is writing about the castrato voice in which the registers could very well have functioned in a different way. He adds that he has sometimes heard a female soprano "entirely *di petto*" but among the male sex "it would be a great Rarity, should they preserve it after having past the age of Puberty." [12] The *voce di testa,* or head voice, is described as having great volubility with "more of the high than the lower notes, and has a quick Shake, but subject to be lost for want of Strength." [13] An annotation by the English translator, Galliard (1687–1749), is of interest:

Voce di Petto is a full Voice, which comes from the Breast by Strength, and is the most sonorous and expressive. *Voce di Testa* comes more from the Throat, than from the Breast, and is capable of more Volubility. *Falsetto* is a feigned Voice, which is entirely formed in the Throat, has more Volubility than any, but of no Substance.

He defines "register" as "a Term taken from the different Stops of an Organ." [14]

Mancini does not agree entirely with the opinions of Tosi with regard to registers. According to him the voice ordinarily divides itself into two registers, one called chest register, and the other, head register or falsetto. He agrees with Tosi that in rare cases a singer may be found who sings only "di petto," but every other student whether he be soprano, contralto, bass or tenor can easily tell the difference between the registers merely by singing the scale. He also agrees with Tosi that the change occurs in the soprano voice at about D in the treble clef while lower voices will experience the change at successively lower pitches. Below this place in their scale the "tones are sonorous and come out with strength and clearness and without effort because they come from the chest." The tone where the change occurs is weaker than the other notes of the scale and can easily be recognized by an experienced teacher.[15] "The great art of the singer consists in acquiring the ability to render imperceptible to the ear, the passing from the one register to the other." According to the author the ideal for any singer, and one most difficult to achieve, was to unite the two, with each tone being of the best and purest and with perfect quality throughout the whole range.

> This is art and it is not easy to reach the goal. It takes study, work and industry to correct the defects originated from the more or less strong constitution of the vocal organs, and it requires ability and such a careful use of the voice to render it equally sonorous and agreeable, that few students succeed.[16]

Many teachers are at fault because of not knowing how to correct these difficulties and the offended student should bring complaint against such a teacher. Mancini says that natural instincts should be followed but that Nature should never be forced. Moreover it is impossible to acquire virtuosity without the registers being blended. In some singers this is more difficult than others since Nature has not treated us all alike. First of all he advises that the voice must be classified as to range so that it will not be forced beyond the limit intended by Nature. Many good voices have been ruined by neglect in this respect.

> Art consists in one's ability to know what Nature intended one to be. When once the gifts of Nature are known, cultivating them easily makes man perfect. . . . The teacher must be careful not to betray their [*sic*] pupils and the pupils not to pay more attention to the teacher than to Nature. If this point is overlooked, all the helps of the precepts of art will be completely void. Take for instance a student who has a strong chest voice, and head tones out of proportion, weak and feeble. In such a voice the break between the two registers comes between C and D [treble clef]. . . . The way to correct it is to have the pupil at once undertake and fix in his mind in his daily study, to keep the chest tones back as much as he can and to force the

voice little by little against the head just there where it seems to be most unfriendly to him and thus fix it and develop it with the same strength that the chest tones have already naturally developed.[17]

The pupil is warned to keep under very careful control that part of his voice which is naturally strong and robust and to make strong that part of the voice which is by Nature weak. The teacher is advised, after keeping the pupil on head tones until they have more strength and flexibility, to have the pupil sing out the chest voice with the usual fullness so as to see how they compare. In the event that the desired evenness has not yet been achieved both the teacher and pupil are urged not to give up faith for by continuing in such a manner "the difficulty will in time be completely mastered and all the other tones of the voice will be benefited greatly by this exercise." [18] Mancini goes on to say that this same rule should be followed in the reverse case, that is, when the student has weak chest tones but a strong head register. Then the latter must be held back until both registers are even. "Arrived at this point, the student will be glad for the achieved success of having the two registers blended, and with patience and industry, he will then undertake the work that leads to the acquisition of the "portamento di voce" so necessary in every style of singing." [19]

Teachers are warned that the registers must be perfectly blended before there is any attempt to acquire agility. Much harm could result from carelessness at this point in the training of the pupil "because the agility would undoubtedly be uneven, where the registers change, and thus be defective in strength and clearness, and also out of proportion." [20] A perfect even scale throughout the entire range is Mancini's ideal.

In our time [1774] teachers wish to enlarge the range, and by forcing Nature, they bring out from the throat even a larger number of tones. Thus, today, the tendency is to judge a singer's merits by the range of his voice. In my opinion, however, the worth of a voice will always depend upon its evenness of quality throughout the whole register, and perfect intonation. The strength of the medium and chest tones must also be equivalent to those of the head, in order to form an even register. The medium and low tones are naturally more homogeneous, sonorous, and pleasing, because they come from the chest, while the head tones are more difficult to perfect because they are more shrill. . . .

Great care must be taken by the student to attack the high tones with the required sweetness and proportion, in order that he can command his entire range to perfection.[21]

Like Mancini, Manfredini speaks only of two registers, and calls the head voice and falsetto one and the same. The heading for his section on the blending of registers is as follows: "On combining the chest voice with the head voice, the latter being vulgarly called falsetto." [22] The chest voice rarely exceeds twelve or thirteen tones according to this writer and sometimes there are more tones in the head register than in the chest. Therefore it is necessary not only to blend them but it must be done in such a way "that the voice seems to consist of one register, that is to say equal throughout." [23] This is achieved by causing the uppermost chest tone, usually C of the treble clef, to be united with the first note or tones of the falsetto,[24] in such a way that the difference in the two is barely noticeable, or even better yet, not noticeable. "This is to be accomplished not by forcing the high chest tones but rather by reinforcing the low tones of the falsetto, or else doing the opposite, if the chest tones should happen to be weaker and deficient, and the falsetto tones plentiful and strong." [25] Manfredini adds that certain weak tones, either of the chest or head registers, can always be strengthened if the exercise be persistent but moderate. Vocal fatigue must be avoided and the tones must never be forced for then the tones will decline in strength and may even be lost.

German Sources

While Calvisius does not mention the word register, head voice, or chest voice, he warns against forcing the high voice or relaxing the low voice. Voices shouldn't stay too much on the high notes.[26] Praetorius mentions the "falsetto" as being a half tone and forced; also it is one that is not bright nor loud.[27] Mattheson is of the opinion that all voices including sopranos can sing falsetto. Tenors and basses get it by contracting and forcing the throat, called "fistulieren." [28]

Agricola, in his translation of Tosi's *Observations,* has added some extensive notes especially with regard to voice registers.[29] First of all he disagrees with the Italian conception that the head voice and falsetto are the same and in order to prove his position he presents a physiological and acoustical analysis of his conception of the processes of phonation.[30] Next he offers somewhat speculative reasons for the differences in the three registers and describes each. The chest voice is the strongest, therefore the opening of the windpipe [glottis] is stronger, harder and larger; also there is more movement of air, and putting all these together it means "that the chest voice can never sing as high as the head voice" (*dass die Bruststimmen niemals so hoch singen könnten als die Kopfstimmen*). This speculation of Agricola's is based on pre-Ferrein theories of voice production[31] and it leads him to complications from which he can only extricate himself by saying that human wisdom cannot judge since it is all manipulated by Nature. But he insists that of two voices of the same range, the one with a chest and the other with a head voice, the glottis of the chest voice has to be a little larger although indistinguishable to the human eye. The possessor of the chest voice is advised to sing more in the middle range while the head voice should remain on the higher tones. An aria should be sung about one tone lower by the former than by the latter.

While it is more difficult for the chest voice to execute rapid passages than the head voice, Agricola insists that the opinion that the chest voice is incapable of fast singing can be contradicted by the great ability of certain singers. The awkwardness in the rendition of fast notes by some chest voices is due to laziness and lack of practice. Many head voices do not sing the fast passages with clarity, sliding over tones too feebly and softly, due to the fact, Agricola says, that the windpipe is not sufficiently elastic to give each tone its proper accent and sharpness. Trills and other little ornaments are usually harder for the chest voice but with diligence and practice these may also be perfected. This author warns that the head voice, due to the ease with which it can perform them, may ruin them because of singing flat, bleating or even singing a "third-trill" (*Terzentriller*).

The chest voice is more durable because the fibers of the glottis are stronger, the windpipe is wider, and the lungs larger, hence the singers with chest voices will keep them until a much later age. Agricola mentions the singers Orsini (d. *ca.* 1750) and

Carestini (*ca.* 1705–*ca.* 1760) as examples of chest voices that maintained their beauty to an advanced age.

The properties of the head voice are held to be the result of a more flexible and less elastic larynx, with a tighter windpipe and less expandable lungs. Agricola says this should all be deduced from what has already been said about the chest voice and need not be discussed further.[32]

After repeating his contention that the Italians, including Tosi, have often mistaken the head voice for the falsetto, Agricola offers a detailed discussion of the "Fistel-stimme." It is better to present his argument in his own words than to try to condense and interpret them.

> Most scientists as well as musicians describe falsetto tones, which may occur in any voice in the highest and lowest notes, and the falsetto voice as a forced voice. But how are these forced tones brought out? Let us first examine the high falsetto tones. It is known that, exerting a certain perceptible force in the throat when singing, many more high notes can be brought out than are in the ordinary range of a voice. Whoever sings in his natural voice, no matter what it may be, as high as he can without forcing, he will find that finally there are no more tones to be heard and one would then believe that the windpipe is completely closed, that no more air can come out and therefore no sounds can be produced. But if one makes a little more effort to sing a few notes higher, it may be noticed that still higher tones are possible which, however, unless artistically done, are a little different in sound than the former, and it will be noticed that the air escaping from the glottis strikes farther back in the roof of the mouth. There can be no other cause for the production of these tones than this, that the entire head of the windpipe [larynx] is stretched higher and drawn farther behind the cavern of the palate and under the bones of the tongue [hyoid bone]. In this position the glottis, which is stretched even more, begins anew to contract the still remaining opening as the tones grow higher until it closes completely and no further tone can come out. Through this stretching upward of the head of the windpipe, the length of the cavern of the mouth which adjusts itself to each tone is still more shortened. Returning from these falsetto tones to the lower tones, the singer who takes notice will observe that upon reaching a certain tone, the head of the windpipe will again leave its high stretched position and return to its original place.[33]

The difficulty of changing from the natural voice to the falsetto is discussed and diligent practise recommended to strengthen those tones where the change occurs. Women are often not bothered with a break but with tenors and basses the break is usually noticeable and sometimes very difficult to hide. Some men sing nothing but falsetto tones and these are known as falsettists, but "all and each of the natural voices, even if they do not make a profession of falsetto singing, can produce some falsetto tones in the higher range."[34] Agricola says that with chest voices the falsetto usually begins in soprano on $\overline{\overline{g}}$, in tenor on $\overline{a}$ and alto and bass are in the same proportion. But with head voices falsetto tones usually start with $\overline{\overline{d}}$ or $\overline{\overline{e}}$ for sopranos and $\overline{e}$ or $\overline{f}$ for tenors. Just as no two people are alike so does each voice vary from every other in many little ways. The less these changes and variations are understandable "the more we must admire and honor in deepest humility the omnipotence and wisdom of the Creator."[35]

The advantages of joining the head voice and the falsetto voice are stressed. The one tone where the change is made should be equally strong and clear in either voice and it should be sung in the lower voice when singing up the scale and vice versa when singing down the scale. This is not possible for everyone, "but it is artistic and naturally advantageous to those whose voices sound equal throughout."[36]

Agricola goes so far as to say that the lowest tones of the voice are also falsetto. They are very few, are weaker than the natural deep tones and are created by just the reverse process as the high falsetto tones, i.e. by dropping the larynx. He observes that those who wish to produce these lower tones forcefully usually have recourse to lowering the head and dropping the jaw but this puts obstacles in the way of the free emission of air from the mouth, therefore these tones cannot have the strength and beauty of the natural tones. High voices trying to produce such tones are in danger of being ruined. Moreover, these tones cannot be heard well. "But the high falsetto tones of many singers, who know how to use them, are just as strong and beautiful as the natural high tones."[37]

Marpurg has abbreviated the foregoing discussion by Agricola on registers except that the head voice is entirely dispensed with.

There exists only the natural or the chest voice and the artificial or falsetto voice and one may sing in either of these on low or high tones. In his opinion, singers should use the Italians as models by bringing out all the tones in either voice purely and clearly without nasal or throaty qualities. The falsetto and chest tones must be perfectly joined and equally strong so that they cannot be differentiated. Because of Agricola's important and fundamental annotations to Tosi's text, Marpurg thinks these should be translated into Italian.[38]

Hiller also refers the reader who wishes to find a complete discussion of registers to Agricola's annotations to Tosi's text. He, too, says there are two voices, the chest or natural and the falsetto or artificial. Whenever the term head voice is used it may be assumed to be identical with the falsetto although frequently with boys and often with young women the falsetto is to be found as a natural voice. On the higher tones the difference is not so noticeable: "At least the joining of the falsetto with the natural is here far easier and the change-over from one to the other more difficult to observe." [39] The blending of these two registers is interestingly discussed in the next paragraph.

> By the addition of a few falsetto tones the range of the natural voice is extended. But the singer must see to it that one would not notice too much the transition from one kind of voice to the other. The limits of the one must still extend a couple of tones into the region of the other; and the sopranist who sings from $\bar{\bar{c}}$ to $\bar{\bar{\bar{e}}}$ up as far as $\bar{\bar{a}}$ with the natural voice and then adds the rest of the tones with the falsetto voice should be able to enter even as early as $\bar{\bar{f}}$ without any drop [in volume] of the voice being noted. Of course, to give to the lower tones of the falsetto voice a fullness corresponding to that of the chest voice causes a certain amount of difficulty.[40]

Any singer should learn to use the falsetto which some call the "fistula-voice" [41] according to Petri. The falsetto which is called "head-voice" by the Mannheim school, should be equalized with the chest voice so that the transition from one to the other is unnoticeable. The falsetto is used when the singer is called upon to perform an aria too high for his voice. Petri says it is better to sing in falsetto voice than to transpose the aria downward when the result is often "an unharmonious or ill-sounding reversion of the same." [42] Since the use of the falsetto is a necessity, explicit directions are given for its acquisition. The singer is advised to find out very carefully how high the natural voice will go without forcing and how low the falsetto voice can be used. The overlapping tones must be practiced slowly over and over again within the range or compass of a fifth, until all the tones are strengthened in either voice, and until the change-over is unnoticeable. This change-over should not always occur at the same place but should be used sometimes higher, and sometimes lower. It is preferable to change too high than too low since the chest voice can be retained in the higher tones whereas the falsetto voice gets too weak on the lowest notes and the transition is therefore evident.

> If I know, for instance, that I am able to go down to $\bar{c}$ with my falsetto voice, then I ought to change over already at $\bar{e}$ or $\bar{d}$, if I am descending; but when ascending I should use my chest voice still as far as $\bar{c}$ or $\bar{d}$. The high basses thus become, through the falsetto, employable for singing the best tenor arias, which is of no small advantage at least in case of an emergency. But still I must admit that only a few learn to use a good falsetto which is not differentiated appreciably from the chest voice.[43]

Aubigny discusses the problem of registers very much as the foregoing sources and refers the reader to Tosi and Agricola. Every voice consists of two kinds of tones, chest and head, the former being lower and more natural. The main problem, says Aubigny, is to unify these two and these naturally weak tones where unification takes place may be fortified by careful and patient practise. It is harder to join these two voices in ascending scales than in descending scales and the change is most difficult for the alto voice.[44]

Lasser also considers the head voice and the falsetto as one and the same. When the teacher examines the voice of a pupil he should try to find that place "where the chest voice ends and the falsetto, or the so-called head voice begins." [45] Any teacher of singing should easily be able to tell the difference between the chest or natural voice and the falsetto or artificial voice. This author says that some singers are able to produce ten or twelve tones, or even more, with the chest voice but most ordinarily in the soprano voice it ends with $\bar{\bar{e}}$ or $\bar{\bar{f}}$, with the other voices proportionately lower. When a singer changes to falsetto in going from $\overline{\overline{f}}$ to $\overline{\overline{g}}$ the difference is readily noticeable, "it being—to use the expression of the Italians—as though one would pull two different stops on the organ." [46] It therefore becomes evident to Lasser why it is so necessary to join these two properly, an accomplishment just as difficult for some as it is easy for others, depending on whether the vocal organs are flexible or rigid. The ability to make such a transition as nearly imperceptible as possible "is achieved most certainly if one endeavors and accustoms oneself to give or produce both the last tone of the chest voice and the first of the falsetto voice in both ways." [47]

French Sources

The French sources on vocal registers are few and even these are not voluminous. Only one of these is by a native Frenchman and his is only a passing comment on the falsetto voice which he describes as being unnatural and forced. It is achieved by the singer forcing his lungs, "just as one draws higher notes from a flute by making the breath enter with more force." [48]

The other two French sources are by authors of German and Italian birth. The German, Martini (born Schwartzendorf), says that each of us has three kinds of voices, the chest voice, or "voix de poitrine" for making low tones, the throat voice, or "voix du gosier" for making the most facile and brilliant tones, and the head voice or "voix de tête" which produces the very high tones but which can only be done easily in staccato.

> The great difficulty consists in making imperceptible the passage from the chest voice to the throat voice and from the throat voice to the head voice, in such a manner that these three voices sound as one, that is to say, all the tones in going through their area should have the same volume, the same quality and the same facility.[49]

The Italian, Mengozzi, is somewhat more explicit. He defines the term register in reference to its use in organs and describes it as the difference in character of a certain group of tones from that of another group of tones. As to vocal registers he says:

All the sounds proceeding from the chest, for example, form a particular division in the compass of the voice and this division is called register. As those sounds from the chest differ in character from the sounds which have their origin in the head, these latter, in their turn form another division or register in the compass of the same voice. . . . We have, therefore, adopted the word *register* from the Italians since it seems to us to explain in a concise manner the different characters of sound which are found in the range of voice.[50]

According to Mengozzi, male singers have two registers, the one, chest, and the other, head, improperly called falsetto. In producing the chest tones, which sounds are always low and medium in the voice, the impetus should be given by the chest, while the head tones should be induced in the frontal sinus and the nasal cavities.[51] It is so difficult for the bass voice to unite the head or falsetto voice with the chest tones and those who can do so are so rare, that this author does not consider it necessary to discuss the problem. Baritones, on the contrary, are advised to use the head voice beginning with $\bar{f}$ while the tenor voice should start the head tones at $\bar{a}$.[52]

As for women's voices, Mengozzi says that the contralto corresponds to the bass voice in range, except that it is an octave higher and has the same difficulty with head tones. The mezzo or lower soprano voice has the same range as the baritone and also can use the head voice. But the soprano has a two octave range with three registers: first, the chest, from $\bar{c}$ to $\bar{f}$; second a medium voice, the tones of which come from the upper part of the larynx and extend from $\bar{g}$ to $\bar{\bar{f}}$; and third, the head voice, the tones of which come from the frontal sinuses and nasal cavities, and the compass being from $\bar{\bar{f}}$ to $\bar{\bar{\bar{c}}}$. Some very high voices may go on up to $\bar{\bar{\bar{g}}}$ but "such a gift of nature is very rare."[53] These registers must be joined in such a way that the passing from one into the other is insensible. In order to accomplish this Mengozzi suggests singing a prolonged tone on the note where the change occurs and cause it to pass over into the next higher register and back again to the lower. This must be done "without a certain very disagreeable break" (*sans un certain hoquet très désagréable*) which results when the inexperienced and untrained singer attempts such a passage.[54]

English Sources

There is very little to be found among the English writers on singing concerning vocal registers. Bayly repeats the opinions of Tosi in saying that the *di petto* (chest) and *di testa* (head) registers must be perfectly united so they "may not be distinguished, both in going up to the highest artificial notes and in returning to the real," for if they do not perfectly unite "the voice will be of different sounds, or as Tosi says, diverse registers, and consequently cannot be heard with delight." [55] Tenducci, the Italo-Anglican voice teacher writes briefly:

> Rule IX. Never to force the Voice, in order to extend its compass in the *Voce di petto* upwards; but rather to cultivate the *Voce di testa* in what is called *Falsetto,* in order to join it well and imperceptibly, to the *Voce di petto* for fear of incurring the disagreeable Habit of singing in the Throat or through the Nose;—unpardonable Faults in a Singer.[56]

There is no attempt by either writer to explain or describe the registers or to suggest how they may be united.

Comparisons and Summations

The early years of the *bel canto* period saw the Italians shunning the head voice, generally considered by them to be unnatural and false and hence it was given the name of falsetto. This may have been due to the fact that the declamatory style of the *Nuove Musiche* did not call for a wide vocal range. It was not many decades before opinions began to change and by the time of Tosi, the head voice was essential for anyone who pretended to be a singer. Also by this time the necessity and importance of blending the registers was fully recognized and in the later works we are given careful instructions as to the means of its achievement. Mancini is especially explicit and warns that virtuosity, the one quality of singing most highly developed in the age of *bel canto,* was impossible without the registers being perfectly blended, in fact, he is positive in saying the registers must be blended before there is any attempt to acquire agility. The ideal voice was one of evenness in quality throughout the entire range, with perfect intonation.

The Germans agree with the Italians until we come to Agricola who insists that the head voice and the falsetto are not one and the same and instead of there being only two registers, chest and head or falsetto, there are three, chest, head, and falsetto. His arguments as to why there are three registers and why high voices differ from low ones seem to be of a speculative nature since they are based on inadequate investigation. While Agricola's opinions on the registers were referred to by later writers in Germany, they are unanimous in rejecting his separation of the head and falsetto registers, all saying that the head and falsetto tones are the same. All agree with the Italians both as to the desirability of a perfect union of the registers and the means of acquiring this end.

Neither the French nor the English sources are of much consequence except to show that, for the most part, their ideas directly stemmed from Italy. Even the German born Martini borrowed and excerpted his work on singing from Hiller [57] who was indebted to Tosi through Agricola. Two exceptions may be noted here since Martini credits every voice with three registers, chest, throat and head while Mengozzi attributes three registers to the soprano voice only, chest, middle, and head, all others having but two. It should be added that the French and English also stress the perfect union of the registers and that this can be attained through careful, persistent, and proper vocal exercises.

XII. VOCAL ORGANS

The voice is nothing but beaten air.[1]

Italian Sources

The statements made by the Italian writers on singing during the *bel canto* period concerning the actual physical organs of phonation do not go much beyond the superficial. Moreover, much the same thing had been said by the ancients and repeated many times since. A table by Artusi lists as "natural instruments" of music, the throat, palate, tongue, lips, teeth, and lungs.[2] Caccini mentions only the throat and this is in connection with learning to execute the trill which was performed on one note with a sort of bleating sound "by beating the throat on the vowel." [3]

Cerone gives us a naive explanation of voice production. After saying that the necessary and natural instruments of voice are the lungs and the throat, we are told that the air which the lungs emit comes up with a certain force and strikes the uvula, thus forming the voice. Plato, Priscianus, Saint Isadore, Rosetus, and others are his sources.[4] Later he says that force of chest and disposition of throat are required for singing vocal ornaments, the first to carry song or passage to its proper end, and the second to utter it easily and without labor.[5] Avella repeats that, according to Albertus Magnus, the vocal organs are the throat, tongue, palate, four front teeth, and two lips together,[6] while Berardi merely says, "The voice is a striking of air which is breathed, upon the vocal passage." [7]

The opinions of Giovanni Bontempi should prove of particular interest since he was not only a castrato and a composer of some eminence but was learned in the history of music as well, especially as to what was then known about ancient music. He defines voice as the sound made by any living thing, when the air, driven out by the lungs is struck by the glottis.[8] Later we are told that the voice comes out of the lungs, involves the windpipe, the muscles of the larynx, the scutiform or cricoid cartilage,[9] the membraneous body, the muscle which serves in swallowing, and many other parts. Physiologists (*Fisici*) teach that the principal instrument of the voice is the larynx, and that the glottis, with the operation of thirty muscles, brings it forth and expresses it.[10] We are further told that the size and shape of the larynx and the windpipe affect the voice, but the following statement is of real import.

The physiologists expound these differences, caused by position, passage, shape, air, expiration, and all the conditions of the larynx; based on the immutable foundation of incontestable reason. Our opinion is, that everything which is derived from experience has no need of reasoning. If this is not admitted by the physiologists, it is their task to give another interpretation of it. Now that this principle has been set forth for their attention, while they go on investigating nature in order to find it out with reason, we, without philosophising further upon it, shall be content to understand it with the teaching of experience itself.[11]

Tevo is important for at least one reason, that is, he was the first musical authority to include a plate showing the cartilages and musculature of the larynx in a musical text-book. First he tells us that the instruments of the voice are the tongue, throat, palate, two lips, four teeth, and lungs.[12] Then follows a reasonably detailed description of the anatomy of those parts concerned with phonation. The bronchia and trachea are barely described, the upper part of the latter being the larynx. Five cartilages necessary to formation of voice are listed: the thyroid or scutiform, cricoid or ring-form, two arytenoid and the epiglottis. The position of each together with the attached muscles is explained, and the hyoid bone and tongue with their musculature are also discussed.[13] The plate, as mentioned above, shows simplified drawings of various cartilages, trachea, attachment of tongue, hyoid bone, sternothyroid and cricothyroid muscles. There is nothing exceptionally detailed or remarkable about this plate and its description except that it is found in a book devoted to music. The probability is that it had been taken from a contemporary manual of anatomy.[14]

Nassare also lists the lungs, windpipe, larynx, epiglottis, and uvula as being the natural instruments forming sound. He considers the strength or weakness of the muscles as important because light, agile muscles moving the epiglottis can work very quickly and since some people have less flexible muscles or a heavier epiglottis the speed of motion is reduced. Also, the singing voice cannot produce such variations as can the fingers used on artificial instruments because the internal muscles are weaker than those of the fingers, and besides, the breath may falter.[15]

Although Tosi ignores the whole problem of phonation, Mancini sees fit to examine it in some detail. According to him, the act of breathing causes a flux of air in the throat which forms the voice. The lungs merely furnish the air, the real organs of the voice being the larynx, glottis, uvula, tongue, soft palate, hard palate, teeth and lips. By means of all these organs the voice is given its many and diverse modulations, so that the better organized these are the more perfect, clear and strong the voice will be. Mancini says that the manner in which the larynx compresses this air causes the various pitches of the voice, and in singing, these organs are in a continuous state of action and excitement. But he holds that it is the larynx which carries the greatest burden, the muscles of which contract strongly on high tones and relax on lower ones. Mancini emphasizes that it is not enough for a singer to have a big chest and the ability to make a big noise. There must be a harmonious disposition of all the vocal organs, and if there are imperfections by nature or as the result of disease, they will cause the voice to be imperfect. "The more perfect the organs of the voice, the more certainty the aspirant can have of becoming a successful singer, if guided by an experienced teacher." [16]

If the teacher of singing in the eighteenth century followed Mancini's advice, he was careful to see that there were no physical impediments in the way of a prospective singer. The teacher was urged to examine the thyroid, and salivary glands, as well as the tonsils to find if there were any swelling or hardening due to disease, for if so, the larynx would not be free. The most careful observations must be made that the uvula or soft palate was free of growth or abnormal openings, that the tongue was flexible and the lips closed symmetrically, that a protruding chin did not mar the symmetry of the mouth, that the teeth were free from irregularity and that the nose was neither too flat nor too long. If the teacher found all these physical features favorably disposed and harmonious as Nature intended, then the pupil could be accepted with a fair chance of success. On the other hand, if he were found to be too defective in one or several of the points listed the teacher could not hope to make him a successful singer. "Imperfect organs of voice are incurable and hence will inevitably result in imperfect singing." The parents were also given the responsibility of finding out the physical defects of the contingent singer over and beyond those directly concerned with singing because, even though they might not have any direct connection with the vocal organs, they could nevertheless greatly influence the success of the student.[17] Mancini speaks of the rare instances when nature bestows all these gifts on one person ". . . so, it seldom happens that we find one person gifted with all those harmonious conditions of vocal organs that form a perfect voice." But voices may be admired for a wide variety of qualities for while some voices are strong, vigorous, and bright, others are flexible and sweet; some are wide in range and sonorous while others are admired because of purity of tone, evenness, and color.[18]

Arteaga offers a very few general comments on voice production and these must be labeled unscientific. "Voice considered in itself is nothing but air pushed upward by the lungs. This air, coming through the canal which is called the trachea, being thinned out through the slit of the glottis, and reverberating in the cavity of the mouth, then comes out of the lips making a noise or inarticulate sound." [19] He is equally indefinite when he says that singing differs from speech by a certain agitation of the larynx which changes its position upward or downward as the pitch varies, also there is a reciprocal oscillation of the lips of the glottis, like strings.[20] Manfredini does not say anything about voice production *per se*. He only mentions the importance of the pupil being endowed with a beautiful and flexible voice, also the rarity of one singer possessing all the natural gifts conducive to good singing.[21]

German Sources

Calvisius says simply that "the voice is formed in the throat, not with lips nor cheeks." [22] Galen is the authority for the statements of Praetorius. According to him the former showed the innervation in the muscles of the larynx and when these hairlike nerves were severed, loss of voice resulted. The windpipe was also of service to the voice since it is a pipe or reed which goes down from the mouth to the lungs and by means of it air is taken in and expelled. However, the head of the windpipe or larynx is considered the proper instrument of voice, which is produced in a little opening of the larynx called the glottis or "little tongue." The tighter it is, the higher the voice; the more dilated, the lower the voice. The various cartilages, three in number, plus the tongue and teeth are also instruments of voice.[23] Kircher likewise refers to Galen. He argues that since the pitch of pipes varies according to size of opening, the larynx functions in the same manner. Therefore the longer the glottis or the opening where the striking of the air causes the sound, the lower the pitch. The shorter and more closed they are, the higher the pitch; consequently, those whose larynx is wide and long are accustomed to sing with a deep, low voice; those whose larynx is tight and narrow, with a high, sharp voice.[24] In still another work he explains that the voice is a species of sound, its material is air, its cause the body of a living animal, its principal instrument the larynx, especially that part which is called the glottis or epiglottis.[25] The lungs, tongue, throat, lips, teeth, and palate are not the cause of voice although they are instrumental in shaping it.[26]

A rather detailed description of the vocal processes is offered by Mattheson which is quite elementary, partly incorrect, and obviously meant for the lay reader, at least as far as physiological matters are concerned. He says the windpipe consists of a number of rings of cartilage, one on top of the other, and are connected by "thin-skinned movable bands" (*dunn-häutige bewegliche Bände*). These cartilages are softer and somewhat more flexible than bone but harder than sinews. The upper two are smaller and by contracting form the head of the larynx and are the glottis or little tongue, "the cleft of which, through very subtle openings and movements, produces the sound." [27] The glottis is compared "to the spout of a small watering can (*mit der Mundung eines Giess-Kannleins*), and above it is another 'upper tongue' called the epiglottis," "the substance of which may be much softer, perhaps like parchment." [28] It is shaped like a three-cornered leaf, raised toward the mouth and hollow on the other side. The epiglottis contributes much to the finer and softer adjustments of tone, especially in trills, turns, and other ornamentations, perhaps even more than the uvula,

notwithstanding it is certain that the glottis itself contributes most and noblest, and therefore neither the lungs, nor the tongue, nor the throat nor the palate are the real cause for the tone, much less the teeth and lips, all of which have no part in it, except that the first produces the air and the others let pass the tone, round, noble, correct, and unhindered, after it has been produced by the cleft of the little tongue on top of the larynx, by thirteen muscles. Therefore the human glottis is the instrument most tuneful, most pleasant, most perfect and correct, or better said, the only and sole correct instrument amongst the large number of tools to produce sound, be they produced artificially or by nature; because all these instruments, be they wind or string, the violin excepted, are all faulty compared to the human voice, even if they be tuned to the highest point of perfection.[29]

It is most interesting to see how Agricola first gives us a very careful description of phonation according to the principles of Galen as further explained by Dodart, with which he seems to agree and then proceeds to report the experiments of Ferrein in detail and find room for agreement here also.[30] All natural scientists, both old and new, agree that the human windpipe has the acoustical qualities of a hollow tube in which sound can be produced by air moving through a small opening, just as with wind instruments. This glottis is in the larynx, which is entirely elastic, because it is made up of cartilages and membranes, each of which is elastic in itself. The text of Agricola follows:

The little opening of the windpipe, which is called *rima glottidis* is surrounded by two of these upper cartilages and by two fixed bands [vocal cords] which go forward from them [cartilages] in front, and it [rima glottidis] is covered by another one [cartilage] which lies above it and which is, in front, attached to the scutiform cartilage, but in the rear it is free, and therefore can open and close. This latter one is called *epiglottis* or throat-lid. All these cartilages of the head of the windpipe are bound together by means of elastic ligaments. But, so that the air which is necessary for the movement of these cartilages and ligaments may always be present, therefore the lung is able, not only to draw it [the air] in from the outside by way of the windpipe and the many little branches which go out from it at the lower end into the whole substance of the lung, but also to drive it [the air] out of it with many degrees of force. Since the above described opening of the windpipe, adjusted to certain muscles, can be widened and drawn together so can it thus produce high and low tones.

Both sides of the opening of the throat stand, at the most, about a *line* or the tenth part of an inch from one another. Yet this very small opening allows a person to produce comfortably with his voice twelve whole tones. It follows then when one sings a whole tone or a major second higher or lower, the opening of the throat is about $\frac{1}{120}$ wider or narrower. The scientists have demonstrated concerning this, that the voice can divide a whole tone at the very least into a hundred small parts [tones] and therefore a human being who has the vocal range of twelve whole tones can produce 2400 different pitches, which, nevertheless, his ear, developed to the finest point, must be able to differentiate (as can be perceived if a string [violin] be made only a hundredth part shorter). They [the scientists] have further shown that if one does not take good care in this differentiation, the number of pitches which a human being can produce become almost infinite since the opening of the windpipe, as with a line, can be divided into an infinite number of parts, which really happens when the sound of one tone changes gradually to that of another, without the sound ceasing. For then the opening of the throat itself draws together, thus its movement takes place through all degrees of its width.

If one would sing a pitch too low, then the throat would become open to such an extent that the air would find an entirely free passage through the same. Then there would result no vibrating movement and, moreover, there would be no sound. However, if one would sing a pitch too high, then the opening of the throat would be entirely closed, the air could not go out, and could therefore not produce a sound.[31]

When one wishes to make sound intelligible, then the uvula, palate, tongue, teeth and lips have to play a part, and "when one wishes to sing, these movements which serve only to produce sound must be skillfully combined and remain in the most friendly relationship." [32] According to the theory outlined above, Agricola argues that the opening in the glottis of the alto is larger than that of the soprano, with the tenor's larger than the alto's and the bass's largest of all. If one sopranist has a range both higher and lower than others, then his glottis must be capable of wider expansion and greater contraction than others.[33] Our author comes forth with an interesting piece of reasoning in explaining the mutation of the male voice. It is due to the throat muscles growing stronger, whereas because the muscles of the castrato remain weak his voice does not change. But women mature and get stronger, yet their voices remain high, and here he refuses to press his rationalizing and merely adds, "This question we shall leave to the natural scientists for further investigation." [34] The arguments proving that the glottis widens as the pitch descends and narrows as the pitch rises are repeated,[35] and then we are offered a full description of the experiments of Ferrein [36] together with the conclusions of the latter.[37] The interesting point here is that Agricola took so much care to explain and prove a theory of voice production which Ferrein had already shown to be entirely incorrect. His real attitude toward the whole problem of voice production is revealed in the following statement:

> While the natural scientists remain silent, it is not up to us, who do not consider the organs of the voice from the point of view of the anatomist or physician but from the point of view of the singer, to decide whether Mr. Ferrein's discoveries through his many experiments are correct or not, as little can be said against his conclusions derived therefrom.[38]

The last of the German sources on voice production, Hiller, has nothing to say about the actual mechanics of the larynx. He is only concerned with keeping the mouth open, with the lips, teeth, tongue and palate out of the way in order that the voice may come "freely out of the chest" (*frey aus der Brust*), and thus produce a good tone.[39]

French Sources

Mersenne accepts the dictum of Galen in saying that the opening of the glottis is "somewhat like the figure of an oval," [40] while Jumilhac repeats the statement of Aristotle and many scientists after him, that the voice "is produced by the air which is pushed from the lungs and chest and by . . . the vibration which is thus made by means of the larynx, glottis, palate, teeth and lips." [41]

A most inaccurate and unscientific explanation of voice production is offered in *Nouvelle Méthode.* All the inflections of the voice as to pitch, clarity, volume, etc., depend on the uvula. It not only opens the windpipe so that the air which forms the voice can come out, but "it is upon the flexibility of the uvula which depends all the variety of sounds of the voice." [42] Somewhat more accurate information is presented by Carré. After saying that a voice is the gift of nature, this author adds that all voices can be improved by exercise, faults may be corrected, voices strengthened, etc.; "nevertheless, from nothing one can make nothing." [43] His ideas on phonation are sketchy. Although the throat is considered the principal vocal organ because "it is by the diversity of movement of its cartilages that it produces the diversity of sounds of the voice (*c'est par la diversité du mouvement de ses cartilages, qu'il produit la diversité des tons de la voix*), nevertheless the windpipe (*trachée-artère*) is "the most proper organ of the voice (*la plus propre organe de la voix*)," since it is maintained that "it is it which, in widening or narrowing, with the arytenoid and the aid of the muscles of the larynx and by means of the epiglottis, makes the voice of the soprano or the bass, of the contra-bass or the contra-tenor." [44] When the windpipe is smooth, clean, and correctly proportioned then the voice is sweet and graceful, while the contrary causes it to be heavy and discordant. This writer goes completely astray when he says:

> Finally it is certain that the uvula or the little cartilagenous membrane resting on the windpipe as the fingers on a flute or on a flageolet, when it is correctly proportioned (that is to say when it is neither too large and heavy, nor too small), contributes greatly to the strength and beauty of the voice; because, governing the amount of air in inhaling and exhaling, it sets forth the voice, more or less, according to the cause and conditions, giving it its ornamentations, rhythms, cadences and trills." [45]

There is some further discussion of the chest, muscles of the chest, breathing, lips, jaws, teeth, mouth, tongue, palate, nares, etc., but it is all very much in the manner of a layman.

Blanchet cites the studies of the ancients, i.e., Aristotle, Cicero, Pliny, and Quintilian as being evidence proving that we also should study the voice. He considers such an investigation to be a necessity for every one and especially for the singing master. "He should not only reflect upon his own organs but still more on those of his pupils and if he succeeds in understanding them he will cause the most inept student to sing with success." [46] The teacher, says Blanchet, cannot go too far in research of this kind. The instrument of the voice is "extremely simple," and consists of the lungs, windpipe and larynx, all of which cooperate in forming the voice. He proposes to give a detailed description which turns out to be quite superficial. The larynx is made up of different cartilages bound together and of some muscles and is square on top and round on the bottom.[47] He is equally bland in his "detailed" description of the glottis, which "is the narrowest and the lowest part of the opening of the larynx; it is a horizontal cleft terminated by two lips, one on the right and the other on the left." [48] All these parts work together as follows: the lung is united to the windpipe and the latter to the larynx where the glottis is found. Blanchet offers a drawing which he says will make "sensible to the eyes that which I have tried to make sensible to the mind." [49] This figure is simple and shows the lungs, trachea, larynx, and lips of the glottis. The view is frontal and exterior, the larynx being very crudely drawn. What purports to be the lips of the glottis seems to be cartilages. Obviously the glottal lips could not be seen by an external-frontal view which showed the various cartilages. After describing Ferrein's experiments, Blanchet compares the tuning of the violin string to that caused by the action of the laryngeal muscles in varying the tension of the vocal bands, also the action of the violin bow on the string is compared to the action of expiration on the vocal bands. The first causes pitch changes while the latter changes the volume, and since the vocal bands are capable of a considerable change in tension the singer may extend the range of his voice accordingly. "If the glottal lips could be tightened *ad infinitum,* then one could produce an infinite number of different sounds." [50] Differences in vocal range depend on the thickness, length, and stiffness of the vocal bands and therefore, Blanchet argues, the voice that can sing through eighteen different pitches has to have glottal lips that are eighteen times as supple as one whose range would be limited to a single degree of pitch.[51] This writer reduces the art of singing to two principles, (1) "to cause the larynx to rise and fall properly" (*à faire monter et descendre à propos le larinx*), and (2) "to correct inhalation and exhalation" (*à bien inspirer et expirer*).[52]

The opinions of Rameau are most interesting. "We cannot do as we please with the larynx, windpipe, and glottis nor can we see their different motions and changes at each sound we wish to produce, but we know, at least, that it is not necessary to force them in making these changes, that it is necessary to allow them the freedom of following their natural movements."[53] As long as the breath lasts one can feel the tones follow the opening of the glottis, but if there is even a little concern about this glottal action, then there is pinching instead of dilation and that which one should feel at the opening of the throat is felt instead at the bottom. This must be carefully watched in all singing exercises. Moreover, the most ornamented singing can become natural to us when we observe the proper means of producing it correctly.[54]

We have already mentioned that the study by Kempelen was concerned with diction, and although it comes well toward the end of the *bel canto* period (1791) some of his opinions should be mentioned. "A little air, impelled by the lungs through the cleft of the glottis, produces the voice; several obstacles such as the tongue, teeth and the lips, oppose this resonant air causing the inflexion and the variety of sounds, each of which has its proper significance."[55] Later we are warned that a complete physiological study would go too far afield. Such a procedure, he says, if applied to violin teaching, would begin by giving the student a description of all the parts of that instrument, how they are connected, the kinds of wood used in each, the construction of the sounding board, strings, bridge, pegs, etc., as well as the muscles and tendons used in fingering and all the other complicated mechanics of violin-playing.[56] A general description of the organs of phonation and speech follow, with references to Galen, Dodart, and Ferrein. He repeats the theory of the latter that the air from the lungs causes the bands of the glottis to vibrate as the bow on a stringed instrument,[57] but again he seems to return to Galen when he says that the voice ceases when the glottis is too wide open or when it is too tightly closed.[58]

Our last French source, Mengozzi, says at the start:

A scientific definition of this organ [the voice] would not enter usefully into the organization of a singing method; however, for the knowledge of the different precepts which should be stated therein, it is necessary to establish the principal ideas of the means which help in the action of the voice.[59]

The palate, tongue, teeth and lips are held to be useful to the mechanism of the voice, while the lungs, windpipe, larynx, frontal and maxillary sinuses, and nasal passages all unite in its formation or modification. A very elementary and brief description is offered of all members of the latter group and we quote only his delineation of the larynx.

The *larynx* is one of the organs of breathing and the principal instrument of the voice. It is the upper part of the windpipe and it has the form of a short cylindrical canal which is opened by an oval cleft which is called the *glottis.* By means of this cleft the air descends and rises when we breathe, sing or speak. It has the faculty of being narrowed or widened at will and its more or less full expansion produces all the variety of sounds of the human voice. The glottis is protected by a very thin and very flexible cartilage called the *epiglottis.* This cartilage is mobile and has the shape of a leaf of ivy. It is inwardly concave and outwardly convex, and its chief purpose is to cover up the glottis when necessary.[60]

Mengozzi finishes by saying that all the parts mentioned have direct connections and are necessary in the production and modification of the voice.

English Sources

Only one of our English sources discusses the vocal organs *per se* and this comes late in time, 1811.[61] Corri makes an interesting statement as follows: "The late celebrated Dr. Arnold[62] very sensibly observed, that the anatomy of the voice would, perhaps, never be clearly explained till some physician should study the subject—who was also a good musician." [63] A short description of the vocal organs follows which is quoted from William Kitchiner, M.D. (1775–1827).[64] Corri, himself, merely says, that the physical requisites of a good singer are "spacious lungs, muscular larynx, wide mouth, with regular teeth." [65]

Comparisons and Summations

The voice teachers of the *bel canto* period were apparently interested in the processes of phonation but only to the extent of repeating the long-standing statements of the natural scientists or of giving simplified descriptions of current physiological treatises. Their interest seems to be motivated more by curiosity than by a desire to find information that would aid them in training the singing voice. Bontempi, the most learned of the Italians, takes a purely empirical attitude in eschewing what the physiologists have to say and relying entirely upon experience. Mancini was not so peremptory in denying physical influences. He examined the prospective student carefully, but only to find defects that would preclude a successful singing career. The Germans must be considered somewhat more accurate in their scientific statements. Kircher, Mattheson, and Agricola offer progressively more and more detail but much of their arguments are speculative and Agricola in the end admits that his responsibility lies in considering the voice from the standpoint of the singer and not the natural scientist.

Although there is also much speculation in evidence among the French, they seem to be the most scientific in their analyses of voice production. In Blanchet we have an arch-exponent of the scientific study and control of the vocal processes, well in advance of his time, even though he had little influence either with his contemporaries or later. When he speaks of the extreme simplicity of the vocal organs, skepticism enters and it may be understood why he was suspect. More impressive are Rameau's insistence on free vocal action and Mengozzi's statement that scientific vocal definitions have no place in a singing method. The English sources make no further contribution.

XIII. VOCAL HYGIENE

A discreet Person will never use such affected Expressions as, 'I cannot sing Today;—I've got a deadly Cold'; and in making his Excuse, falls a Coughing. I can truly say, that I have never in my Life heard a Singer own the Truth, and say, 'I'm very well today': They reserve the unseasonable Confession to the next Day, when they make no Difficulty to say, 'In all my Days my Voice was never in better Order than it was Yesterday.' [1]

If singers don't watch their diet, they become beggars in old age.[2]

The healthier the body, the sounder is the voice.[3]

Italian Sources

PROPER diet, regular sleep, and good physical care of the body were already recognized as having a salutary effect on the voice at the beginning of the *bel canto* period. These, as well as most of the therapeutic agents in use had been known since antiquity [4] and the seventeenth and eighteenth century singing manuals refer with some frequency to these hygienic practices which, by and large, were considered important for singers. After a number of general comments on the importance of good health and how best to maintain it,[5] Cerone suggests that singers should exercise frequently, avoid satiety in eating and drinking, choose light food, easy to digest, avoid spicy stew, cold oil, nuts, and fruits with thick rind. As to drinking, trebles, falsettos and contraltos must drink well-diluted wine while tenors and basses, if they are young, should put a little water in their wine, especially in the summer-time. In winter they should drink pure wine because, if watered, wine chills the stomach and tightens the chest. Elderly singers should drink pure wine because they do not have the natural heat of the stomach which young people have, and there should be "little converse with Madame Venus," especially in spring and autumn. There follow remedies for throat ailments: raw garlic, myrrh under the tongue, etc.[6]

Uberto merely offers the general statement that according to the teaching of the ancients, moderate eating and temperate living were important for singers,[7] while Doni argues that if Nero, the most luxury-loving and voluptuous of princes could abstain from foods harmful to the voice, then present-day (1647) singers should be able to do likewise. On the contrary, he reports that "modern" singers indulge in strong drink and all kinds of luxuries so injurious to the voice as to cause him to blush.[8] A rather similar regimen was recommended by Avella. Since a good voice is the prerequisite for singing, it is necessary to maintain good health for one cannot have a good voice free of all indispositions without good health. In order to conserve his voice a singer should be free to go about in his own way.[9] One should take rather strenuous exercise (*usque ad sudorum*—until one sweats) before eating, which should be done in moderation, avoiding all coarse foods.[10] One must not begin to sing too high nor too low for then the passages are injured and the windpipe becomes inflamed.

Lorente suggests the following for the preservation of a voice that is naturally good, clear, and sweet. Never begin singing with violence of spirit for this endangers the passages, impedes the windpipe, and puts the natural tone of the voice out of tune. Constant use of the voice is recommended since this is very effective in purifying, conserving, purging, and perfecting the voice, but this exercise should be undertaken before eating, or after the food is digested. There follows the usual advice about moderation in eating and drinking, also the kinds of food (light and easy to digest) as well as how and when wine should be drunk and by whom, in almost the same words used by Cerone and others. Remedies for hoarseness, cough, catarrh, etc., used by medical doctors are also given. Raw garlic clarifies the voice, benzoin dissolved in water and drunk is good for roughness of the throat and refines a husky voice, as does sweet-gum or gum of the storax tree. Congestion of blood in the head may spoil the voice and for this the singer should drink the fluid from crocodile root (*raiz del crocodilio*) boiled in water, which treatment causes nose bleeding. When a solo singer has to sneeze he may put it off by rubbing the upper gum vigorously. "All these remedies which we set forth here are very good and easy to do, for the conservation of the human voice, using them with moderation and with the advice of a medical doctor."[11]

Tosi only gives a few, but very pertinent, general maxims. "He that studies Singing must consider that Praise or Disgrace depends very much on his Voice which if he has a mind to preserve he must abstain from all manner of Disorders, and all violent Diversions.[12] . . . The best Time for Study is with the rising of the Sun; but those who are obliged to study, must employ all their Time which can be spared from their other necessary Affairs.[13] . . . Let him [the singer] shun low and disreputable Company, but, above all, such as abandon themselves to scandalous Liberties." [14] Mancini is even more brief, his references to vocal hygiene being more by implication than by direct advice. The young singer should not be started out too early because he is apt to associate himself with persons "not in love with moral living." Such a mode of life "injures his health and ruins forever chest and voice." [15] That he was aware of the effect of sickness or intemperate eating is shown by the following statement: "Among the temporary causes from which one sings out of pitch, is weakening of chest resulting from disease or temporary illness, or it is sometimes caused by indigestion, by eating too much or at no regular time or from other similar disorders." [16] One feels from these terse remarks of both Tosi and Mancini that they regarded vocal hygiene and good health as being so obvious as not to require extended discussion.

German Sources

Praetorius, the first of the German sources, writes about the aid to health in general to be derived from daily vocal practice. It is wonderful exercise, good for health, and well-being, works like a massage for athletes, warms internal organs, keeps passages open and prevents superfluity or coagulation of humors.[17] All of his authorities on vocal hygiene are from antiquity, viz., Scepsius, Pliny, Suetonius, Cicero and Quintilian.[18] Not until a century later do we find further comment on the care of the voice. Printz only advises against singing too loudly. "A singer should not shout excessively like a village sexton and a farmer but should sing, although loud and with some strength, pleasingly and delightfully." [19]

According to Mattheson, the first duty of the student of singing is to put the voice in good condition and preserve that condition. "Whoever wishes to sing well must examine diligently everything pertaining to the voice, must take care of it and pause, practice, guide, direct, control, and preserve it."[20] He adds that there are external and internal means of caring for the voice, to eliminate roughness due to excessive humors, to smooth out, moderate, strengthen, and preserve it. The ancients made a special profession of this science but at the time Mattheson was writing (1739) scarcely any of the music masters, with the exception of the Italians, understood and profited by it.[21]

> Among the German singers I have not known a better vocalist than the renowned concert master, Bimmler, who, when he had to sing in the evening, did not eat in the middle of the day, taking only now and then some fennel, as a tea, and practiced at the clavichord, singing his part with quiet, low voice, and with so much concentration that he brought out every time, new, well-selected ornamentations.[22]

A very excellent English singer, Abel, is mentioned as having maintained his voice until late age mostly due to his moderation in eating and drinking.

Just as correct singing will cause the voice to develop and improve, Mattheson says that it can be helped by a good diet and now and then by a little medicine. The diet is up to the individual while the medicine may be left to the doctors. Singers lack knowledge of their bodies (a great evil), and lack moderation in living habits, but the Plenus Venter (full belly) is about as helpful for singing as for studying. He considered wine, especially undiluted, to be harmful to the voice, as it contracts the throat and injures the chest. Well-brewed beer is better for the male voices than for the female and, finally, snuff and all fat and rich foods must be avoided. The good teacher, while he is not necessarily obliged to follow the same regimen, should know all the dietary and living regulations for singers. "A good general does not only think of giving orders to his soldiers, but also looks after their welfare."[23] As to medicines, caution is urged that, at least some of them be avoided or used sparingly as possible. Laxatives serve the best but julep and sweet lubricating syrups should never be used because, while they produce a certain smoothness, they leave the lungs and larynx coated with a slimy, tough, unclean, slippery matter. Mattheson advises instead a little zwieback or a spoonful of vinegar because they clean, sharpen, cool, and dry the throat. He knew a couple of famous women singers,

one of whom only took biscuit, the other something sour such as lemon or the like, when their throats were to be clean and they had to sing. Many who thought otherwise and preferred raisins or something sweet were astonished about such indelicate remedies, refused to imitate them, particularly with regard to the sour, and always came out on the losing end. In this matter each has to test the circumstances and the peculiarities of his temperament and reject that which does not agree with him.[24]

In a later book, Mattheson boils all this down to a few words. Good singers must lead a simple life—it is observed everywhere that singers eat very sparingly on the day of performance. The voice needs care—Germany has produced many good basses with beer-drinking, but wine is harmful since it contracts the throat and larynx.[25]

Marpurg warns that if a singer wishes to preserve his voice he should avoid air that is impure, foggy, too cold, too hot, smoky, and dusty. He should protect his chest well and stay out of the north wind.

He should not . . . sing directly after eating, he should observe a reasonable diet in eating and drinking and avoid everything bitter, pungent, salty, acid, and harsh, or take these at least very moderately and rarely. Lastly, he should neither sing too much nor shout because this makes the throat hoarse and ruins the voice.[26]

In his opinion schools should not give singing lessons from one to two o'clock in the afternoon since it is not good to sing on a full stomach. These should be shifted to some more suitable hour. "The most convenient hours for practice in singing are the hours of the morning." [27] When the boys' voices are changing, also during the period of puberty with girls, exercises should be made somewhat easier and with softer tone so that no harm may be done.[28]

After some very positive warnings against forcing the voice,[29] Hiller discusses in detail the proper *modus vivendi* for singers. Since high voices are more easily harmed than low voices, he says that they must have more attention and care. Especially is this true of boys between the ages of fifteen and seventeen. The singer should not strain his voice at this mutation, least of all he should try to sing high notes, which nature has begun to take from him, by forcing, otherwise he takes the risk of losing his voice entirely. The same consideration is required of girls' voices at the age of fourteen or fifteen, if they wish to properly preserve the voice. "But one does not need omit singing entirely: it must only be done less often and with a moderate tone." [30]

As to diet, Hiller says that anything deleterious to general health harms the voice. The singer must avoid impure, cold, and foggy air, especially in spring and autumn, so as to escape coughs and head colds, and in general, anything that might cause hoarseness. Smoke and dust are bad as are sharp, salty, sour, tart, fat, and overly sweet foods, although if any of these are taken moderately and not too often, no great harm will occur.

In short, moderation in eating and drinking, in which connection one should watch not so much what one eats and drinks, as *how much* one eats and drinks, together with a way of living that is good in all other respects, are for the person who cares for his health, and for the singer who wants to preserve his voice, of equal importance.[31]

Further, we are told that habitually sitting, as some do, in a stooped position with the abdomen pressed together is harmful to the voice, as are too violent exercises such as rapid running, excessive dancing, strenuous horse-back riding and the like. At least one should not try to sing immediately after such excitements or agitations, just as one should drink nothing, or very little, after singing. Singing in the cold open air or in apartments that are poorly ventilated or are too cold or too hot is also harmful.[32] A careful singer will refuse to sing immediately after eating "since the lungs have not all the freedom necessary for taking breath when the stomach is full." [33] Hiller refers to Marpurg's suggestion that lessons should not be given during the hour of one to two in the afternoon and agrees with him that the morning is the best time for singing practice, or at least a few hours after eating.

The usual stern warnings against forcing the voice too high and too loud, especially during the mutation years, are given by Petri, as well as the penalties resulting therefrom.[34] The singer should avoid cold and stormy weather, dust, smoke, and fatty vapours, and this author takes to task the cantor who sends his best singers out in all kinds of weather to sing at public affairs. Also more ordinary voices should be trained for this kind of work as well as other occasions in order that the best voices need not sing too loud, too much, nor too long for their natural strength.[35]

Like Hiller, Petri is not radical with regard to diet. "The singer should be careful, but not anxious, about his diet, for eating of unfavorable food is not so much harmful; it is rather its excessive eating that is wrong. The healthier the body, the sounder is the voice." [36] Strong beverages are most harmful to the lungs and hence to the voice. One should not offer them to a singer immediately after a performance. "How many have already gone to the cemetery in this manner!—Could one not better allow them to rest for a full hour, so that they could fully regain a quiet pulse and free lungs?" [37]

According to this author the best foods for singers are those containing little or no spices, salt, sugar, vinegar, and that are not overly fat. Over-baked and cooked fats and butter are most harmful, as are nuts and fresh wine, although if taken in moderation the results are not too harmful. Singing lessons and exercises or choir practice immediately after eating cause great damage both to health and voice because the lungs should always be able to breathe freely before one undertakes to sing. All violent exercises should be shunned such as climbing stairs, horse-back riding, dancing, fencing, nor should one sing after being excited by anger or other unruly passions.

> Finally, after singing one should sit completely still for awhile without drinking anything whether warm or cold. Later, one takes a very small sip, and then after a few minutes one takes more, but however strong the thirst may be, one should not satisfy it. Solomon says that preaching tires the body, but I believe that singing fatigues the body much more, and that one should, in this respect, exercise all possible care, lest one should do injury to the health, and besides, ruin the voice at the same time.[38]

If we wish to preserve the voice we should both eat and drink non-phlegm producing foods and drink, according to Kuerzinger.

Cold and fatty foods as well as "guzzling" are very harmful to the voice, and overheating from jumping, running, etc., will finish off the voice pretty quickly, and especially gulping down drinks while overheated and devouring victuals, fruit, cheese, and sweet stuff.

> There are excellent singers who take a little salad rather than anything sweet; for it is well known that sugar produces and increases phlegm. But fresh eggs eaten raw, also tea from fennel or anise-seed is beneficial to one's voice. A small glass of good wine for the soprano and an old brown beer, where available, for the alto, can do no harm.[39]

This author also warns the singer against forcing the voice, listing it as one of the chief errors in singing.[40]

The following points are made by Aubigny. The diet is most important to a singer; there should be no greasy foods, nuts, almonds and milk. One should never sing after a meal. Clothing should be worn that allows physical freedom, for the chest is a delicate organ and should not be restricted by clothing. A singer should accustom himself to changes in climate.[41] Too much smoking is bad.[42]

The advice of Lasser, the last German source, would seem to be a fair résumé of the general attitude of the German voice teacher on the care of the voice. He says that the teacher should enjoin upon the pupils that they carefully guard themselves against any excess in eating and drinking, and against all other excesses of whatever nature, against constant violent physical exercises and against over-heating, for only a regular way of living enables one to preserve the voice. Keeping the neck and chest moderately protected during inclement winter weather is necessary, but anyone who accustoms these parts to an over-delicate and weakening care will quite certainly be more subject to head colds, catarrh, and hoarseness. The hours of the forenoon are best for singing, but do not by any means exclude the afternoon and evening. However, singing immediately after eating is injurious to the voice and even harmful to health.[43]

French Sources

Mersenne, the great French musical savant of the seventeenth century, saw fit to stress the various means by which a singer should attend to his voice. One way is bodily exercise, before meals, until a good sweat is worked up, while a second is by singing as often as possible in the choirs of the church. The third consists in abstinence from all sorts of immoderate pleasures "and particularly from women as noted by Quintilian and Cornelius Celsus . . ." [44] As to the selection of food he is less specific since the varied circumstances of living oblige one to eat whatever is at hand. However he considers leeks and onions to be good for the voice because they clear the throat, and the same is true of crushed cabbage seed mixed with a little sugar of licorice, and of the syrup of tobacco (?). He cites the belief that a leaden plate placed on the stomach makes the voice clear and more agreeable. But he passes up all such extraordinary remedies and customs which may be used by performers and preachers to maintain their voices, and turns to the remedies for sickness, especially colds and inflammations which diminish the voice and render it hoarse, rough and disagreeable. Barley water and licorice with a little sugar is excellent to fight these inflammations. If this is not available a decoction of figs, or some syrup of violetts [*sic*], of waterlily, of *iniubes* (?) or of licorice; honey and water seems to be helpful. The reader is referred to Condronchius [45] for further remedies and advice on diet.[46]

Bacilly merely repeats the advice about singing in the morning before eating for then the voice is better disposed and there is less danger of colds and hoarseness.[47] Carré on the other hand offers detailed advice and arguments. After a lengthy harangue on the benefits of wine [48] he finishes with the statement, "But in order that it be just as beneficial to the voice as to the health, it is necessary that one drink only in moderation, wisdom, and discretion." [49] Then follows a tabulation of the ill effects of too much wine which causes the voice (as well as all other organs) to become weak and indisposed.[50] Nine rules are offered for those who wish to preserve their voices for a long time, to always be in good vocal state, and to avoid hoarseness. These "are absolutely necessary":

1. Never allow the feet to become cold, much less the head, and one must take great pains to keep the latter covered during the night.
2. Avoid as much as possible intemperate air, above all that which is too

hot or too cold; also the rays of the sun and of the moon, snow, winds, fogs, the evening damp and morning dew, and generally everything that taints the air.

3. Take care not to cry out too much nor to speak lengthily and with ardor.

4. Consume as little as possible of things that are cold and bitter, such as radishes, salads, sour grapes, vinegar, oranges, lemons, apples, etc., and in general of all kinds of fruits, or rough vegetables.

5. Never wash the mouth with, nor drink, water that is too cold and likewise beware of eating ice or snow.

6. Refrain, when at all possible, from the eating of oil or things containing it, or the swallowing of it unnecessarily.

7. Refrain from eating nuts and from using their oil, also that which is made from unripened olives.

8. Do not eat eels, because they are oily, slimy, and pituitous; they cause clogging and load the stomach.

9. Refrain from too much drinking, because the perfection of the voice consists in a moderate dryness of its organs: the throat which is one of them, is for that reason composed of a durable and cartilaginous substance, for the purpose of helping the air thrust by the lungs, making the voice clearer, louder, and more sonorous.[51]

To these "absolutely necessary" rules Carré adds some further precautionary advice. Take care in eating and drinking that nothing falls down the windpipe as this causes violent coughing, thus making the voice hoarse. Sneezing is just as bad and both are unfortunate for the throat should not be excited especially when one has to sing or speak in public; this disturbance often lasts from morning till night. These and many other things which are learned from experience are detrimental to the voice. Also the voice naturally degenerates with age and as these organs become weak and loose, the voice becomes lower, less sonorous and loud than those of younger singers.[52]

In the following chapter Carré discusses the causes of hoarseness and laryngitis along with remedies for the same. The principal causes are a chilled head, cold and wet feet, eating of fruit and raw vegetables, oil in general, nuts—especially old and rancid ones, eels, excessive drinking, and the straining of the voice in speaking or singing. A great number of remedies in the nature of drugs, liquids, and medicines together with how they are prepared, mixed, and applied, finishes the chapter.[53]

Only a few general rules are offered by Martini. The voice is the most beautiful, also the most fragile, of all instruments and has disorders that are sometimes temporary and sometimes incurable. Of all the prescriptions to preserve it "the best is to refrain from all excesses, from all beverages that are too strong, to protect oneself from too much heat and cold, and from passing too suddenly from one to the other; and from singing too high, too loudly, and too long at a time." [54]

The strictest precautionary measures for the care and preservation of the voice are urged by Tomeoni.[55] Since the voice is a most delicate and frail instrument and therefore susceptible to deterioration and even complete loss, it is necessary to give it the most serious care. Both virtuosi and amateurs should refrain from doing anything harmful to it. According to Tomeoni this includes all excesses of whatever kind, singing opposite an open fire or in moving air, singing in a room where there is a carpet or too much furniture, or which is too resonant (because the former causes one to sing too loudly, the latter, to sing off pitch), singing in the open air, before a mirror or too near a wall, or immediately after eating. Those who have colds should avoid singing entirely and should study harmony and accompanying for the time being. All kinds of nuts, raw artichokes, and all the fruits dried in the oven or in the sun are harmful and make the voice rough and unpleasant. He cautions the teacher against allowing a young voice to sing too high for too long a period of time. "It is a young plant whose nature and kind are unknown, and one must be content to water it daily with care so that it may grow and expand until the time when its established character will reveal the method of training that should be followed." [56]

Further advice against tiring the chest and damaging the voice of the child follows, especially during the years of mutation, when it is very profitable to emphasize the corollary music studies such as theory and piano.[57] Even the mature singer is urged to learn his music, using only half-voice.[58]

The eighth chapter of Mengozzi's *Méthode de Chant* is entitled "On the Preservation of the Voice." In it he says, in essence, what we have noted in preceding writers. The voice is subject to indispositions and maladies that may end in the loss of this organ of speech and song. In order to prevent this he insists that it is necessary for those in the singing profession to habituate themselves to a routine which will prevent as much as possible such difficulties. First of all it is necessary to avoid prolonged singing of exercises that are either too high or too low, at all times, as it is the middle ranges that are less tiring, and when the voice tires, it is then time to stop. Even the practice of another instrument for excessively long intervals does harm to the voice. We are told that one should avoid too violent exercises such as running, wrestling, fencing, and even lively and prolonged dancing. Sitting at a table writing for too long in one position is dangerous. Care should be taken not to change suddenly from hot to cold temperatures, and to avoid draughts, since colds and inflammations of the head and throat are the result. All excesses should be shunned and especially that of staying up at night for it is an absolute truth that immoderation destroys the voice and the results of long planning and hard study are then lost.[59]

English Sources

There is nothing to be found in the English singing manuals on vocal hygiene. Tenducci warns against forcing the voice especially on high tones, and suggests that it is best to sing a little at a time and often.[60] An anecdote by Kelly on a remedy for sore throat is pertinent.

> One day I was saying to him [Lord Howth] that I had a very bad sore throat; he told me he had a never failing recipe for a sore throat. His directions were,—just before going to bed, to get scalding water, and the finest double-refined sugar, with two juicy lemons, and above all, some good old Jamaica rum; and when in bed, to take a good jorum of it, as hot as bearable.
>
> 'Why, my lord,' said I, 'Your prescription seems to be nothing more than punch.' 'And what is better for a sore throat than good punch?' said his Lordship; 'good punch at night, and copious gargles of old Port by day, would cure any mortal disease in life.' [61]

Comparisons and Summations

It is obvious that all the writers of whatever nationality placed great emphasis on the proper care of the voice. It is also obvious that they were all in general agreement as to what this care should be. While it is true that some seem to be over-solicitous as to details of bodily care, diet, and methods of practice, it is however an indication of the seriousness with which they considered the profession of the singer and the preparation necessary for such a career. The earlier Italians appear to have been more solicitous in this respect while the eighteenth century sources reveal, only in passing, their concern. Tosi and Mancini are brief while Manfredini says nothing at all. The Germans and French, on the other hand, are quite explicit for the most part and, although extremes of physical caution and diet are sometimes counselled, there is much good advice and common sense to be found. The impression is gained that the singing teachers of Germany and France found more resistance to the moderations that were cautioned, because of the fact that singing was not looked upon as the highly specialized art and profession in these countries as it was in Italy. The more rigorous climate of the north must be considered a factor in their insistence on greater physical precautions. But there was general agreement in all countries that moderation in eating, drinking, and living, together with the avoidance of all vocal strain were the cardinal tenets to be followed in the hygiene of the voice.

XIV. GENERAL CONCLUSIONS

WITHIN the limits of this study the following conclusions appear to be defensible:

1. Italy was the wellspring of everything concerned with the art of singing. The writers of the singing manuals in other countries pay frequent homage to the singers and teachers of Italy. In Germany we find Mattheson, Agricola, Hiller, Marpurg, Petri, Lasser, and Aubigny acknowledging their debt to the Italians. In France the list of authors includes Rameau, Martini, Mengozzi, Blanchet, Tomeoni, and Fetis, while Burney, Bayly, Corri, Lanza, and Tenducci, in England, testify clearly to the influence from the south. It is of importance to note that Tomeoni and Mengozzi in France and Corri, Lanza, and Tenducci in England were all transplanted Italians while Tosi's *Osservazioni* was translated into English, German, and French, and Mancini's *Riflessioni* was published in German and French editions. There is no evidence of any counter-movement of German, French, or English influences on the singing style of Italy.

2. The vocal pedagogy of the bel canto period was based on empirical methods. There is a wealth of evidence that the singing experience of the teacher was a most important part of the teaching method. All the great teachers in Italy had been singers and the two great writers, Tosi and Mancini, were famous both as teachers and singers. Among the Germans, Mattheson, Petri, and Hiller were singers and together with Marpurg and Agricola were thorough students of the Italian opera and the Italian methods of singing. Tomeoni and Mengozzi in France and Tenducci, Corri, and Lanza in England were singers of note. The teacher set himself up as an example to be observed and imitated by the pupil, and further, the student was urged to see and study the performances of actors as well as singers. The words of Bontempi most accurately epitomize this attitude. "Our opinion is, that everything which is derived from experience has no need of reasoning. . . . We . . . shall be content to understand it [singing] with the teaching of experience itself" (see above, p.

127). Three-quarters of a century later Mancini wrote to the same effect:

> In giving the precise rules to a student let the teacher not only tell him and explain to him, but let him illustrate his meaning by making himself an example. . . . Let the experienced teacher follow this method and he will soon be convinced how much more preferable are practical demonstrations to general rules. (See above, pp. 103 f.)

3. There was, at all times, great stress placed upon the natural methods of singing, as well as the natural gifts necessary before a person should even attempt to become a singer. These latter included a pleasing appearance, adequate breathing capacity, no malformations of face, mouth, or body, a good ear, etc. The posture must be natural, the tone must be produced naturally, there must be no distortion of mouth or facial features, and in short the entire process of singing must be free of anything that might interfere with ease in the production of the voice. Any kind of artificiality or affectation was looked upon with scorn and was discouraged from the start.

4. Theories of phonation were based on incomplete or incorrect information. The anatomy of the throat was for all practical purposes well understood but the physiology of the vocal organs was by no means complete. Before the experiments of Ferrein in 1741 the theories of phonation were based on the incorrect speculations of Galen and even after this time there is considerable doubt that Ferrein's theories were ever instrumental in affecting teaching methods. Even Agricola, who gives the most complete exposition of phonation theories, both pre- and post-Ferrein, of any of the authors of singing manuals, says:

> It is not up to us, who do not consider the organs of the voice from the point of view of the anatomist or physician but from the point of view of the singer, to decide whether Mr. Ferrein's discoveries . . . are correct or not. (See above, p. 133.)

Most of the writers present simplified, superficial, and often incorrect descriptions of the vocal organs that were apparently included to satisfy the curious. Therefore it may be safely assumed that physiological knowledge had little or nothing to do with the vocal technique of the *bel canto* period.

5. There were no attempts at the conscious control of particular muscles. The singer was urged to keep a natural and free muscular balance of all his physical faculties in order that they could respond naturally and quickly to the sense and idea of the music and the text. All the external mechanical forces as well as the inward nervous and muscular controls were given a set of relationships that encouraged their free and unhampered functioning. These relationships were of the greatest aid in allowing virtuosity to triumph and they enabled the artists of the *bel canto* period to develop the technical skills for which they were acclaimed. There was only one exception, Blanchet (see above, pp. 97 f., 135 f.), who insisted that by muscular control of the larynx, even the tone-deaf could become perfect singers. His theories never gained recognition; moreover, he was not a musician, but had conducted considerable research on phonation.

6. On vocal hygiene, advice varied from the practical and useful to the nonsensical, much as today. Although some writers urged a regimen of living that amounted to pampering, the majority insisted that moderation and temperance in all things was the best for singers. Whatever encouraged good health also encouraged good singing and it was unlikely that a sound voice could be found in an unsound body. The greatest care was always taken to avoid overtaxing the voice and as a consequence the voices usually retained their freshness and beauty to an advanced age. This is quite contrary to present-day conditions.

7. There was general agreement on the broad precepts of singing, and more important, on the means by which these ends were to be reached. It is really notable to find the identical phrase or sentence turning up in book after book, even in the different languages. This made it possible for standards to be established and to be maintained, a condition impossible at the present time when there is almost a complete lack of agreement on method. A few minor differences are to be found such as whether a wind, string or keyboard instrument is best for developing the ear, and what and how many vocal registers exist. But the means of blending registers were agreed upon as was the necessity for acquiring a good ear.

IN FINE

THE all-important question finally arises: What are the implications for the teacher and student of singing?

First of all, the popular conception that the teaching methods of the *bel canto* period were secret and have been lost is proven to be a myth. Too many teachers have trafficked thus, albeit claiming at the same time to possess the secret themselves. Quite to the contrary, the methods appear to be so obvious, easy, and natural as to preclude the efficaciousness of the usual line of nostrums peddled in the average studio. It is only by means of the latter that pupils are held in a state bordering on hypnotism. The evidence is at hand. All that is needed is the light of musicological investigation on each aspect of *bel canto*. As far as this study goes it reveals an amazingly direct and simple approach to the business of singing.

It must be admitted that the particular vocal technique and virtuosity of the *bel canto* artists may be impossible to achieve today. The peculiarly singular and unnatural gifts of the castrati due to a bizarre custom now uncountenanced for the purposes of the art of song lifted vocalism to an apogee no longer within the realm of probability. But their twin ideals of beautiful tone and florid line are still highly desirable in performance and when achieved in substantial measure are greatly enjoyed even by the musically unsophisticated. The means by which these were attained is no secret. Granted that much of our music calls for more declamatory, dramatic, and subjective treatment, still the vocal masterpieces of the seventeenth and eighteenth centuries will not reveal their true worth except when performed with the lyrical and florid qualities of *bel canto*. The harrowing performances by oratorio soloists today are grim testimony that these qualities are either misunderstood or totally ignored.

There were no short cuts or "open sesames" to the art of singing. Lessons were begun at an early age and they were continued without interruption, although with the greatest care, until mastery was reached. There was no attempt to make a voice "big" unless it was meant by Nature to develop in that way. Voices were noted for their sweetness, brilliance, vigor and virtuosity, and performers were noted for their intelligence and taste, but there was seldom mention of great volume and quantity. It is safe to say that the shouting and bellowing so frequently heard now would have received short shrift at the hands of the eighteenth century opera audience. As already noted, the methods were simple and direct. Once the prospective pupil was conceded to have the necessary natural gifts, he was taught to sing easily and naturally and by direct example from his teacher as well as from artists already successful.

It may be argued that it is no longer possible for the would-be artist to begin his training at such an early age nor can he study under the circumstances that obtained in the conservatories of eighteenth century Italy. This must be admitted, however: modern psychological studies have given strong evidence that long years spent in formalized drill are no longer necessary for the acquiring of advanced muscular techniques, and a great saving in time may result when technical problems are taken from the music itself. Another important time-saver would be the establishment of standardized precepts for the study of singing and the scrapping of the great welter of utterly intangible and thoroughly confusing theories that spring eternal in the voice studios across the land. Perhaps no other one thing could contribute so much to the raising of the calibre of vocalism today as the acceptance of formulae and the methods of putting them into practice.

In our opinion the methods of teaching voice in the *bel canto* period are clearly delineated in the instruction manuals of the times. The unexcelled vocal artistry of those performers and their influence on singing throughout the Western World are more than sufficient evidence that a sympathetic and thorough study of the entire subject would indicate positive means for the restoring of an improved art of singing in the studios, concert halls and opera houses of today.

NOTES

Preface

1. James L. Mursell and Mabelle Glenn, *The Psychology of School Music Teaching,* New York, Silver, Burdette Co., 1938, p. 278.

2. The reader is referred to W. J. Henderson, *Early History of Singing,* New York, 1921; G. Fantoni, *Storia universale del canto,* Milan, 1873. 2 vols. in 1. These have been of little value in this study.

3. Francis Rogers, Article in Educational Department of *Musical America,* Dec. 25, 1940, p. 35.

4. L. J. DeBekker, *Music and Musicians,* New York, Nicholas Brown, 1925, p. 58.

II. Definition of Terms

1. *Harvard Dictionary of Music,* ed. Willi Apel, Cambridge, Harvard University Press, 1944.

2. "The term is nowadays in use in the announcements of a large number of singing masters, each of whom (and he alone) possesses the secrets of the great Italian teachers." P. A. Scholes, *The Oxford Companion to Music,* London, Oxford University Press, 1943, p. 85.

3. See *Musical Courier,* Jan. 15, 1946, pp. 14 f. Advertisements of voice teachers in Sunday Music Section of New York *Times,* etc.

4. Cf. T. Baker, *Dictionary of Musical Terms,* 25th ed., New York, G. Schirmer, 1939; Scholes, *op. cit.,* pp. 85, 871.

5. Cf. Hugo Riemann, *Musik-Lexikon,* 11th ed. Berlin, M. Hesse, 1929, 2 vols.; Hans Moser, *Musiklexikon,* Berlin, M. Hess, 1935, 2 vols.

6. Rene Vannes, *Essai de Terminologie Musicale,* Paris, Eschig, 1925.

7. Cited above, note 4.

8. Benelli, *Regole per il Canto Figurato,* Dresden, 1819, 16.

9. Andrea Costa, *Considerazione sopra L'Arte del Canto in Generale,* London, 1824, pp. 7 f.

10. F. Florino, *Breve Metodo di Canto,* Naples, 1840 [dedicated to Crescentini].

11. *Ibid.,* p. 1.

12. *Ibid.,* p. 2.

13. *Ibid.,* p. 4.

14. *Ibid.,* p. 6.

15. *Ibid.,* p. 7.

16. This collection was published in Milan shortly after Vaccai returned from London in 1838. The exact date has not been established.

17. See Giulio Vaccai, *Vita di Nicola Vaccai,* Bologna, 1882, pp. 141 f.

18. Francesco Lamperti, *Guida teorica-pratica-elementare per lo studio del canto,* Milan, Ricordi, 1864. "E una triste ma innegabile verità che il canto trovasi oggigiorno in uno stato di deplorabile decadenza."

19. *Op. cit.,* Preface, p. ix.

20. Francesco Lamperti, *A Treatise on the Art of Singing,* transl. by J. C. Griffith, London, Ricordi, *ca.* 1877.

21. G. A. Biaggi, "Considerazioni della Musica Italiana," in *Regio Istituto Musicale,* Florence, 1865, pp. 41–55.

22. G. A. Biaggi, Pietro Romano, and Luigi Casamorata, "Relazione delle commissione," in *Regio Istituto Musicale,* Florence, 1866, pp. 33–39. Report signed July 7, 1865, p. 37.

23. *La Scena,* Trieste, May 4, 1865.

24. Ed. Tommaseo and Bellini, Turin, 1865, I, pt. 2, 920, entry 42.

25. Cesare Perini, "Quale sia il miglior metodo da adottarsi onde il bel canto possa riottenere il suo primato in Italia." In *La Scena,* Trieste, Dec. 14, 21, 28, 1865, nos. 33, 34, 35.

26. F. I. Polidoro, "Alcuni pensieri sull'insegnamento del Canto." In *La Scena,* Nov. 22, 1866, Trieste.

27. P. 117. "E doloroso a dirsi . . . ma pur troppo è vero che pochi sono coloro che conservano e propagano le vere tradizioni del bel canto."

28. M. Francesco D'Arcais, "Memoria sulla pratica conoscenza della musica in tutto quello puo interessare l'esercizio dell'arte del canto." In *Regio Istituto Musicale,* Florence, 1868, pp. 61–65.

29. *Ibid.,* p. 62. "Le cure degli allievi e dei maestri erano rivolte più all'educazione della voce che alla scienza musicale propriamente detta."

30. G. A. Biaggi, "Della vita e delle opere di Gioacchino Rossini." In *Regio Istituto Musicale,* Florence, 1869, pp. 15–46.

31. G. A. Biaggi, "Del Melodramma e del *Lohengrin* di R. Wagner." In *Regio Istituto Musicale,* "Luigi Cherubini," *Atti dell' Accademia,* 1872, pp. 31–44. See p. 34, where the author says that this style abandons the procedures of melodic discourse and *bel canto.* He echoes Rossini's laconic comment: "abbaiamenti." Also attention may be called to Biaggi's preface to the *Vita di Nicola Vaccai* (cited above), pp. xv, xxiv.

32. Adolfo Baci, "Osservazioni sul teatro di musica in Italia." In *Regio Istituto Musicale,* "Luigi Cherubini," *Atti dell' Accademia,* 1872, pp. 58–69, esp. p. 66.

33. *Ibid.,* p. 67.

34. F. Lamperti, *L'arte del Canto,* Milan, 1883, p. 30.

35. G. N. Carozzi, *Guida ant'igenica di ginnastica vocale,* Milan, 1890.

36. "Oggi queste tradizioni del nostro *bel canto* sono sbaragliate, e non solo dal nuovo indirizzo del l'opera drammatica basato sulla declamazione, ma delle stesse condizioni deplorabili dell'arte lirica, caduta in balia dell'ignoranza e del mestiere." *Ibid.,* p. 3.

37. H. D. Mannstein [real name Steinmann], *Geschichte, Geist und Ausubüng des Gesanges von Gregor dem Grossen bis auf unsere Zeit,* Leipzig, 1845.

38. *Ibid.,* p. 139.

39. "Der schöne Ton ist allein das Material, woraus der Sänger seine Bildungen schaffen darf," p. 144.

40. ". . . die Schöpfer des schönen Tones," p. 145.

41. F. S. Gassner, *Universal-Lexikon der Tonkunst,* Stuttgart, 1849.

42. ". . . schöngebildeten Ton."

43. Gassner, *op. cit.,* pp. 343–46.

44. C. F. Nehrlich, *Die Singkunst,* 2d ed., Leipzig, 1853.

45. ". . . die Klangschönheit ist ihr 'Ein' und 'alles.' "

46. Nehrlich, *op. cit.,* pp. 58 ff.

47. F. Wieck, *Klavier und Gesang,* Leipzig, 1853.

48. *Ibid.,* pp. 40–59.

49. "Wenn ich überhaupt vom Gesang spreche, so meine ich nur den schönen Gesang, die Basis der feinsten und vollendetsten musikalischen Darstellung," p. v. The words "schönen gesang" are to be noted here as they are the German equivalent of *bel canto.*

50. F. Sieber, *Vollständiges Lehrbuch der Gesangskunst,* Berlin, 1858.

51. "Bildung des schönen Tones." Pp. 72–74.

52. "Während unsere angehenden Opernsänger sofort auf den dramatischen Ausdruck losstenern, bilden die Italiener vor allem die selbständige Schönheit der Stimme, die allseitige Technik des Singens; zuerst gilt ihnen der schöne Ton." *Deutsche Musik-Zeitung,* Vienna, May 12, 1860, p. 60.

53. *Loc. cit.*

54. Martin Haertinger, *Das Grundgesetz der Stimmbildung für den Kunstgesang,* Mainz, 1872, pp. 4 ff., and elsewhere.

55. H. Mendel, *Musikalisches Conversations-Lexikon,* Berlin, 1870–1879, 11 vols. Cf. IV (1874), 212–24.

56. Cited above.

57. "Es triumphirt in unsern Opernhäusern meist nur noch die Lunge, Geschmacksrohheit, Unnatur, Karrikatur, sinnloses Outriren, somit der verwerflichste Missbrauch der menschlichen Stimmen." p. 191.

58. "Sie haben kein Gefühl für's Schöne, sie können nicht einmal einen natürlichen, seelischen, reizenden, vornliegenden Ton von einem kalten, hässlichen, gepressten, forcirten, kehligen Ton uterscheiden." p. 192.

59. Hugo Riemann, *Musik-Lexikon,* Leipzig, 1882.

60. *Ibid.*, p. 304.

61. F. Bremer, *Handlexikon der Musik,* Leipzig, 1882. See "Gesangmethode."

62. Julius Hey, *Deutscher Gesangs-Unterricht,* Mainz, 1886. 4 parts.

63. *Ibid.*, part 3, p. 160.

64. "Die Zeit der italienischen Oper scheint gründlich vorüber zu sein." *Allgemeine Musik-Zeitung,* 1885, p. 170.

65. Cf. *Allgemeine Musik-Zeitung,* 1885, p. 20; 1888, pp. 127, 462; 1889, p. 409; 1890, pp. 45 ff., 130, 228; 1891, p. 130.

66. F. Sieber, *Il Bel Canto.* 2 vols. Berlin, ca. 1887.

67. "In unserer Zeit, wo sich das widerwärtigste Schreien aller Orten unter der beschönigenden Devise 'dramatischen Gesanges,' breit macht, wo die unkundige Menge viel mehr darauf zugeben scheint, wie laut als wie schön gesungen wird, ist vielleicht eine Sammlung von Gesängen willkommen, welche—wie der Titel besagt—dazu beitragen möchte, dem bel canto wieder zu seinem recht zu verhelfen."

68. F. J. Fétis, "Examen de l'état actuel de la Musique en France," in *Revue Musicale,* 1827, p. 444.

69. ". . . la tradition de l'excellente école italienne de cette époque et retarda de près de trente ans la connaissance de l'art du chant en France." *Loc. cit.*

70. F. J. Fétis, *Biographie Universelle,* Brussels, 1844, VIII, 382. Article on Tosi.

71. "L'époque de Rossini a été celle où le beau chant italien a jeté son dernier éclat." A. C. E. Boisson, *Petite Encyclopédie,* 1884, II, 82.

72. "Les interprètes de Rossini, de Bellini, et de Donizetti furent les derniers élèves des maitres du *bel canto* ou de l'art de chanter du XVIII siècle." H. Lavoix, *Histoire de la Musique,* Paris, 1884, p. 299.

73. Sabrina H. Dow, *Artistic Singing,* Boston, 1883, Cf. pp. 42, 67, 69 ff.

74. A. B. Bach, *Musical Education,* London, 1884. Cf. p. 247 and pp. 150 ff.

III. Laryngology

1. Gordon Holmes, "History of the Progress of Laryngology from the Earliest Times to the Present," in *The Medical Press,* London, July 15, 1885, p. 49, and subsequent issues to Sept. 9, 1885. This was translated into German and published as a book in the following year. A more recent, but less detailed treatment, based on the work of Holmes, is that of Jonathan Wright, *A History of Laryngology and Rhinology,* Philadelphia, Lea and Febiger, 1914.

2. Holmes, *op. cit.*, p. 49.

3. Aristotle, *De Anima,* transl. by W. S. Hett. Loeb Classical Library. New York, Putnam, 1935, p. 420b.

4. Aristotle, *De Audibilibus,* in *Minor Works,* transl. by W. S. Hett. Loeb Classical Library. New York, Putnam, 1936, pp. 800a–803a.

5. Aristotle, *Problemata,* transl. by E. S. Forster. Loeb Classical Library. New York, Putnam, 1932. Book XI, "Problems on the Voice," and Book XIX, "Problems connected with Harmony."

6. Holmes, *op. cit.,*.p. 72.

7. *Ibid.,* pp. 72 ff.

8. *Ibid.,* p. 73.

9. *De Vitiis Vocis,* Francofonte, 1597.

10. *Historia anatomica,* Lugduni Batavorum, 1597; *De Visione, Voce, Auditu,* Venice, 1600; *De Voce, de Gulo, de Respiratione et ejus Instrumentis,* Venice, 1601.

11. *De Larynge Vocis Organo Historia Anatomica,* Ferrara, 1600.

12. *De Vocis Auditusque Organis Historiae,* Ferrara, 1600.

13. Holmes, *op. cit.,* p. 120.

14. Cf. M. S. Murrich and J. Playfair, *Leonardo da Vinci, the Anatomist,* Baltimore, Williams and Wilkins (Published for Carnegie Institute of Washington) 1930, chap. 15, pp. 191–97.

15. Marin Mersenne, *Harmonie Universelle,* Paris, 1636. Cf. Prop. III, XIII, XVI, and XXXVI of the part entitled, "De la voix, Des Parties qui servent, à la former, de sa definition, de ses proprietez, e de l'oüye."

16. Denis Dodart, "Mémoire sur les causes de la voix de l'Homme," in *Mémoires de l'Académie de Sciences,* Paris, 1703, pp. 1–50.

17. *Ibid.,* p. 42.

18. Holmes, *op. cit.,* p. 121.

19. Antoine Ferrein, "De la Formation de la Voix de l'Homme," in *Académie Royale des Sciences,* Paris, 1741, pp. 409–32.

IV. Vocal Hygiene Before 1600

1. Synesius, in Migne, *Patrologiae Cursus Completus,* Series Graeca, Vol. LXVI, col. 1148.

2. Cf. Holmes, *op. cit.,* p. 74.

3. St. Jerome, Commentary on Epistle to the Ephesians, III, 5:19, in Migne, *op. cit.,* Series Latina, Vol. XXVI, col. 528.

4. Antiphon, *Oratio de Choreuta.*

5. Aristotle, *Problemata,* 901b.

6. *Ibid.,* 904b.

7. Quintilian, *Institutio Oratoria,* XI, iii, 19.

8. Aristotle, *op. cit.,* 900a.

9. *Ibid.,* 901a.

10. *Ibid.,* 904b.

11. *Ibid.,* 903b.

12. Isidorus, "De Ecclesiasticis Officiis," ii, 12, in Migne, *op. cit.,* Vol. LXXXIII, col. 792. Rabanus Maurus, "De Institutione Clericorum," ii, 48, *ibid.,* Vol. CVII, col. 362.

13. Clearchus apud Athenaeum, xiv, c. 19.

14. Beroaldus: *Commentarius ad Suetonium.* London, 1548. In "Nerone," p. 533.

15. Suetonius, Life of Nero, c. 20.

16. Athenaeus, iii, 18, 19. Here is an account of how the abstinence from eating figs for eighteen years resulted in one person becoming a famous actor.

17. *Ibid.,* ii, 42.

18. Cicero, *De Oratore,* I, ii, 70.

19. Quintilian, *op. cit.,* transl. by H. E. Butler. Loeb Classical Library. London, Heinemann, 1921. XI, iii, 19–20. (Henceforth, "Loeb Classical Library" will be referred to simply as "Loeb.")

20. *Ibid.,* XI, iii, 22–23.

21. *Ibid.,* XI, iii, 28.

22. In Martin Gerbert, *Scriptores Ecclesiastici de Musica Sacra.* St. Blasius, 1784, III, 233.

23. See pp. 30 f.

24. Camillo Maffei, *Delle lettere del S*[or] *Giov. Camillo Maffei da Solofra, Libri due: Dove tra gli altri bellissimi d'apparar di cantar di Garganta, senza maestro,* Napoli, 1562. Quoted by Franz Haböck, "Die Physiologischen Grundlagen der Altitalienischen Gesangschule" in *Musik* (*Die*) VIII (Sept., 1909), 343.

25. See pp. 15 f.

26. *Op. cit.,* Introduction.

27. *Ibid.,* Bk. I, chap. 13, p. 64.

28. *Ibid.,* chap. 14, p. 68.

29. *Ibid.,* Bk. II, chap. 1, p. 88.

30. *Ibid.,* p. 90.

31. Cites Celsus, Bk. 7, chap. 25.

32. I have not been able to identify this plant.

33. *Ibid.,* p. 92.

34. *Ibid.,* p. 93.

35. *Ibid.,* pp. 98 f.

36. *Ibid.,* pp. 93 f.

37. *Ibid.,* p. 113.

38. In A. Lavignac, *Encyclopédie de la Musique et Dictionnaire du Conservatoire,* Paris, Libraire Delgrave, 1926, Part II, 871–904.

39. *Ibid.,* p. 874.

V. Development of Singing Technique Prior to 1600

1. In this chapter extensive use has been made of the writer's master's thesis, *The Art of Singing in Antiquity and the Middle Ages,* Columbia University, 1943.

2. Homer, *The Odyssey,* transl. by G. H. Palmer, Cambridge, Mass., Houghton, Mifflin, 1929. Cf. Book VIII, pp. 11, 43–45, 63, 67, 262–67, and *ad passim.*

3. *Homeric Hymns,* transl. by H. G. Evelyn-White (Loeb), London, W. Heineman, 1914, p. 543.

4. *Op. cit.,* pp. 566–97.

5. These were, in large measure, singers.

6. Plato, *Laws,* transl. by R. G. Bury (Loeb), New York, Putnam, 1926, p. 660.

7. Plato, *Republic,* transl. by Paul Shorey (Loeb), New York, 1930, pp. 568B, 595A, 607–8.

8. *Laws,* p. 659.

9. *Laws,* p. 669F.

10. Aristotle, *Politics,* transl. by H. Rockham (Loeb), New York, Putnam, 1932. Cf. pp. 1337b–1342a.

11. *Op. cit.,* 1339b, 8.

12. *Loc. cit.*

13. *Melopoeia* included both composing and singing.

14. Aristotle, *Poetics,* transl. by W. H. Fyfe (Loeb), New York, Putnam, 1927, Book VI, pp. 1–7.

15. *Loc. cit.*

16. Cf. *op. cit.,* p. 1461b.

17. Aristotle, *Rhetoric,* transl. by J. H. Freese (Loeb), New York, Putnam, 1929, p. 1403b.

18. Aristotle, *De Audibilibus,* in Minor Works, transl. by W. S. Hett (Loeb), New York, Putnam, 1936.

19. *Ibid.,* p. 800a.

20. *Ibid.,* p. 801a.

21. *Ibid.,* p. 803a.

22. *Ibid.,* p. 800b.

23. *Ibid.,* p. 803a.

24. *Loc. cit.*

25. Aristotle, *Problemata,* transl. by E. S. Forster (Loeb), New York, Putnam, 1932.

26. *Op. cit.,* p. 918b.

27. Dionysius of Halicarnassus, *De Compositione Verborum,* ed. with translation by W. Rhys Roberts, London, Macmillan, 1910.

28. *Op. cit.,* p. 127.

29. *Ibid.,* p. 269.

30. *Ibid.,* p. 283.

31. Plutarch, *Moralia,* transl. by several hands, ed. W. W. Goodwin, Boston, 1870, 5 vols. (*De Musica,* 102–35).

32. Gustav Reese, *Music in the Middle Ages,* New York, 1940, p. 18, says that the authenticity of his authorship is open to question.

33. *De Musica,* chap. 15.

34. *Ibid.,* chap. 31.

35. Quintilian, *Institutio Oratoria,* transl. by H. E. Butler (Loeb), London, 1921. XI, iii, 19.

36. *Ibid.,* XI, iii, 22–24.

37. Augustine (Saint), *De Musica,* transl. by R. Catesby Taliaferro, Annapolis, St. John's Bookstore, 1939 Bk. VI, superscription, p. 148.

38. Cf. Martin Gerbert, *Scriptores Ecclesiastici de Musica Sacra,* St. Blasius, St. Blasius Press, 1784, I, 38–39, 246; II, 25, 225, 233; III, 120. Boethius, *De Institutione Musica,* ed. G. Friedlein, Leipzig, 1867, I, 34.

39. "Is vero est musicus, qui ratione perpensa canendi scientiam non servitio operis sed imperio speculationis adsumpsit." *Loc. cit.*

40. Gerbert, *op. cit.,* II, 253.

41. *Ibid.,* III, 235–36.

42. *Ibid.,* III, 68.

43. *Ibid.,* III, 317.

44. Gerbert, *op. cit.,* III, 68.

45. Gerbert, *op. cit.,* III, 344.

46. E. De Coussemaker, *Scriptorum de Musica Medii Aevi Nova Series,* Paris, A. Durand, 1864, I, 8.

47. *Ibid.,* II, 2.

48. De Muris, in Gerbert, *op. cit.,* III, 216, 236; "A Certain Carthusian Monk" in Coussemaker, *op. cit.,* II, 470; Philip de Vitry, in *ibid.,* III, 45; Simon Tunstede, in *ibid.,* IV, 233; Adam de Fulda, in Gerbert, *op. cit.,* III, 352.

49. Coussemaker, *op. cit.,* I, 158.

50. *Ibid.,* I, 93.

51. Cf. "A Certain Carthusian Monk," Coussemaker, *op. cit.,* II, 446; Simon Tunstede, *ibid.,* IV, 259; Bull of Pope John XXII, in *The Oxford History of Music,* Vol. I; "The Polyphonic Period," by H. E. Woolridge,

London, Oxford University Press, 1929, p. 294; Ornithoparcus, "Of the Ten Precepts Necessary for Every Singer," from Dowling's translation (1609), reprinted in Hawkins, *General History of the Science and Practice of Music,* London, 1776, II, 404 ff., precept #9.

52. Cf. Gerbert, *op. cit.,* I, 173.

53. *Ibid.,* II, 249.

54. Quoted in Paul Henry Lang, *Music in Western Civilization,* New York, Norton, 1941, from Andre Pirro, p. 140.

55. Cf. Coussemaker, *op. cit.,* IV, 344.

56. *Ibid.,* 382.

57. Cf. *Ibid.,* II, 193.

58. Cf. Gerbert, *op. cit.,* III, 233–34.

59. *Ibid.,* 352.

60. *Loc. cit.*

61. Gerbert, *op. cit.,* III, 316.

62. *The Oxford History of Music,* Vol. I, "The Polyphonic Period . . . 330–1400," by H. E. Woolridge, London, Oxford University Press, 1929, pp. 293 ff.

63. Lang, *op. cit.,* 140.

64. Cf. *Oxford History,* I, 294.

65. August W. Ambros, *Geschichte der Musik,* Breslau, 1862–1878, II, 345.

66. Coussemaker, *op. cit.,* IV, 129. Bk. II, ch. 20 of the *Liber.*

67. Cf. *Sammelbände der internationalen Musikgesellschaft,* IX (1907–1908), 538; *Revue Musicale,* June, 1932, p. 10; A. Schering, *Beispiele,* #166, p. 176.

68. G. W. Lanfranco, *Scintille di Musica,* Brescia, 1533, p. 33, cited in Bernhard Ulrich, *Die Grundsätze der Stimmbildung während der a capella-Periode und zur Zeit des Aufkommens der Oper, 1474–1640,* Leipzig, B. & H., 1912, p. 112.

69. G. C. Maffei, *Discorso della Voce,* Naples, 1562, cited in Ulrich, *op. cit.,* pp. 33 f.

70. G. Zarlino, *Istitutioni Harmoniche,* Venetia, 1573, p. 240.

71. G. C. Zacconi, *Prattica di Musica,* Venetia, 1592, facing p. 54.

72. *Op. cit.,* facing p. 55.

73. Bragio Rossetti, *Libellus de rudimentis musicas,* Verona, 1529, cited in Ulrich, *op. cit.,* pp. 59–63.

74. Johann Frosch, *Rerum musicarum opusculum rarum ac insigne,* Argentorati, 1535. Cf. ch. 19.

75. Cited in Ulrich, *op. cit.,* p. 59.

76. *Ibid.*, p. 38.

77. *Op. cit.*, facing p. 59.

78. Cf. G. B. Bovicelli, *Regole, Passaggi di musica,* Venice, 1594, cited in Ulrich, *op. cit.*, pp. 59–60.

79. A. P. Coclicus, *Compendium Musices,* Nuremberg, 1552, cited in Ulrich, *op. cit.*, p. 9.

80. *Organo* here might mean any musical instrument, as Latin *organum* usually does.

81. Nicola Vicentino, *L'antica musica ridotto alla moderna prattica,* Rome, 1555. Facing p. 55.

82. G. Zarlino, *op. cit.*, p. 240.

83. Cf. *op. cit.*, p. 425.

84. *Op. cit.*, pp. 43–44.

85. *Op. cit.*, p. 58.

86. Cf. *op. cit.*, p. 59.

87. ". . . non fractis et remissis vocibus muliebre quiddam de more sonantes, sed virili sonitu et affectu." Cf. S. Poisson, *Traité théorique et pratique du plain-chant,* Paris, 1750, pp. 408–10; J. Bona, *Opera Omnia,* Antwerp, 1723, p. 540.

88. "Viros de cet virili voce cantare, et non more femineo tinnulis, vel, ut vulgo dicitur, falsis vocibus histrionicam imitari lasciviam," in Migne, *Pat. Lat.*, vol. CLXXXI, col. 1737.

89. M. Gerbert, *De Cantu et Musica Sacra,* San Blasianis, 1774, I, 318; cf. also II, 206, for the comment of J. Busch (1400–1479), Abbot of the Monastery Novum Opus. The text of Busch's comment may be read in his *De Reformatione Monaster* (no date), II, 502, 859, 863.

90. *Op. cit.*, p. 79.

91. *Op. cit.*, p. 80.

92. *Op. cit.*, p. 79.

93. *Op. cit.*, pp. 81 f.

94. Cf. Vicentino, *op. cit.*, pp. 80 (so numbered, but should be p. 84), 92 f.; cf. also, O. Tigrini, *Il compendio della musica,* Venetia, 1588, pp. 112–15.

95. Zacconi, *op. cit.*, facing p. 56.

96. It has been the contention of the writer that the Spanish falsettists were really castrati masquerading as falsettists because of the ecclesiastical and popular feelings against the institution of castration, feelings that were not long in being reconciled.

97. Max Kuhn, *Die Verzierungskunst in der Gesangs-Musik des 16.–17. Jahrhunderts,* Leipzig, B. & H., 1902, ch. III, pp. 52 ff.

98. Friedrich Chrysander, *Lodovici Zacconi als Lehrer des Kunstgesanges,*

in *Viertaljahrschrift für Musikwissenschaft,* VII (1891), pp. 337–96; IX, (1893), 249–310; X (1894), 531–67.

99. "La musica éstata bella sempre, et ogni hora piu per la dilligenza, et per la studio che ci fanno i cantori si abellisce: la quale non si rinova, à si muta per via delle figure, che sempre le sono d'una sorte; ma con le gratie, et gl'accenti la si fa parer sempre piu bella." Zacconi, *op. cit.,* p. 58.

100. Other studies of the vocal art of the sixteenth century besides those of Chrysander, Kuhn and Ulrich already cited are: Kurt Huber, *Ivo de Vento,* 1918, ch. 3, pp. 87 ff.; Giulio Silva, "The Beginning of the Art of 'Bel Canto,'" in *Musical Quarterly,* New York, VIII (1922), 53–68; Hugo Goldschmidt, "Verzierungen, Veränderungen und Passaggien," in *Monatshefte f. Musikgeschichte,* 1891, pp. 110–28.

VI. The Castrati

1. The castrati have been widely investigated in the following studies by Franz Haböck: *Die Gesangskunst der Kastraten,* Wien, Universal-Edition, 1923; *Die Kastraten und ihre Gesangskunst,* Stuttgart, Deutsche Verlags—Anstalt, 1927. The untimely death of the author in 1921 prevented further planned publications. The present survey is based largely on these sources.

2. Perhaps the most complete is in the possession of The New York Academy of Medicine. It consists of about 70 unpublished manuscripts which were written during the 1930's by E. D. Cummings. His death in 1941 prevented the completion of this monumental work.

3. C. Burney, *Present State of Music in France and Italy,* London, 1771, pp. 301 f.

4. Cf. Haböck, *op. cit.,* p. 238.

5. Herodotus, Book VIII (*Urania*), ch. 105.

6. Haböck describes in detail the statue of an infibulated singer in the Museo del Collegio Romano; cf. *op. cit.,* p. 72.

7. Theodorus Balsamon, Annotations to "Canones Sanctorum Patrum qui in Trullo . . . convenerient," in Migne, *Pat. Graeca.,* vol. CXXXVII, col. 532.

8. For a recent commentary on the state of the eunuch in the Byzantine world the reader is referred to Steven Runciman, *Byzantine Civilization,* London, Edward Arnold & Co., 1923, pp. 703–4. The author says: "For a boy to be really successful it might be wise to castrate him, for Byzantium was the eunuch's paradise. Even the noblest parents were not above mutilating their sons to help their advancement, nor was there any disgrace in it."

9. Haböck, *op. cit.,* p. 149.

10. G. Fantoni, *Storia Universale del Canto,* Milan, 1873.

11. Although Haböck believes they were used in Spain before 1557, he

considers the question still an open one as to whether the Italian or the Spanish Church employed them first.

12. Palestrina was dismissed as a result of this edict.

13. The writer has been unable to find the exact source of this quotation. It is quoted by the following: A. B. Marx, *Gluck und die Oper,* Berlin, 1863, p. 161; C. F. D. Schubart, *Ideen zu einer Aesthetik der Tonkunst,* Vienna, 1806, p. 43; Haböck, *op. cit.,* p. 165; Francis Rogers, "The Male Soprano" in *Musical Quarterly,* V (July, 1919), p. 414.

14. Ludwig Spohr, *Autobiography,* London, 1865, I, pp. 297 ff., p. 312; II, pp. 35 ff.

15. See letter to Fanny dated April 4, 1831; also letter to Zelter, dated June 16, 1831. There are a number of editions available, one of the best known being Felix Mendelssohn, *Letters from Italy and Switzerland,* transl. by Lady Wallace, Philadelphia, 1863.

16. Those who wish to find a full discussion of this attitude toward the problem are referred to Haböck, *op. cit.,* pp. 4–10.

17. The anatomical background of this problem is discussed in detail in Haböck, *op. cit.,* ch. 3, pt. 1, p. 75, under the title "Das Wachstum des Kehlkopfes." His sources extend from Aristotle, *Historia Animalium,* Bk. IX, 50, 631b, on down to those of J. Tandler and S. Gross, Vienna, 1907, concerning members of the Skoptzi, a religious sect believing in self-mutilation. They include dissections of the throats of castrati by different anatomists, e.g. Dupuytens, Paris, 1811, who found the larynx to be about a third smaller than normal, and W. Gruber, 1847, who dissected the larynx of a 65-year-old castrato and found it about a fourth smaller. One important general conclusion resulted from these researches, viz., the earlier the operation, the higher the voice was likely to remain. Most of the *soprani* castrati were operated on during the ages of 7 and 11 while those who suffered it later, 11–14, were more likely to be *mezzi* or *contralti.*

18. "Ils deviennent pour la plupart grands et gras comme des chapons, avec des hanches, une croupe, les bras, la gorge, le cou rond et potelé comme des femmes. Quand on les rencontre dans une assemble, on est tout étonné, lorsqu'ils parlent, d'entendre sortir de ces colosses une petite voix d'enfant." Charles de Brosses, *Lettres familières écrités d'Italie en 1739–40,* second authentic ed., Paris, 1858, 2 vols., p. 239.

19. Cf. Haböck, *op. cit.,* p. 254.

20. Cf. Francisco Caffi, *Storia della Musica Sacra nelli gia Cappella ducale di S. Marco in Venezia dal 1318 al 1797.* Venezia, 1854, II, 36 f.

21. François Raguenet, *Parallèle des Italiens et des François en ce qui regarde la musique et les opéras,* Paris, 1702, pp. 75 ff. For a modern translation see *Musical Quarterly,* XXXII (July 1946), pp. 425 ff.

22. Haböck, *op. cit.,* pp. 257 f.

23. Goethe, *Italiänische Reise,* Stuttgart, 1862, I, pp. 518 ff.

24. Haböck, *op. cit.,* p. 261.

25. Haböck, *op. cit.,* pp. 263 f.

26. Rousseau, *Dict. de Musique,* 1767.

27. Tatler, January 3, 1709.

28. Nicolini had sung in Italian while the rest of the English cast had used a translation.

29. Spectator, June 4, 1712.

30. P. F. Tosi, *Observations on the Florid Song,* transl. by Mr. Galliard, London, 1743 (original, Bologna, 1723). See note, p. 152.

31. F. W. Marpurg, *Historisch-Kritische Beytrage,* 1755, I, p. 36.

32. Goethe, *op. cit.,* p. 413.

33. Cf. also *op. cit.,* p. 607.

34. Schopenhauer, *Reisetagebücher,* Leipzig, 1923, p. 268.

35. Fétis *Biographie des Musiciens,* II, p. 390.

36. Charles Burney, *A General History of Music,* new ed. New York, 1935, II, pp. 528 ff.

37. Especially in England where controversies had continually raged round and about them.

38. Tosi, *op. cit.,* p. 152.

39. Manuel Garcia, *Hints on Singing,* New York, 1894. Preface VI.

VII. Appearance and Pose

1. Cicero, *Orator,* XVIII, 60.

2. Quintilian: *Institutio Oratoria,* Bk. XI, iii, 12–13.

3. For detailed consideration the reader is referred to M. F. Bukofzer, *Music in the Baroque Era,* New York, Norton, 1947, chaps. 1, 2; D. J. Grout, *A Short History of Opera,* New York, Columbia University Press, 1947, I, 3–59. A more widely integrated discussion may be read in Lang, *op. cit.,* pp. 314–64.

4. Grout, *op. cit.,* pp. 40 f. See also *Revue Musicale,* June, 1932, p. 10.

5. Durante, *Arie Devote,* 1608, in Ulrich, *op. cit.,* p. 33.

6. ". . . sopra tutto il canto sia pieno di maiestà, più o meno secondo l'altezza del concerto gesteggiando, avvertendo però ch'ogni gesto e ogni passo caschi su la misura del suono e del canto," M. Da Gagliano, *Dedicatoria a prefazione alla Dafne,* 1608, in Angelo Solerti, *Le origini del Melodramma,* Turin, 1903, p. 83.

7. Girolamo Diruta, *Il Transilvano,* 1609, in Ulrich, *op. cit.,* pp. 33 f.

8. ". . . digo que siempre a gradaran mas à los que dan audiencia un puro

y simple Cantor que sec modesto, que el artificioso y diestro sieudo contrahecho." Cerone, *Melepeo,* 1613, p. 67.

9. Scaletta, *Scala di Musica,* 5th ed., 1656, pp. 9, 23.

10. ". . . fanno tante smorfie, ed atti vezzosi son la bocca, e con gli occhi, che, pare propriamente si svenghino per dolcezza." Doni, *Trattati,* 1635, in Ulrich, *op. cit.,* p. 48.

11. Donati, *Motetti* II, 1636, in Ulrich, *op. cit.,* p. 34.

12. Penna, *Primi Albori,* 1684, p. 49.

13. P. F. Tosi, *Opinioni de'cantori antichi e moderni o sieno osservazioni sopra il canto figurato,* Bologna, 1723. Translations were published in English (1743), German (1757), French (1774), while there have been reprints in Italian (1904) and English (1906).

14. Pp. 25 f. All page references here are to the reprint of the English translation by Mr. Galliard, London, 1743.

15. *Op. cit.,* p. 56.

16. *Op. cit.,* pp. 61 f.

17. *Op. cit.,* pp. 88 f.

18. *Cantus diversi ex antiphonario Romano Avenione,* 1777. Rule 9. "Éviter tout ce que peut causer du dégout aux autres, comme les mouvemens [*sic*] extraordinaires du corps, de la tête, des livres, du gosier." Excellent advice on use of the body and arms in gesture together with careful details urging the performer to be natural, judiciously avoiding studied artificiality, is offered by Planelli. One should use a mirror to test oneself and should study painting and sculpture as models for learning proper gestures. Antonio Planelli, *Dell' opera in Musica,* Naples, 1772. Pp. 152–82.

19. G. B. Mancini, *Pensieri e riflessioni pratiche sul Canto Figurato,* 3d ed., Milan, 1777. The first edition appeared in 1774. All references throughout this study are to the translation by Buzzi. See Bibliography.

20. Cf. *op. cit.,* pp. 249 f.

21. *Op. cit.,* p. 56.

22. *Op. cit.,* p. 93.

23. *Op. cit.,* pp. 97 f.

24. *Op. cit.,* pp. 95 f.

25. *Op. cit.,* p. 183.

26. *Op. cit.,* p. 184.

27. *Op. cit.,* pp. 164 f.

28. *Op. cit.,* pp. 165 f.

29. Vincenzo Manfredini, *Regole Armoniche,* 2d ed., Venice, 1797.

30. *Op. cit.,* pt. III, pp. 53–75.

31. ". . . senza gusto, e senza colorito; e recitano con tanta indolenza, che sembran figure di stucco." *Op. cit.,* p. 54.

32. "Come in atto di sorridere; nè si ha da sporger la lingua sulle labbra." *Op. cit.*, p. 59.

33. "Quando si canta va sempre tenuta la testa alta, ferma, e diritta; nè va fatto nessun molto sconvenevole colle spalle, le braccia; o altra parte del corpo; ma bisogna tenersi in una nobile attitudine, e cantare in piedi acciò la voce esca fuori più facilmente; soprattutto quando si studia, e allorchè si ha impegno, e premura di farsi sentire." *Op. cit.*, p. 66.

34. Cf. Charles Burney, *Memoirs of the Life and Writings of the Abate Metastasio*, London, 1796, 3 vols.

35. Cf. J. Müller-Blattau, *Die Kompositionslehre Heinrich Schützens*, Leipzig, 1926, p. 37.

36. "*In Summa*, ein Sänger soll nicht durch die Nasen singen. Er soll nicht Stammlen, sonst ist er unverständlich. Er soll nicht mit der Zung anstossen oder lispeln, sonst versteht man ihn kaum halb. Er soll auch die Zähne nicht zusammen schliessen, noch den mund zu weit aufthun, noch die Zung über die Lefzen herausstrecken, noch die Lippen aufwerfen, noch den mund krümmen, noch die Wangen und Nasen verstellen wie die Meerkatzen, noch die Augenbraunen zusammen schrumpfen, noch die Stirn runtzeln, noch den Kopf oder die Augen darinnen herumdrehen, noch mit den selben blinzen, noch mit den Lefzen zittern, etc." *Op. cit.*, p. 39.

37. ". . . wie ein Kutscher auf dem Bock." Cf. Johann Mattheson, *Der Volkommene Capellmeister*, Hamburg, 1739, pp. 98 f.

38. "Mancher wendet das Gesicht im Singen so weit zur rechten Hand, dass ihn die Zuhörer auf der lincken Seite gar nicht vernehmen. Ein andrer kehret es um. . . . Einige werffen bey dem Singen das Haupt im Nacken, wodurch der Klang in die Höhe steiget, da kein Zuhörer ist; andre neigen es fast auf die Brust herunter, singen im Barte, wie man sagt, und verfehlen ebenfalls des wahren Zweckes dadurch, sie mögen sonst so fähig seyn, als sie wollen. Viele können die Hände nicht still halten, welches wol, bey dem Abgange guter Geberden, am besten wäre; sondern müssen, wenn sie ja sonst keine alberne Bewegung damit machen, den ungebetenen Tact auf eine und andre Art führen: welches doch eine Sache ist, die den Weg zu der Zuhörer Hertzen nimmermehr bahnen wird. Die meisten aber halten die Charteke, entweder aus Ubersichtigkeit, welche zu entschuldigen, oder aus Gewohnheit, die zu tadeln, so nahe am Munde und vor die Augen, dass sich die Stimme daran stösset, und von niemand, als dem singenden selbst, absonderlich in grossen Kirchen, deutlich vernommen werden kan." *Op. cit.*, p. 99.

39. "Er muss dabey wohl aufgerichtet stehen, und nicht den Kopf zur Erde hangen, und dadurch den Hals zudrücken." F. W. Marpurg, *Anleitung zur musik überhaupt und zur Singkunst inbesondere*, 1763, p. 10.

40. "zu deren Verbesserung der Spiegel und ein guter freund zu Rathe gezogen werden muss, in Acht zu nehmen. Hieher gehöret besonders das Verdrehen des Kopfes; die Verkehrung der Augen; das Nicken mit dem Kopfe den jeder note; das Schütteln mit dem Kopfe; das Wanken und Poltern mit den Fussen; das Legen der Hand hinters Ohr; die Berührung des Munder mit der Hand; die Krummung desselben; das Zittern desselben bey einem Triller, und so weiter. Wer kann alle Grimassen zählen: Eine anständige Leibestellung; weder ein zu süsses noch zu saures Gesicht; weder ein haselirendes noch zu ernsthaftes Amtswesen; und weder ein zu furchtsames noch zu freyes Betragen, ist, so wie jedern Redner, also auch jedem Sänger aufs nachdrücklichste zu empfehlen." *Op. cit.,* pp. 23 f.

41. J. A. Hiller, *Anweisung zum Musikalisch-richtigen Gesange,* Leipzig, 1774. Cf. p. 6. It is harmful to the voice for a singer to sit habitually "with a pressed together abdomen" (mit zusammengedrücktem Unterleibe). Cf. *op. cit.,* p. 14.

42. "Auf alle unanständige Bewegungen des Leibes, als hin und herwanken, Scharren mit den Füssen, Schütteln des Kopf's u. s. w. auf alle Grimassen des Gesichts, als Verzerren des Mundes, Blinzen mit den Augen u. d. g. muss man genau Achtung geben, weil man sich leicht so etwas angewöhnt. Ich habe eine italiänische Sängerinn gekannt, die bey ihrer sonst sehr guten Stimme, und bey ihrer nicht zu verachtenden Art zu singen, doch das Unangenehme hatte, dass sie den Kopf zurück warf, die Augen immer nach der Decke richtete, und das Gesicht so verzog, dass man hatte glauben sollen, sie bekäme Convulsionen. Sich vor dergleichen unanständigkeiten zu bewahren, giebt man den Rath, bisweilen vor dem Spiegel zu singen; und gewiss, wem daran gelegen ist, stets mit der vortheilhaftsten Mine aufzutreten, dem kann kein besserer Rath gegeben werden." *Op. cit.,* p. 27.

43. Johann Samuel Petri, *Anleitung zur praktischen Musik,* Leipzig, 1782, cf. p. 197. An earlier edition in 1767, about one-third as large, is less useful.

44. "Wenn man durch die Nase, mit zusammengebissenen Zähnen, oder im Gegentheil wie ein Müllerlöw mit gar zu sehr aufgesperrtem Maul und dergleichen garstigen Umständen singt, daraus nicht nur ein sichtbarer Eckel bey den Zuhören, sondern auch eine Unvernehmlichkeit im Verstand entstehet." Ignaz F. X. Kuerzinger, *Getreuer Unterricht zum singen mit Manieren,* Augsburg, 3d ed., 1793, p. 51.

45. P. Jumilhac, *La Science et la pratique du plainchant,* 2d ed., 1847. This is a reprint of first edition, 1673, with added notes. Cf. p. 264.

46. Jean Blanchet, *L'art, ou les principes philosophiques du chant,* Paris, 1756. A similar treatise had been published a year earlier under the author-

ship of Jean Antoine Berard, an opera singer, but Blanchet claimed authorship, saying that he had sold the ms. to Berard. Eitner has established Blanchet's claims.

47. Cf. *op. cit.,* pp. 79 ff.

48. "On doit, debout ou assis, se tenir de bonne grace, le corps droit et la tête elevée sans affection. Il ne faut pas gesticuler en chantant ni faire des grimaces de la bouche des yeux et du front. Il ne faut pas marquer la mesure de la tête ni du corps . . . On s'éviteroit la peine de battre la mesure, si on avoit la valeur des nottes et le mouvement bien imprimés dans la tête." Antoine Bailleux, *Solfege pour apprendre facilement la musique vocale,* etc., 3d ed., Paris, 1760, p. 122.

49. Jean Philippe Rameau, *Code de Musique pratique ou méthodes, etc.,* Paris, 1760. Cf. pp. 14 f.

50. *Op. cit.,* p. 20.

51. Raparlier, *Principes de musique, les agréments du chant,* Lille, 1772, p. 30. Nothing further is known of this author.

52. Jean Paul Egide Martini, *Mélopée Moderne; ou, L'art du chant, reduit en principes,* Paris, *ca.* 1792. Cf. p. 4.

53. Florido Tomeoni, *Théorie de la musique vocale,* Paris, 1799. Cf. p. 87. The reader interested in a discussion of stage fright and its cure is referred to chap. 10, p. 76. The author places great emphasis on singing according to Nature, i.e., naturally, and insists on the superiority of the Italian method. In chap. 13, pp. 110–114, he discusses the advantages of having opera texts translated into the vernacular.

54. "Plusieurs raisons physiques empechent le pied de battre exactement la mesure; la principale est que le repos et l'aplomb du corps sont nécessaires pour l'exécution de la musique; le mouvement du pied ne peut que leur etre contraire." *Op. cit.,* p. 103.

55. *Loc. cit.,* pp. 103 f.

56. B. Mengozzi, *Méthode de chant du Conservatoire de Musique,* Paris, 1803.

57. "Pour se préparer à bien faire la gamme, l'élève doit se tenir, 1°: dans une attitude naturellement droite, et sans faire le moindre effort; 2°: Il tiendra la tête levée sans la pencher trop en arrière, car si les muscles de la gorge étaient trop tendus, ils ne pourraient point agir librement; 3°: La bouche doit être comme souriant et convenablement ouverte, autant du moins que la conformation de celle de l'élève le comportera, afin de prononcer sans l'altérer, la voyelle sur laquelle il doit chanter la Gamme; 4°: Il faut que l'élève prenne garde qu'en ouvrant la bouche, sa physionomie n'emprunte un caractère sinistre; id doit éviter aussi de faire aucune grimace avec les parties

mobiles du visage; 5°: Il doit appuyer légèrement la langue derrière les dents inférieures; 6°: La machoire supérieure doit être perpendiculairement, et médiocrement détachée de la machoire inférieure." *Op. cit.,* pp. 8 f.

58. C. Burney, *The Present State of Music in Germany, the Netherlands and United Provinces,* London, 1775, 2d ed., corrected, I, p. 149.

59. *Op. cit.,* I, p. 129.

60. *Op. cit.,* I, p. 92.

61. *Op. cit.,* I, p. 150.

62. *Op. cit.,* I, p. 246.

63. Domenico Corri, *The Singer's Preceptor,* or *Corri's Treatise on Vocal Music,* London, 1811. Cf. pp. 1, 4.

64. Gesualdo Lanza, *Lanza's Elements of Singing in the Italian and English Styles,* London, 1813, 4 vols., I, p. 81.

65. *Op. cit.,* III, p. 170.

VIII. Breathing

1. "Chi sa ben respirare e sillabare, saprá ben cantare." According to Francesco Lamperti this statement was written in his "Memoirs" by the famous eighteenth century castrato and singing teacher, Pacchiarotti. Cf. Lamperti, *Guida teorico-pratica-elementare per lo studio del canto,* Milan, Ricordi, 1864, Preface. Manuel Garcia gives credit to Pellegrini Celoni, Anna Maria. Cf. Garcia, *Hints on Singing,* London and New York, 1894, p. 13. Steinmann offers a similar quotation credited to Pacchiarotti without giving any source. It is as follows: "Project the voice well, breathe correctly, pronounce clearly, and your song will be perfect." (Mettette ben la voce, respirate bene, pronunciate chiaramente, ed il vostro canto sarà perfetto.) H. F. Steinmann, *Die grosse Italienische Gesangschule,* Dresden, 1848. Intro., III.

2. P. 39.

3. This style of singing is described by Caccini as having "contempt" for the strict rhythm of the music or the written note values, making some shorter by half while others were made longer, according to the meaning (conceit) or emphasis of the words. It marks the beginning of recitative and was one of the most important stylistic features of the *Nuove Musiche.* Giulio Caccini, *Le Nuove Musiche,* prefazione a cura di Francesco Vatielli, Roma, Reale accademia d'Italia, 1934. This is a reprint of the original 1601 edition. Cf. pp. 8 f. This preface is also printed in Angelo Solerti, *Le Origini del Melodramma,* Milan, 1903, pp. 53–75. Cf. p. 68.

4. "E di essa è pur necessario valersi per dar maggiore spirito al crescere e scemare della voce, alla esclamazioni e tutti gli altri effetti che habbiamo mostrati; facciasi, che non gli venga meno poi ove è bisogne . . . senza

valersi della respirazione per altro, che per mostrarsi padrone di tutti gli affetti migliori, che occorono usarsi in sì fatta nobilissima maniera di cantare." G. Caccini, *op. cit.*, pp. 8–9.

5. Cited in Ulrich, *op. cit.*, p. 61.

6. Cf. Cerone, *op. cit.*, p. 68.

7. Cf. Ulrich, *op. cit.*, p. 65.

8. *Ibid.*, p. 128.

9. G. B. Doni, *De Praestantia Musicae Veteris*, Florence, 1647, p. 108. There was not so much objection to the breaking up of long passages in the following century, especially in the music of Händel. Note Tosi's comments that follow.

10. P. F. Tosi, *op. cit.*, pp. 24–25.

11. Francesco Maria Vallara, *Primizie di canto fermo*, Parma, 1724, p. 2.

12. G. B. Mancini, *op. cit.*, pp. 53 f.

13. *Ibid.*, pp. 112 f.

14. Cf. C. Burney, *Present State of Music in France and Italy*. London, 1771, pp. 326 f. He speaks of the special care given to the young castrati at the Conservatory of St. Onofrio in Naples.

15. *Ibid.*, p. 120.

16. *Ibid.*, p. 121.

17. *Ibid.*, p. 145.

18. *Ibid.*, p. 154.

19. Cf. *ibid.*, p. 157.

20. *Ibid.*, p. 161.

21. *Ibid.*, p. 153.

22. *Ibid.*, p. 157.

23. *Ibid.*, p. 163.

24. Cf. V. Manfredini, *op. cit.*, p. 59.

25. *Ibid.*, p. 61.

26. ". . . la quale consiste principalmente nel prender fiato con gran prontezza, e in un modo che nessun se ne possa accorgere." *Ibid.*, p. 62.

27. "Se poi la debolezza della voce, o la qualità della cantilena, obbligasse tavolta di dover prender fiato a mezza parola, si prenda anche così, ma con gran cantela, affinche si faccia sentire men che si può lo spezzamento delle parole." *Loc. cit.*

28. "Bisogna però osservare attentamente, non solo di non prender fiato a mezza parola; lo che, come ho detto, può farsi solamente in qualche caso particolare, ma nemmeno dopo il trillo; ne prima di aver finito il sentimento di una cantilena, e di aver terminato una cadenza." *Op. cit.*, pp. 62 f.

29. Cf. Forkel, *Algemeine Geschichte der Musik*, Leipzig, 1788–1801.

Footnote, 65; Albert Allerup, *Die Musica Practica des Johann Andreas Herbst,* Kassel, Barenreiter—Verlag, 1931, pp. 32–34.

30. Cf. Michael Praetorius, *Syntagma Musicum,* Wolfenbüttel, 1619, III, p. 82.

31. Cf. *op. cit.,* III, p. 181.

32. "Wenn er vor der Figur Athem holet und den Vortheil einen langen Athem zu haben weiss." Wolfgang Caspar Printz, *Compendium Musicae Signatoriae et Modulatoriae vocalis, Dresden,* 1714, Pt. II, chap. 6, ¶ 26, # 7.

33. ". . . mit gemässigter Stimme immer in einem Athem so lange wegzusingen, als nur ohne Beschwerlichkeit möglich ist." Mattheson, *Vollkommene Cap'm'ter,* p. 97.

34. ". . . so kan man doch durch fleissige Übung den Vortheil zu Wege bringen, dass der Athem länger aushalte, als gewöhnlich, wenn die eingezogent Lufft nicht auf einmahl, oder nicht zu häuffig, sondern auf das sparsamste nur nach und nach, wieder heraus gelassen wird, indem man sie mit grosser Aufmercksamkeit in etwas zurück und wol zu Rathe hält. Dieses ist eine Kunst, durch welche ein Sänger vor andern trefflich hervorragen kan, und worauf sich die Welschen Ton-Künstler meisterlich verstehen; andre Völcker aber wenig oder gar nicht sich legen." *Loc. cit.*

35. ". . . alsdenn mit wolabgemessener Austheilung desselben, durch die Glottis und ihre zarte Spalte, dem Ton seine rechte Gestalt gegeben werde." *Loc. cit.*

36. *Op. cit.,* p. 111.

37. Johann Friedrich Agricola, *Anleitung zur Singkunst.* Aus dem italienischen des Herrn Peter Franz Tosi, mit erläuterungen und zusätzen von J. F. Agricola, Berlin, 1757.

38. Cf. Burney, *Present State of Music in Germany,* II, p. 91 f.

39. *Op. cit.,* p. 25.

40. "Es ist allhier gut, dass der Meister seinen Schüler mit den Einschnitten der Melodie etwas bekannt machet, als nach welchen man am bequemsten frische Luft einziehen kann: ob es gleich, wenn viele kurze Einschnitte, die etwann nur einen halben Tact ausmachen, auf einander folgen, im geringsten nicht bey jedem nöthig ist. Ueberhaupt kann gemerket werden, dass bey jedem unterbrochnen Fortgange des Gesanges . . . die beste Zeit Athem zu holen ist. Wenn es nöthig ist, solches in einer langen Passage zu thun, so muss man alle vorhergehende Umstände gehörig erwägen, um den rechten Ort zu treffen. Dass man zwischen einem triller und der folgenden Note nicht Athem schöpfen müsse, ist schon vor langen Zeiten verboten gewesen." Marpurg, *Anleitung zur Musik,* 1763, pp. 29 f.

41. ". . . und zwar bald mit schwacker, bald mit gemässigter und bald mit starker stimme." *Loc. cit.*

42. ". . . um sich nach und nach einen langen Athem zu verschoffen, ohne der Lunge Schaden zuzufügen." Cf. *op. cit.,* p. 30.

43. Cf. Hiller, *Anweisung zum musikalisch-richtigen Gesange,* Leipzig, 1774, pp. 8 f.

44. ". . . es ist eine von den Hauptflichten eines Singmeister, seine Schüler zur Ersparrung des Athems gleich Angangs zu gewöhnen." Cf. *op. cit.,* p. 9.

45. "Denn geschichte Lehrmeister werden in den Übungstunden bey den Arien ihren Schülern *in praxi* diese Vortheile am besten zeigen können, wenn sie des wahren Gesangs selbst mächtig sind." Cf. Petri, *Anleitung zur praktischen Musik,* 1782, pp. 192 ff.

46. "Wenn durch gar zu oft wiederholtes unzeitiges Athemholen die Worte und Gedanken des Vortrages getrennet, und die Läuffe zerbrochen, und zerrissen werden." Kuerzinger, *Getreuer Unterricht,* 1793, p. 51.

47. ". . . denn auch in diesem Stücke kommt viel auf Übung und Gewohnheit an." J. B. Lasser, *Vollständige Anleitung zur Singkunst,* Munich, 1805, p. 60.

48. ". . . zudeme wird selbst den zuhörern darüber bange, wenn sie den Sänger so mühsam und mit Geräusche Athem holen hören." *Loc. cit.*

49. ". . . wirkt auf die Lunge und das Stimmwerkzeug gleichmächtig." *Loc. cit.*

50. "Ein bischen Dreistigkeit, die aber nicht in eine sträfliche Zufriedenheit mit seinen Fehlern ausartet, ist hierinn von besten Nutzen." *Loc. cit.*

51. Cf. *op. cit.,* p. 62.

52. "Il est constant qu'elle s'acquiert et s'augmente par l'exercise, aussi bien que les autres circonstances du Chant." Benigne de Bacilly, *Remarques curieuses sur l'art de bien chanter, et particulierement pour ce qui regarde le chant françois,* Paris, 1668, p. 50.

53. Jumilhac, *La Science et la pratique du plain-chant,* 1673. Cf. p. 263.

54. Cf. *op. cit.,* pp. 266 f.

55. Blanchet, *L'Art du chant,* 1756. Cf. pp. 7 ff.

56. "Pour bien inspirer, il faut élever et élargir la poitrine, de maniere que le ventre se gonfle: par cet artifice, on remplira d'air toute la cavité du poumon. Pour bien expirer, il faut faire sortir l'air intérieur avec plus ou moins de force, avec plus ou moins de volume, selon le caractère du Chant." *Op .cit.,* p. 26.

57. From these statements it would seem that Blanchet borrowed his ideas from the Italians and passed them on to his students.

58. ". . . dans la manière de pouffer l'air des poumons sans gene et sans contrainte." Rameau, *Code de Musique,* 1760, p. 15.

59. "Oui, toutes les perfections du chant, toutes ses difficultés, ne dépendent que du vent qui part des poumons." *Op. cit.,* p. 16.

60. ". . . maîtres que du vent, et que par conséquent c'est à nous de savoir si bien le gouverner, que rien ne puisse en empecher l'effet." *Op. cit.,* p. 16.

61. *Ibid.* It is most important to mention a footnote which Rameau has inserted here *a propos* the word "glotte" or glottis. He says, "I call the glottis that which perhaps can, at times, be applied to other organs that are contiguous; but this is of no consequence whatever with regard to that which is of importance." (J'attribue à la glotte ce qui pourroit peut-être, en certain cas, s'appliquer aux autres agens qui lui sont liés; mais cela n'est d'aucune conséquence pour le fait dont il s'agit.) This betrays a very superficial understanding or appreciation of the physiological processes of singing.

62. Here again Rameau's misunderstanding of the process of phonation leads him to say that the glottis becomes dilated. "C'est que la glotte se dilate pour lors à l'aise sans se roidir."

63. Cf. *op. cit.,* pp. 16 f.

64. Cf. *op. cit.,* p. 18.

65. Cf. Raparlier, *Principes de musique,* 1772, p. 42.

66. "Lorsque par la respiration les poumons sont bien remplis d'air il faut le garder avec le plus grand ménagement et n'en laisser sortie que la portion nécessaire pour donner de la vibration à la voix. Cette manière de respirer donne la force d'enfler et de diminuer les sons a volonté; elle augmente le volume de la voix dans les sons graves et dans les sons aigus; elle procure de la facilité et de la légèreté dans les passages difficiles, ainsi que de la durée pour pouvoir bien terminer les longues phrases de chant; elle donne de plus aux chanteurs une assurance imperturbable." Martini, *Melopée Moderne,* 1792, p. 6.

67. "Si par hasard on était obligé de suspendre le sens par la respiration, il faudrait alors le faire avec beaucoup d'adresse et d'une manière presque insensible, afin que l'auditeur ne s'en apercut pas." Tomeoni, *Théorie de la Musique Vocale,* 1799, p. 25.

68. Cf. *op. cit.,* pp. 26 ff.

69. "Il faut observer que l'action de respirer pour chanter, diffère en quelque chose de la respiration pour parler. Quand on respire pour parler, on pour renouveller simplement l'air des poumons, le premier mouvement est celui de l'aspiration, alors le ventre se gonfle et sa partie supèrieure s'avance un peu; ensuite il s'affaisse, c'est le second movement, celui de l'expiration: ces deux mouvemens s'opèrent lentement, lorsque le corps est dans son état naturel. Au contraire, dans l'action de respirer pour chanter, en aspirant, il faut aplatir le ventre et le faire remonter avec promptitude, en gonflant et avancant la poitrine. Dans l'expiration, le ventre doit revenir fort lentement à son état naturel et la poitrine s'abaisser à mesure, afin de conserver et de ménager, le plus longtems [*sic*] possible, l'air que l'on a introduit dans les poumons; on le doit le laisser échapper qu'avec lenteur, et sans donner de se-

cousses à la poitrine: il faut pour ainsi dire qu'il s'écoule." Mengozzi, *Méthode de Chant,* 1803, p. 2.

70. *Op. cit.,* pp. 9 f.

71. Cf. the statutes of Stoke-College, founded by Archbishop Parker, 1535, Strype's Parker, p. 9: "Which said queristers [choiristers], after their *breasts* [voices] are changed," etc. Cf. Fiddes' *Life of Wolsey,* Appendix, p. 128: "Singing-men, well-breasted." Also *Tusser's Husbandrie, ca.* 1550, ed. P. Short, p. 155: "The better *brest,* the lesser rest, to serve the queer [choir] now there, now here," i.e., the better the voice, the more the chorister was called upon to sing. In Shakespeare's *Twelfth Night,* Sir Andrew says of the Clown who has been asked to sing, "By my troth the foole has an excellent breast." (II, iii, 22.) Also in Fletcher's, *The Pilgrim,* III, vi: "Let's hear him sing, he has a fine breast."

72. Anselm Bayly, *A Practical Treatise on Singing and Playing,* London, 1771, p. 39.

73. Sir John Hawkins, *A General History of the Science and Practice of Music,* London, 1776, note, Bk. 12, chap. 112.

74. Giusto Ferdinando Tenducci, *Instruction of Mr. Tenducci, to his Scholars,* London, *ca.* 1785, p. 1.

75. Cf. Lanza, *Elements of Singing,* III, p. 44 f.

76. *Op. cit.,* III, p. 170. This is a direct quotation and indicates a lack of ability on the author's part to express himself clearly in English.

77. Cf. also Hiller, *Anweisung,* footnote p. 165, where Tosi's book is recommended as the best for the study of ornamentation.

IX. Ear Training

1. Job, XXIX, 11.

2. Thomas Dekker, *The Gull's Hornbook,* III.

3. Cf. Tosi, *Observations,* p. 36.

4. ". . . recitare"—the word includes reading aloud, singing, etc.

5. ". . . piu con le orecchio, che con la voce." Giovanni Maria Artusi, *Delle imperfettioni della Moderna Musica,* Venetia, 1600, p. 2.

6. *Op. cit.,* facing p. 3.

7. Allesandro Guidotti, *Prefazione alla rappresentazione di Animo e Corpo di Emilio de Cavalieri,* 1600. In Solerti, *Le Origini,* p. 5.

8. "Per procedere adunque con ordine dirò che i primi, e i piu importanti fondamenti sono l'intonazione della voce in tutte le corde, non solo, che nulla non manchi sotto, ò cresca di vantaggio, ma habia la buona maniera, come ella si debba intonare." Caccini, *Le Nuove Musiche,* p. 3.

9. These opinions of Caccini may also be found in Solerti, *Le Origini del Melodramma,* p. 62.

10. Diruta, *Il Transilvano,* 1609, Pt. II, Bk. 4, p. 24.

11. "El perfecto cantante mas canta con la oreja, que con la boca." Cerone, *Melopeo,* 1613, p. 70.

12. Doni, *De Praestantia Musicae Veteris,* 1647, p. 99.

13. Avella, *Regole di Musica,* 1657, p. 112.

14. Tosi, *Observations,* p. 19.

15. Mancini, *Riflessioni,* p. 61.

16. *Op. cit.,* p. 63.

17. *Op. cit.,* pp. 63 f.

18. Cf. *op. cit.,* pp. 66 f.

19. *Op. cit.,* p. 67. It is of interest to note Mancini's use of the masculine gender in speaking of sopranos. Even as late as 1777 the term *soprano* meant the high castrato voice whereas the female soprano was usually called *cantatrice.*

20. Cf. *op. cit.,* pp. 69 ff. The author goes into some detail and quotes Tosi to explain the actual mathematical differences between C♯ and D♭, etc.

21. Cf. *op. cit.,* p. 155.

22. *The Martellato* or the "Hammer" was a vocal ornament consisting of a series of repeated staccato tones.

23. *Op. cit.,* p. 156.

24. *Op. cit.,* p. 157.

25. *Op. cit.,* pp. 158 f.

26. *Op. cit.,* p. 162.

27. ". . . perchè certamente non arrivera mai ad essere un perfetto cantante." Manfredini, *Regole Armoniche,* 1797, pp. 43 ff.

28. ". . . perchè non v' è cosa nella musica, che dispiaccia tanto, quanto una falsa intonazione." *Op. cit.,* p. 59.

29. ". . . premesso però sempre il dominio assoluto di un orrechio idoneo e favorevole alla musica; essendo questo il requisito principale per eseguire una giusta, e perfetta intonazione." *Op. cit.,* p. 60.

30. Cf. *op. cit.,* p. 75.

31. See above, p. 90.

32. Praetorius, *Syntagma Musicum,* 1619, III, 181.

33. "Wenn ein Gesang angefangen werden soll, soll ein jeder Sänger seinen Ton entweder aus dem Preambuliren des Organisten, oder aus der Intonation des Directoris erlernen, damit er recht anfange und nicht bald anfangs einen Fehler begehe." W. C. Printz, *Compendium Musicae Signatoriae,* 1714, chap. 4, ¶ 9.

34. "Wenn man in den Schriften einiger alten Sangmeister lieset, dass die Musiker unter sich night einig sind, ob man mit dem rechten Ton, oder mit einer Secunde, Terz oder Quarte, ec. tiefer oder höher, intoniren solle: so siehet man daraus, dass der Fehler des Tonsuchens vorzeiten für eine musi-

kalische Tugend muss seyn gehalten worden. Heutiges Tages haben keine andere Personen, als die alten Mütterchen, Kinderwärterinnen, u.s.w. die Erlaubniss, sich den Sprung einer Note in ihren Liederchen auf solche Art zu erleichtern. Der Vocalist muss, in Ansehung der Intonation, die Instrumente, die sonsten in einer andern Aussicht Copien der Singstimme seyn müssen, zu seiner Vorschrift nehmen." F. W. Marpurg, *Anleitung zur Musik,* 1763, pp. 21 f.

35. Cf. J. S. Petri, *Anleitung zur practischen Musik,* 1767, p. 196.

36. ". . . damit der Schüler bald anfänglich zu einer reinen Intonation angeführet werde." *Op. cit.,* p. 197.

37. "Man kan sie also erkennen, wenn man ihnen Töne vorsingt, die sie nachstimmen sollen, und da wird man gemeiniglich bemerken, dass die, die nach etlichen Lehrstunden immer in Tonsuchen bleiben und unter zehn Probetönen dennoch kaum einen treffen, sind meistentheils zum Gesange ganz untüchtig, und haben gar kein musikalisches Gehör." *Op. cit.,* p. 213.

38. "Ob er einige vorgesungene Noten sogleich fassen, und genau nachsingen könne, sonst möchte es mit seiner Fähigkeit nicht zum besten stehen, und alle Mühe vergebens seyn." I. F. X. Kuerzinger, *Getreuer Unterricht,* p. 5.

39. ". . . massen die menschliche Stimme ohne Begleitung eines Instruments stets zum sinken geneigt ist." *Loc. cit.* This difference of opinion as to the use of the violin could be accounted for in two ways. Petri placed the violin in the hands of the beginning student where the pitch would likely be uncertain whereas Kuerzinger would have the teacher accompany the singer with the violin and we are to assume that the intonation would likely be true. Moreover, the latter was also a violinist and the title of his instruction book was as follows: *Getreuer Unterricht zum singen mit Manieren, und die Violin zu spielen.*

40. "Ein Singmeister muss ein feines Gehör haben, fehlt es ihm daran, oder singt er selbst unrein, wie will er andere rein singen machen?" Lasser, *Vollständige Anleitung,* p. 11.

41. "Er untersuche vor allen das Gehör . . . seiner Lehrlinge." *Loc. cit.*

42. "Da die Stimmung der Klaviere, Orgeln und Instrumente in der musikalischen Welt so ungleich ist, so rathe ich dem Meister, viel lieber nach höherer Stimmung zu unterrichten, weil es jenem Sänger, der an die tiefere Stimmung gewöhnt ist, alsdann sauer wird, by einer höhern zu singen." *Op. cit.,* p. 12. There was no internationally accepted standard of pitch until a half century or more later.

43. B. Bacilly, *Remarques,* chap. 9, pp. 51–59.

44. "Disposition du Gosier." The first is the voice itself.

45. "C'est par elle que la Voix se rectise quand elle est fausse; s'adoucit

quand elle est rude; se modere quand elle est trop forte; se soutient quand elle est tremblante. C'est par elle que le gosier s'accoutume à marquer ce qu'il faut, et à couler ce qu'il ne faut marquer que légèrement; et pour tout dire, c'est par elle que l'on paruient à bien comprendre tout ce qui se prattique dans l'Art de bien Chanter; mesme on peut dire qu'avec beaucoup d'Oreille, on peut acquerir de la Voix, et la faire quasi sortir du neant, par le travail, et sur tout estant secondé d'un bon maistre, comme je diray dans le Chapitre suivant." *Op. cit.,* p. 54.

46. *Op. cit.,* pp. 55 ff.

47. ". . . le commun proverbe qui porte qu'il vaut mieux chanter de l'oreille que de la bouche." See Cerone p. 90 f.

48. "De mesme c'est l'oüy qui connoist et discerne tous les sons, et tous leurs intervalles, leur bonne ou mauvaise suite, leurs consonances ou dissonances, leurs temps et leurs mesures, leurs cadences et leur silences, leur ton moderé ou excessif, l'accord ou discord des diverses voix; et universellement toutes les autres choses qui concernent les sons et les voix qui sont l'object de cette science." Pierre Jumilhac, *La Science et la pratique,* pp. 259 f.

49. "Enfin il n'y a rien que l'on doive tout consulter en tout ceci que l'oreille qui est audessus des Regles de l'Art même puisque c'est elle qui en doit juger." *Nouvelle Méthode très facile pour apprendre le plein-chant,* Rouen, 1719, p. 21.

50. Blanchet, *L'Art du Chant,* 1756. Cf. chap. 7, pp. 37–41.

51. "La Méthode que ju viens d'enseigner ne contribuera pas peu à étendre l'empire du Chant, en multipliant les talens de bien des personnes: les Dames qui ont de la voix sans avoir de l'oreille, pourront avec le secours de me régles ajouter à leurs charmes, s'assurer une ressource contre les disgraces de l'age, et espérer d'etre encore agréables, quand elles auront cessé d'etre aimables." *Op. cit.,* pp. 102 ff. This smacks of quackery. Fetis says that Blanchet was not a musician but had made researches on the vocal organs and their mechanism all of which have been forgotten. Cf. F. J. Fetis, *Biographie Universelle des Musiciens,* 2d ed., Paris, 1877, I, p. 435.

52. ". . . dans tous les habiles Chanteurs, dont le nombre est infiniment plus grand en Italie qu'en France." Rameau, *Code de Musique,* p. 19.

53. Cf. *op. cit.,* p. 22.

54. ". . . un premier moyen de former l'oreille." *Op. cit.,* p. 21.

55. "On ne scauroit avoir trop d'attention quand on commence à chanter, a sentir et faire sentir l'intervale et les modifications qu'il y a d'un son à un autre. Je ne puis trop recommander de chanter avec des instruments, car je suis très-persuadé que si l'on chante faux si souvent et avec tant d'obstination, cela vient du peu d'habitude d'entendre des accompagnements." Lecuyer, *Principes de l'art du Chant,* p. 6.

56. "Un Écolier enseigné avec un Violon chantera sa partie avec justesse et éxactitude." J. P. E. Martini, *Melopée Moderne*, p. 4.

57. "La Justesse de l'intonation est le premier point dont doivent s'occuper l'Écolier et le Maistre. On ne peut supporter d'entendre chanter faux. Cet accident arrive quelque fois par foiblesse [*sic*] d'estomac; mais un Écolier qui au bout d'un mois ne sauroit saisir avec justesse les sons d'un instrument, ou chanter à l'unisson d'une voix de son diapason, doit etre averti que son défaut d'oreille est un obstacle à ce qu'il puisse jamais chanter, et consequemment fairê des progrès." *Loc. cit.*

58. "On doit attaquer le son franc et juste, sans preparer et sans arriver à ce son par aucune trainée." Mengozzi, *Méthode de Chant*, p. 11.

59. W. Turner, *Sound Anatomized in a Philosophical essay on Musick*, London, 1724, p. 40.

60. Cf. Bayly, *A Practical Treatise on Singing*, 1771, pp. 37 f. We have noted the author's acknowledgment of his debt to Tosi's "Observations." See above, p. 87.

61. Tenducci, *Instruction*, 1785. Rule III, p. 4.

62. Corri, *The Singer's Preceptor*, pp. 1–4, 12–29 includes many exercises for the development of intonation.

X. Resonators

1. Chaucer, *Canterbury Tales*, Prologue, l. 122.
2. Durante, *Arie Devote*. Cf. Ulrich, *op. cit.*, p. 48.
3. Donatí, *Motetti*, Vol. II, Rule III. Cf. Ulrich, *op. cit.*, p. 63.
4. Tosi, *Observations*, p. 88.
5. Mancini, *Riflessioni*, p. 89.
6. *Ibid.*, pp. 90 f.
7. *Ibid.*, pp. 91 f.
8. *Ibid.*, pp. 92 f.
9. "Ogni cantante deve situar la sua bocca, come suol situarla, quando naturalmente sorride, cioè in modo, che i denti di sopra siano perpendicolarmente, e mediocremente distacatti da quelli di sotto."*Ibid.*, p. 93.
10. *Ibid.*, p. 95.
11. *Ibid.*, p. 161.
12. *Ibid.*, p. 96.
13. "La maniera di aprir la bocca è una regola essenzialissima, dependendo molto da essa il formar la voce chiara, e la schietta e chiara pronunzia delle parole. Eppure questa regola tanto importante, pochi cantanti l'osservano con esattezza, per trascuvaggine certamente dei primi loro maestri . . . La bocca dunque, cantando, non si deve aprire nè troppo, nè poco, ma una cosa giusta, tenendola aperta come in atto di sorridere; nè si ha da sporger la

lingua sulle labbra, lo che fa cantare nel naso, e pronunziare da scilinguato." V. Manfredini, *Regole Armoniche,* p. 59.

14. Cf. *op. cit.,* p. 74.

15. ". . . durch die Nasen und mit unterhaltung der Stimme in Halse." Praetorius, *Syntagma Musicum,* III, p. 182.

16. "Die *Vocales* wollen in der *Pronunciation* eine rechts ihnen zukomende Eröffnung des Mundes haben und soll nicht eine in die andere verändert werden. Es stehet greulich wenn man *Dius* für *Deus, nuster* für *noster, gretia* für *gratia* u.s.f. singet. . . . Die Stimme soll nicht zwichen den Lippen oder holen Backen sondern in der Kehle formiret werden." Printz, *Compendium,* chap. 4, ¶¶ 4, 6.

17. Mattheson, *Volk. Cap'm'ter,* p. 97, ¶ 21.

18. ". . . dem sie haben hiebey sonst keine Verrichtung, als nur, dass sie fein bescheidentlich auf die Seite treten." *Loc. cit.,* ¶ 22.

19. Agricola, *Anleitung,* pp. 26 f.; note 14.

20. "Oder sie können auch durch willkuhrlich angenommene Fehler, z. e. wenn man beym Singen die Zunge ohne Noth zurück zieht, und krumm macht, welche doch, so viel als möglich ist, platt und gerade im Munde biegen sollte, ingleichen wenn man den Mund nicht weit genug eröfnet oder die Zähne zusammendrücket entstehen. Aus dem ersten und zweyten Falle nimmt das sogenannte Singen durch die Nase, und aus dem dritten das Singen in der Kehle [il cantar di gola] seinen Ursprung: und dieser Mängel können noch viele andere mehr seyn. Sind es nun Naturfehler so können sie freylich nicht verbessert werden: sind es aber zufällige oder angenommene Fehler; so darf man nur ihre Ursachen aus dem Wege räumen, oder den Theilen des Mundes ihre rechte Stellung zu geben suchen: und hierdurch sind sie gar wohl zu verbessern." *Op. cit.,* p. 30.

21. ". . . um dem Tone nicht am freyen Durchgang hinderlich zu seyn." Marpurg, *Anleitung zur Musik,* p. 23.

22. Our singers of florid passages today rarely observe such a rule. Cf. *op. cit.,* p. 37.

23. "Hell ist die Stimme, wenn sie durch den öffenen Mund, ohne Zwang und Drücken der Kehle, frey aus der Brust heraus kommt." Hiller, *Anweisung,* p. 6.

24. ". . . die anständigste beym Gesange, und die bequemste zur Hervorbringung eines guten Tons der Stimme." *Loc. cit.*

25. Abbe George Joseph Vogler, *Stimmbildungskunst,* Mannheim, 1776. Cf. p. 3.

26. Petri, *Anleitung zur Pracktisches Musik.* Cf. p. 197.

27. Kuerzinger, *Getreuer Unterricht.* Cf. p. 51.

28. Nina D' Aubigny von Engelbrunner, *Briefe an Natalie über den Gesang,* 1803, p. 72.

29. *Op. cit.,* p. 112.

30. *Op. cit.,* pp. 114 f.

31. ". . . denn bey jedem Selbstlauter ist ja die Oeffnung desselben nicht so ganz die nämliche." Lasser, *Vollständige Anleitung,* p. 12.

32. Jumilhac, *La Science,* pp. 263 f.

33. ". . . de crainte que passant dans la tête ou dans le nez elle ne degenere en fausset par sa sourdité." Bailleux, *Solfeges,* p. 121.

34. "La position de la bouche doit être naturelle et un peu riante." Martini, *Melopée,* p. 4.

35. "Le Maitre doit aussi corriger les Ecoliers qui ont le défaut de chanter du nez ou de la gorge. S'il ne peut y réussir, il doit s'en séparer." *Loc. cit.*

36. Cf. Mengozzi, *Méthode,* pp. 8 f.

37. "En Vocalisant, l'élève doit faire attention à tenir toujours la bouche également ouverte, et sur tout à ne jamais mouvois ni le menton ni la langue." *Op. cit.,* p. 11.

38. Bayly, *A Practical Treatise,* p. 31.

39. *Ibid.,* p. 32.

40. *Ibid.,* p. 34.

41. Burney, *The Present State of Music in Germany,* I, pp. 245 f.

42. Tenducci, *Instruction,* Rule IV, p. 4.

43. *Ibid.,* Rule IX, *loc. cit.*

44. Lanza, *Elements,* I, p. 23.

45. Cf. *ibid.,* I, pp. 36–48.

XI. Voice Registers

1. Charles Churchill, *The Rosciad,* 1. 1003.

2. Cf. pp. 40 f.

3. Cf. p. 74.

4. ". . . nel quale possa cantare in voce piena e naturale per i sfuggire le voci finte . . . Ma dalle voci finte non può nascere nobilità di buon canto che nascerà da una voce naturale comoda per tutte le corde." Caccini, *Le Nuove Musiche,* pp. 8 f. Also in Solerti, *Le Origini,* pp. 68 f. Caccini is, in all likelihood, speaking of the masculine voice.

5. Cerone, *Melopeo,* p. 326. It could be that in speaking of "head voice" Cerone had in mind the falsetto voice.

6. F. Rognoni, *Selva di varii passaggi secondo l'uso moderno,* 1620. In Ulrich, *op. cit.,* p. 121.

7. Della Valle, *Della musica,* in Solerti, *op. cit.,* p. 162.

8. Andrea di Modena, *Canto Harmonico,* Moderna, 1690, p. 214.

9. F. S. Santoro, *Scola di canto fermo,* Naples, 1715, p. 20.

10. Cf. Nassare, *Escuela Musica,* II, 436. Also Vallara, *Primizie di canto fermo,* p. 4, Rule 14.

11. Tosi, *Observations,* p. 23.

12. *Op. cit.,* pp. 23 f.

13. *Loc. cit.*

14. *Op. cit.,* pp. 22 f.

15. Mancini, *Riflessioni,* pp. 58 f.

16. *Ibid.,* pp. 59 f.

17. *Ibid.,* pp. 109 f.

18. *Ibid.,* p. 110.

19. *Ibid.,* pp. 110 f.

20. *Ibid.,* p. 148.

21. *Ibid.,* p. 68.

22. "Dell' unire la voce di petto colla voce di testa, la quale volgarmente chiamasi falsett." Manfredini, *Regole Armoniche,* p. 61.

23. ". . . che la voce sembri tutta di un registro, che vuol dire tutta equale." *Loc. cit.*

24. Manfredini uses the word "falsetto."

25. "Questa cosa si fa non sforzando le corde acute di petto, e rinforzando piuttosto le corde basse del falsetto; o facendo il contrario, se le corde di petto fossero mai deboli, e mancanti; e quelle di falsetto, abbondanti, e forti." *Loc. cit.*

26. Cf. Seth Calvisius, *Musicae artis,* Jena, 1612. His eleven rules for singing are quoted in Forkel, *Algemeine Geschichte,* II, 65*n*; also in Albert Allerup, *Die "Musica Practica" des Johann A. Herbst,* Kassel, 1931, pp. 32 ff. Note rules 2, 4, and 6.

27. Cf. Michael Praetorius, *Syntagma Musicum,* III, 181.

28. Cf. Mattheson, *Mithridat wider den Gift einer welschen Satyr,* Hamburg, 1749, pp. 140 f.

29. Cf. Agricola, *Anleitung.* All the discussion that follows will be found on pp. 22, 31–37 under note "o."

30. Cf. below, pp. 131 ff.

31. Cf. below, p. 131.

32. ". . . dass die Eröfnung der Luftröhre geschmeidiger, und folglich weniger elastich, die Luftröhre an sich selbst enger, und die Lunge nicht so ausdehnbar ist, wird man aus der Beschreibung der Bruststimme schon hinlänglich haben abnehmen können. Es ist also nicht nöthig weiter etwas davon zu gedenken." *Op. cit.,* p. 34. It is difficult to follow the author's reasoning here for the statement would seem to be a contradiction. Flexibility and suppleness in the larynx should make it more elastic than less so, but his theory that the head voice lacks the clarity and sharpness of the chest voice must be made to appear reasonable.

33. "Die meisten Naturkündiger sowohl als Tonkünstler beschreiben die

Falsett-töne, welche bey jeder Stimme sowohl in der äussersten Höhe als in der äussersten Tiefe vorkommen können, durch gezwungene Töne, und eine Falsettstimme durch gezwungene Stimme. Aber wie werden denn diese gezwungenen Töne heraus gebracht? Wir wollen erstlich die Falsett-töne in der Höhe untersuchen. Man weis, dass man durch einen gewissen fühlbaren zwang, den man dem Halse im Singen anthut, viel mehrere hohe Töne heraus bringen kann, als sonst ordentlich der Umfang einer jeden Stimme mit sich bringet. Wer mit seiner natürlichen Stimme, es sey was für eine es wolle, so weit in die Höhe singt, als er ohne Zwang kommen kann, du wird finden, dass ihm endlich keiner mehr anspricht; und denn könnte er glauben, dass die Luftröhre nunmehr gänzlich verschlossen sey, dass sie folglich keine Luft mehr heraus lassen, und also auch keinen Ton mehr angeben könne. Bemüht er sich aber ein wenig, noch mehrere Töne hinauf zu singen; so wird er bemerken können, dass ihm noch einige höhere ausprechen werden, welche aber, ohne Kunst anzuwenden, dem Laute nach etwas von den vorigen unterschieden sind; und er wird wahrnehmen, dass die aus der Glottis heraus gehende Luft weiter hinten in der Tiefe des Gaumens anschlägt. Es kann also keine andere Ursache der Hervorbringung dieser Töne seyn, als diese, dass der ganze Kopf der Luftröhre höher gespannet, und weiter in das Hinterste der Höhle des Gaumens, unter dem Zungenbeine, hinauf gezogen wird. Die noch mehr gespannete Glottis fängt in dieser Lage von neuem an, ihre noch übrige Oefnung bey immer höher steigenden Tönen zusammen zu ziehen; bis sie sich endlich ganz und gar schliesst, und weiter kein Ton mehr heraus kömmt. Durch dieses Hinaufspannen des Kopfes der Luftröhre wird also auch die jedem Tone sich bequemende Länge der ganzen Höhle des Mundes noch mehr verkürzet. Geht man im Singen wieder mit dieser Falsett-tönen nach der Tiefe zurück; so wird einer der dabey auf sich selbst Achtung giebt, finden, dass bey einem gewissen Tone, der Kopf der Luftröhre, seine hoch gespannte Stellung auf einmal verlässt, und sich wieder an seinen vorigen Ort setzet." *Op .cit.,* pp. 34 f.

34. "Alle und jede natürliche Stimmen, wenn sie auch nicht vom puren Falsettsingen Profession machen, können in der Höhe einige Falsett-töne angeben." *Op. cit.,* p. 36.

35. ". . . je mehr ist unsere Schuldigkeit, die Allmacht und Weisheit des Schöpfers in tiefster Demuth zu bewundun, und zu verehren." *Loc. cit.*

36. "Es ist aber die Kunst und der natürliche Vortheil derjenigen deren Stimmen durch gehendes egal klingen." *Op. cit.,* p. 37.

37. "Die Falsett-töne in der Höhe hingegen, sind bey vielen Sängern, welche recht damit umzugehen wissen, eben so stark und schön als die natürlichen hohen Töne." *Loc. cit.*

38. Cf. Marpurg, *Anleitung,* pp. 19 f.

39. ". . . wenigstens ist hier die Verbindung der Falsetstimme mit der natürlichen weit leichter, und der Uebergang von einer zur andern schwerer zu bemerken." Hiller, *Anweisung,* p. 10.

40. "Durch die Beyfügung einiger Falsettöne wird der Umfang der natürlichen Stimme erweitert. Nur muss der Sänger darauf Acht haben, dass man den Uebergang von einer Art der Stimme zur andern nicht zu sehr gewahr werde. Die Grenzen der einen müssen sich noch bis auf ein paar Töne ins Gebiete der andern erstrecken; und der Sopranist, der von $\bar{\bar{c}}$ zu $\bar{\bar{\bar{c}}}$ bis ins $\bar{\bar{a}}$ mit du natürlichen Stimme singt, und sodann mit der Falsetstimme die übrigen Töne hinzu setzt, muss mit dieser auch schon in $\bar{\bar{f}}$ eintreten können, ohne dass man einen Abfall bemerkt. Es verursacht aber allerdings einige Schwierigkeit, den untern Tönen des Falsets eine der Bruststimme gemässe Stärke zu geben." *Op. cit.,* p. 11.

41. From the fistula or pipe which sounds high.

42. ". . . eine unharmonische oder misslingende Verkehrung derselben." Petri, *Anleitung,* p. 205. The author here is evidently concerned with the true-tempered scale.

43. "Ich weiss z. e., ich kan bis $\bar{c}$ hinunter mit dem Falsett, so soll ich mit $\bar{e}$ oder $\bar{d}$ schon wechseln, wenn ich absteige; im Aufsteigen aber bis $\bar{c}$ oder $\bar{d}$ noch die Bruststimme gebrauchen. Die höhen Bassisten werden also durch das Falsett zu den besten Tenorarien brauchbar, welches wenigstens im Nothfalle von nicht geringem Vortheile ist. Aber doch gestehe ich, dass wenige ein gutes Falsett lernen, das sich von der Bruststimme nicht merklich unterscheide." *Op. cit.,* p. 206.

44. Cf. Aubigny, *Briefe,* pp. 92–100.

45. ". . . wo die Bruststimme zu ende ist, und das Falsett, oder die sogenannte Kopfstimme eintritt." Lasser, *Vollständige Anleitung,* p. 12.

46. ". . . wie wenn man [um mich des Ausdrucks der Italiener zu bedienen] auf der Orgel zwey verschiedene Register zieht." *Op. cit.,* p. 13.

47. ". . . wird am zuverlässigsten erreichet, wenn man sich bemühet und gewöhnet, sowohl den Letzten Ton der Bruststimme, als den ersten des Falsetts auf beyde Arten anzugeben." *Loc. cit.*

48. ". . . tout comme on tire de la flute des tons plus hauts en y faisant entrer le vent avec plus de force." Kempelen, *Le Mécanisme de la parole,* p. 93. This book is a study in diction and need not be considered too seriously.

49. "La grande difficulté consiste à rendre imperceptible le passage de la voix de poitrine à celle du gosier, et de celle du gosier à celle de tête, de manière que toutes ces trois voix n'en forment qu'une, c'est-a-dire, que tous les tons en parcourant leur espace ayent la même force, la meme qualité et la même facilité." Martini, *Melopée Moderne,* p. 5.

division particulière dans l'étendue de la voix, et cette division s'apelle Registre. Comme ces sons de Poitrine diffèrent pour le caractère des sons qui prennent leur naissance dans la Tête, ceux ci à leur tour forment une autre division ou Registre dans l'étendue de la même voix . . . Nous avons donc adopté le mot *registre* des Italiens parce qu'il nous a paru exprimer d'une manière concise les différens caractères de son qui se trouvé dans l'étendue de la voix." Mengozzi, *Méthode de Chant,* p. 4, note 2.

51. Cf. *loc. cit.*

52. *Ibid.,* p. 5. The actual pitches of these tones were probably from a semi-tone to a whole-tone lower than the standard pitch of today.

53. *Loc. cit.*

54. Cf. *op. cit.,* pp. 12 f.

55. Bayly, *Practical Treatise,* pp. 32 f.

56. Tenducci, *Instruction,* p. 4.

57. Cf. articles on Martini in the music lexicons of Fetis, Mendel, and Eitner.

XII. Vocal Organs

1. "Vox nihil aliud quam ictus aer." Seneca, *Naturales Quaestiones.* Bk. II, sec. 29.

2. Cf. Artusi, *L'Arte del Contrapunto,* p. 1. Hippocrates and Aristotle wrote to the same effect and many others after them.

3. "Il trillo descritto de me sopra una corda sola . . . cioe il comminciarsi dalla prima semiminima eribattere ciascuna nota con la gola sopra la vocale 'a,' fino all ultima breve." Caccini, *La Nuove Musiche,* p. 4. Playford, in his free translation of *Le Nuove Musiche* sees fit to add that "some observe, that it is rather the shaking of the Uvula or Pallate on the throat in one sound upon a note." In order to achieve this skill Playford says, "The most surest [*sic*] and ready way is by imitation of those who are perfect in the same," although some have learned by beating or shaking "with their Finger upon their Throat, which by often practice came to do the same notes exactly without." John Playford, *An Introduction to the Skill of Music in Three Books,* 12th ed., London, 1694. Cf. pp. 43 f. Pp. 31–46 are a translation of *Le Nuove Musiche.*

4. Cf. Cerone, *Melopeo,* pp. 324 f.

5. *Op. cit.,* p. 551.

6. Avella, *Regole di Musica,* 1657. Cf. p. 43.

7. ". . . la voce è una ripercussione d'aria respirata all arteria vocale." Berardi, *Ragionamenti,* p. 42.

8. Cf. Bontempi, *Historia Musica,* Perugia, 1695, p. 84.

9. One is forced to the conclusion that Bontempi regarded the terms

"scutiform" and "cricoid" as interchangeable or else that either one cartilage or the other is involved in each act of phonation.

10. Cf. *op. cit.*, p. 109. There is apparent further lack of understanding with regard to the glottis and the epiglottis.

11. "Espongono queste differenze i Fisici, cagionate dal sito, dal meato, dalla figura, dall' aria, dall' espiratione, e da tutti i temperamenti della laringe; fermate sopra gl'immobili fondamenti della incontestabile ragione. La nostra opinione è, che tutto quello che si raccoglie dall' esperienza non habbia indigenza di ragione. Se questa non venga dei Fisici ammessa, sarà loro ufficio il darne altra sentenza. Et essendo esposto questo gando la Natura per ritrovarlo con la ragione, noi senza filosofarvi sopra saremo contenti di conoscerle con l'insegnamento della propria esperienza." *Op. cit.*, p. 110.

12. Cf. Zaccaria Tevo, *Il Musico Testore*, Venezia, 1706, p. 32.

13. Cf. *ibid.*, pp. 33 f.

14. Cf. *ibid.*, facing p. 35.

15. Nassare, *Escuela Musica*, II, p. 432 f. These comments on voice production can only be considered inept.

16. Cf. Mancini, *Riflessioni*, p. 54.

17. *Ibid.*, p. 55.

18. *Ibid.*, p. 57.

19. "La voce considerata in se stessa non è altro, che l'aria sospinta in su dai polmoni, la quale introducendosi pel canale, che si chiama *trachea*, indi assotigliandosi per la fessura della glottide, e nella cavita della bocca ripercuotendosi, esce poi dalle labra formando un romore, o suono inarticolato." Stefano Arteago, *Le rivoluzioni del teatro musicale italiano dalla sua origine fino al presente*, Venezia, 1785, p. 61.

20. *Ibid.*, p. 65.

21. Manfredini, *Regole Armoniche*. Cf. pp. 54, 75.

22. "Vox in gutture, non labijs vel buccis efformanda." Quoted in Forkel, *Algemeine Geschichte*, II, 65*n*; also in Allerup, *Die "Musica Practica" des Johannes A. Herbst*, p. 32.

23. Praetorius, *Syntagma Musicum*, I, pp. 188 f.

24. Kircher, *Magnes, sive de arte magnetica opus tripartium*, pp. 843 f.

25. Kircher seems vague as to the distinction between the glottis and epiglottis, and repeatedly combines the terms in this way as if he considered them interchangeable.

26. Kircher, *Musurgia Universalis*, p. 20. It should be mentioned that although Kircher was held in great respect by contemporaries, subsequent scholars have gradually diminished his stature.

27. ". . . aus dessen Spalte, mittelst überaus subtiler Oeffnungen und Bewegungen, der Klang hervorgebracht wird." Mattheson, *Der volkommene Capellmeister*, p. 96.

28. ". . . dessen Substantz aber viel weicher seyn mag, etwa wie ein Pergament." *Loc. cit.*

29. ". . . dennoch aber thut die Glottis selbst ganz gewiss das meiste und vornehmste dabey: und ist also weder die Lunge, noch die Zunge, weder die Gurgel, noch der Gaumen die rechte Ursache des Tones; vielweniger sind es die Zähne und Lefzen, welche alle keinen weitern Antheil daran haben, als dass die erste den Wind hergibt, die andern aber, nachdem der Schall durch die Spalte des Züngleins oben an der Lufftröhre, mittelst dreizehn Musceln gezeuget worden, fein hohl, vernehmlich, richtig, und ungehindert heraus lassen. Es ist also die einzige menschliche Glottis das klangreicheste, angenehmste, vollenkommenste und richtigste Instrument, oder besser zu sagen, sie ist das einzige und allein richtige Instrument unter der grossen Menge klingender Werckzeuge, sie mögen durch Kunst verfertiget, oder von der Natur hervorgebracht werden; denn alle diese vom Winde getriebene oder mit Saiten bezogene Instrumente, nur die Geigen ausgenommen, sind mit einander falsch, gegen die menschliche Stimme zu rechnen, und wenn sie auch auf das beste gestimmet wären." *Loc. cit.* The last statement is taken from an article by Dodart in *Memoires de L'Acad. Roy. de Sciences,* 1700, p. 16, entitled "Memoire sur les Causes de la voix de l'Homme." Mattheson is incorrect in giving the pagination as p. 338. The process of phonation described seems to be at least partly deduced from Dodart's *Memoire.* That he really did so is further borne out by his comment on voice production in his *Mithridat,* p. 142. Here he explains that high tones cause a moderate contraction of the windpipe and its sensitive organs while low tones result from the opposite action. If the entire range were to be suddenly sung from bottom to top the glottal opening would quickly contract, which, of course, is the theory of Galen. He also compares the voice to the oboe saying that they are "to some extent" alike.

30. The reader will find the following discussion in Agricola, *Anleitung zur Singkunst,* pp. 25–42.

31. "Von zweenen dieser obern Knorpel, und zween davon vorwärts hin abgehenden festen Bändern, wird die kleine Eröfnung der Luftröhre, welche *rima glottidis* heisst, umgeben, und von einem andern, welcher oben drüber lieget, und vorn an dem schildförmigen Knorpel befestiget, hinten aber frey ist, und folglich auf—und zugehen kann, bedecket. Dieser letztere wird *Epiglottis* oder der Kehldeckel genennet. Alle diese Knorpel des Kopfes der Luftröhre sind durch elastiche Ligamente mit einander verbunden. Damit aber auch die zu der Bewegung dieser Knorpel und Ligamente nöthige Luft immer da sey: so ist die Lunge vermögend, dieselbe, durch den Canal der Luftröhre, und die unten von ihm ab, und in die ganze Substanz der Lunge hinein gehenden vielen kleinen Aestchen, nicht nur von aussen einzuziehen, sondern auch mit vielen Graden der Stärke wieder heraus zu treiben. Weil

die jetzt beschriebene Eröfnung der Luftröhre, vermittelst der dazu bestimmten Muskeln, erweitert und zusammen gezogen werden kann; so kann sie folglich hohe und tiefe Töne angeben.

"Die beyden Seiten der Eröfnung der Luftröhre stehen aufs höchste um eine Linie, oder um den zehnten Theil eines Zolles von einander. Dieser sehr kleinen Entfernung ungeachtet, kann doch ein Mensch mit seiner Stimme ganz bequem zwölf ganze Töne angeben. Folglich wird, wenn ein solcher einen ganzen Ton angiebt, oder eine grosse Secunde höher oder tiefer singt, die Eröfnung der Luftröhre um 1/120 Theil von einem Zolle enger oder weiter. Die Naturkündiger haben aber auch noch über dieses erwiesen, das die Stimme einen ganzen Ton wieder zum wenigsten in hundert andere ganz kleine Töne eintheilen, und folglich ein Mensch, der zwölf ganze Töne singen kann, 2400 verschiedene Töne herausbringen könne; welche alle noch durch ein, im höchsten Grade, seines Gehör, (als welches wahrnehmen kann, wenn eine Saite nur um den hunderten Theil kürzer gemacht wird) müssten unterschieden werden können. Sie haben noch weiter erwiesen, dass wenn man auf diesen Unterscheid nicht mehr Acht haben will, die Anzahl der Töne, welche ein Mensch hervorbringen kann, unendlich gross seyn würde: weil sich die Eröfnung der Luftröhre, wie eine jede Linie, in unendlich viele unendlich kleine Theile eintheilen lässt; welches auch wirklich geschieht, wenn die Stimme von einem Tone nach und nach zum andern kömmt, ohne dass der Schall aufhöret. Denn indem sich die Eröfnung der Luftröhre zusammen zieht; so geschieht ihre Bewegung durch alle Puncte ihres Diameters.

"Wenn man einen allzutiefen Ton hervorbringen will, so wird die Eröfnung der Luftröhre dergestalt gross gemacht, dass die Luft durch dieselbe einen ganz freyen Durchgang findet. Folglich geräth sie dadurch nicht mehr in eine zitternde Bewegung, und folglich auch entsteht kein Schall mehr. Wenn man aber einen allzuhohen Ton angeben will, so wird die Eröfnung der Luftröhre ganz verschlossen, die Luft findet keinen Ausgang mehr, und kann also keinen Schall verursachen." *Op. cit.,* pp. 25 f.

32. "Diese Bewegungen nun müssen, wenn man singen will, mit jenen, welche nur zur Hervorbringung des Tones dienen, aufs geschickteste vereiniget werden, und in der freundschaftlichsten Verbindung stehen." *Op. cit.,* p. 27.

33. *Ibid.,* p. 28. Agricola also uses the masculine when speaking of a soprano. Cf. p. 92, n. 19.

34. "Diese Frage wollen wir den Naturkündigern zu weiterer Untersuchung überlassen." *Ibid.,* p. 29.

35. Cf. *ibid.,* p. 31.

36. Cf. *ibid.,* pp. 30 f.

37. *Op. cit.,* pp. 37 ff.

38. "Uns, die wir Werkzeuge der Stimme hier, nicht sowohl als Anatomisten oder Aerzte, sondern vielmehr als Sänger betrachten, kommt, bey einem allgemeinen Stillschweigen der andern Naturkündiger, über diesen Punct, nicht zu, zu entscheiden, ob die, mit so vielen Versuchen bestärketen Entdeckungen des Herrn Ferrein in allen Stücken ihre Richtigkeit haben, oder nicht: da sonst, wider seine daraus hergeleiteten Folgen, wenig einzuwenden seyn würde." *Ibid.,* p. 40.

39. J. A. Hiller, *Anweisung,* p. 6.

40. "Quasi la figure d'une oval." Marin Mersenne, *Harmonie Universelle,* Vol. II, prop. 3, p. 5.

41. ". . . est produit par l'air qui est poussé du poumon et de la poitrine, et par . . . le battement, qui s'en fait par le moyen de l'artere vocale du larinx, de la glotte, du palais, des dents, et des lèvres." Jumilhac, *La Science,* p. 46. Cf. also p. 48.

42. ". . . c'est de la flexibilité de la luette que dépend toute la varieté des tons de la voix." *Nouvelle Methode,* p. 12. Further explanations are offered as to why this is so but they are too naive to be considered. Eitner suggests that the author was an ecclesiastic of the diocese of Rouen. This "singing method" was a popular one since there were several editions over a period of more than a century.

43. "Mais de rien on ne peut rien faire."

44. ". . . c'est elle qui en se dilatant, ou en s'étrécissant avec l'aritenôïde à l'aide des muscles du larynx, et par le moyen de L'épiglotte fait la voix de *superius* ou de *Basse-taille,* de *basse-contre* ou de *haute-contre."* Rénir Carré, *Le Maistre des novices dans l'art du chanter,* Paris, 1744, pp. 19 f.

45. "Enfin ou assure que la luette ou petite membrane cartilagineuse posée sur la trachée-artère, comme les doigts sur une flute ou sur un flageolet, lorsqu'elle est bien proportionée; c'est à dire lorsqu'elle n'est ni trop grosse et pesante, ni trop petite, contribue infiniment a la force et a la beauté de la voix; parce que réglant le volume d'air qui doit entrer et celui qui doit fortir, elle articule plus ou moins la voix suivant le sujet et les circonstances, lui donne ses agrémens et mesure ses cadences ou tremblemens." *Loc. cit.*

46. "Il ne doit pas seulement réfléchir sur ses organs; mais encore sur ceux de ses Ecoliers: s'il vient à bout de les connaitre . . . il parviendra à faire chanter avec succès les sujets les plus ineptes." Blanchet, *L'art du chant,* p. 5. We have already noted, pp. 97 f., the unusual claims made by this author with regard to ear training.

47. *Ibid.,* pp. 6 f.

48. ". . . est la partie la plus étroite et la plus basse de l'ouverture du larinx: c'est une fente horisontale terminée par deux lèvres, l'une à droit et l'autre à gauche." *Ibid.,* p. 7.

49. ". . . sensible aux yeux, ce que j'ai taché de rendre sensible à l'esprit." *Loc. cit.*

50. "Si les levres de la glotte pourvoient être plus tendens à l'infini, l'on pourroit en tirer une infinité de sons de différentes sortes." *Ibid.,* p. 17.

51. *Ibid.,* p. 23. Blanchet's theory of voice production appears to be sound, based as it was on the experiments of Ferrein, but his speculation carries him astray, as we have already seen in his insistence that pitch could be varied by a conscious control of the rise and fall of the larynx. Cf. p. 498.

52. Cf. *ibid.,* chap. 7, pp. 37–41.

53. "Nous ne pouvons disposer du *larynx,* de la *trachée-artère,* de la *glotte,* nous ne voyons pas leurs diffèrentes configurations, transformations, à chaque son que nous voulons donner; mais nous savons du moins qu'il ne faut pas les contraindre dans ces différences, qu'il faut leur laisser la liberté de suivre leur mouvement natural." Rameau, *Code de Musique Pratique,* p. 16.

54. *Ibid.,* p. 19. From these remarks it is obvious that Rameau was ignorant of or did not agree with the conclusions of Ferrein.

55. "Un peu d'air presse par les poumons à travers la fente étroite de la glotte produit la voix; plusieurs obstacles que la langue, les dents, et les lèvres opposent à cet air resonnant causent l'inflexion et la varieté des sons, dont chacun a sa signification propre." Kempelen, *Le méchanisme de la parole,* p. 27.

56. *Ibid.,* p. 60.

57. *Ibid.,* p. 83.

58. *Ibid.,* p. 106.

59. "La définition philosophique de cet organe n'entrerait pas utilement dans le plan d'une Méthode de Chant; mais, pour l'intelligence des différens préceptes qui doivent y être énoncés, il est nécessaire d'établis les notions principales des moyens qui contribuent à l'action de la voix." Mengozzi, *Méthode de Chant,* p. 1.

60. "Le *Larinx* est un des organes de la respiration et le principal instrument de la voix, c'est la partie supérieure de la trachée-artère, il a la forme d'un canal court et cylindrique qui est ouvert par une fente ovale qu'on appelle *Glotte;* par cette fente l'air descend et remonte quand on respire, chante ou parle: elle a la faculté de s'étrécir ou de s'élargir à volonté, et sa plus ou moins grande dilatation produit toutes les variétés des tons de la voix humaine: la glotte est défendue par un cartilage très mince et très fléxible, appellé *épiglotte;* ce cartilage est mobile et a la forme d'une feuille de lierre, il est concave intérieurment et convexe supérieurement; sa principale attribution est de recouvrir la glotte au besoin." *Ibid.,* pp. 1 f.

61. It is included here only because the author, Corri, was trained in Italy under Porpora and became one of the most influential singing teachers in England.

62. Likely Dr. Samuel Arnold, d. 1802.

63. Corri, *The Singer's Preceptor,* p. 4.

64. His book, "Observations on Vocal Music" was published in 1821.

65. *Op. cit.,* p. 1.

XIII. Vocal Hygiene

1. Tosi, *Observations on the Florid Song,* p. 147.

2. Mattheson, *Mithridat wider den Gift einer welschen Satyr,* Hamburg, p. 48.

3. Petri, *Anleitung zur pracktischen Musik,* p. 214.

4. Cf. above, pp. 19 f.

5. Cf. Cerone, *Melopeo,* pp. 37, 48–52, 60–61, 174.

6. Cf. *ibid.,* pp. 327 ff.

7. Uberti, *Contrasto Musico,* Rome, 1630; cf. p. 9.

8. Doni, *De Praestantia,* p. 100. It must be said that the information concerning Nero was taken from Suetonius and might therefore be considered legendary. A later statement of Doni's is of interest, in which he says that the people of Asia Minor excel in sweetness of voice and aptitude for singing, not only because of luxury and wealth and softness of spirit, and lively and happy disposition, but because of the clemency of the sky and the excellence of the water. *Ibid.,* p. 104.

9. Avella quotes Celsus [fl. 1st c.] to the effect that for a voice to be preserved it is necessary for a man to be now in his villa, now in the city, again hunting, then fishing, and to rest from time to time. Cf. Avella, *Regole di Musica,* p. 127.

10. *Loc. cit.* Again he refers to *Medicina,* Bk. I, of Celsus, where according to Avella it is written that the singer should water his wine well and if he is elderly he should drink natural and good wine. Middle-aged singers will do well to take a little water along with wine, in order to prevent the inflammation which is common at this age, especially in warm weather. In winter, however, drink pure wine, not too strong, and abstain from debauchery. It must be said here that Book I of the *Medicina* referred to does not offer this advice particularly to singers but rather to all. Since Avella considers good health requisite to good singing, he may be pardoned for the liberties he has taken with the written word of Celsus. Since Cerone had already written to the same effect, it is possible that still earlier writers were guilty of misrepresenting the text of Celsus.

11. "Todos estos remedios que aqui ponemos, son muy buenos, y faciles de hazer, para conservacion de la vox humana; usando de ellos con moderacion, y consulta del docto Medico." Lorente, *El Porque de la Musica.* Cf. pp. 727 ff. There is nothing original in this work but it is interesting in that he attaches a great deal of importance to good health for the singer.

12. Tosi, *op. cit.,* p. 80.

13. *Op. cit.,* p. 89.

14. *Op. cit.,* p. 144. The reader is again referred to the quotation from Tosi at the beginning of this chapter in which he advises the singer against feigned indispositions.

15. Mancini, *op. cit.,* p. 44.

16. *Op. cit.,* pp. 70 f.

17. Cf. Praetorius, *Syntagma Musicum,* I, p. 188.

18. Cf. *op. cit.,* pp. 189, 190, 198.

19. "Ein Sänger soll nicht übermässig schreyen, wie die Dorff-Küster und Acker-Studenten, sondern zwar laut, und mit ziemlicher Stärke, doch lieblich und anmuthig singen." Printz, *Compendium,* chap. 4, ¶ 7.

20. "Wer aber wol singen will, der muss nothwendig alles, was zur Stimmes gehöret, mit Fleiss untersuchen, ihrer schonen und warten, sie üben, lencken, regieren, zwingen und unterhalten." Mattheson, *Vollkommene Kapellmeister,* p. 94, ¶ 3. Cf. also ¶ 2.

21. Cf. *op. cit.,* p. 95, ¶ 8.

22. "Unter den Teutchen Sängern habe ich keinen grössern Phonascum gekannt, als den berühmten Capellmeister Bimmler, welcher, wenn er des Abends singen sollte, sich des Tages der gewöhnlichen Mittags-Mahlzeit enthielt, von Zeit zu Zeit etwas Fänchel, wie einen Thee, zu sich nahm, und inzwischen bey dem Clavichord, mit gemähliger und gelinder Durch-singung seiner Partie sich stets übte, auch solchen Fleiss darauf wandte dass er sie allemahl auf eine neue Art, mit veränderten wolgewehlten Zierrathen herausbrachte." *Loc. cit.,* ¶ 9.

23. "Ein guter Feldherr dencket nicht nur auf das Befehlen, sondern auch auf das wehlen seiner Soldaten." Cf. *op. cit.,* p. 98, ¶¶ 23, 24.

24. ". . . deren eine nur Biscuit, und die andre ein wenig saures, von Citronen oder dergleichen zu sich nahm, wenn der Hals recht sauber seyn und sich hören lassen sollte. Viele, die hierin eines andern Glaubens waren, und sich lieber an Rosinen oder Zucker-Werck ergetzten, verwunderten sich über solche unanständige Mittel, wollten es, absonderlich mit der Säure, nicht nachmachen, und kamen immer dabey zu kurtz. Es hat auch in diesem Stücke ein jeder billig die Umstände und Eigenschafften seines Temperaments zu prüfen, und was ihm nicht dienlich ist, auszusetzen." *Loc. cit.,* ¶ 26.

25. Cf. Mattheson, *Mithridat,* p. 46.

26. "Der Sänger muss . . . nicht gleich nach dem Essen singen, eine vermunstige Diät im Essen und Trinken beobachten, und alles Bittre, Scharfe, Salzige, Saure und Herbe meiden, oder wenigstens sehr mässig und selten geniessen. Endlich muss er weder zu viel singen, noch schreyen, weil

solches die Kähle rauh machet, und die Stimme verdirbt." Marpurg, *Anleitung,* p. 34.

27. "Die bequemsten Stunden zur Uebung im Singen sind die Morgenstunden." *Loc. cit.*

28. *Op. cit.,* pp. 34 f.

29. Cf. Hiller, *Anweisung,* pp. 8 f., 12.

30. "Man braucht das Singen eben nicht ganz zu unterlassen: es muss nur sparsamer und mit gemässigterm Tone geschehen." *Op. cit.,* p. 13.

31. "Kurz, Mässigkeit im Essen und Trinken, wobey man nicht so wohl darauf siehet, was, als WIEVIEL man isst und trinkt, nebst einer in allen übrigen Stücken, guten Lebensordnung, sind für den Menschen, der seine Gesundheit liebt, und für den Sänger, der seine Stimme schonen will, von gleicher Wichtigkeit." *Op. cit.,* pp. 13 f.

32. Cf. *op. cit.,* pp. 14 f, ¶ 20.

33. ". . . dass bey vollem Magen die Lunge nicht alle Freiheit zum Athemholen hat." *Loc. cit.,* ¶ 21.

34. Cf. Petri, *Anleitung,* p. 213.

35. Cf. *op. cit.,* p. 214.

36. "In der Diät soll ein Sänger sorgfältig seyn, ob gleich nicht ängstlich, denn nicht so wohl der Genuss eines nicht zuträglichen Nahrungsmittals, als vielmehr sein zu reichlicher Genuss ist schädlich. Je gesünder sein Körper ist, desto fester ist seine Stimme." *Loc. cit.*

37. "Wie viele haben sich damit schon den Kirchhof geholt!—Kan man ihnen nicht eine gute Stunde Zeit lassen, erst vollkommen zu ruhigem Pulse und freyer Lunge zu kommen?" *Loc. cit.*

38. "Endlich nach vielem Singen soll man eine Zeitlang gänzlich ruhig sizzen [*sic*], ohne etwas zu trinken, es sey warm oder kalt. Nachher nimt man nur einen sehr kleinen Mund voll, und so fort nach einigen Minuten ein mehrers zu sich, und wenn gleich der erste Durst noch so stark wäre, so soll man ihm nicht ein Genüge thun. Salomo sagt: Predigen macht den Leib müde, aber ich glaube, dass Singen den Körper weit mehr angreift, und dass man alle Vorsicht dabey brauchen müsse, um seiner Gesundheit nicht Schaden zu thun, und seine Stimme nicht zu gleich mit zu verderben." *Op. cit.,* p. 215.

39. "Es gibt trefliche Singer, die ehender etwas Salat, als von Zucker zu sich nehmen; wie es denn auch eine bekannte Sache, dass der Zucker Schleim mache und vermehre. Aber frisch gelegte Eyer sogleich ungesotten ausgetrunken, auch Thee mit Fenchel, oder Sternaniss ist der Stimme dienlich. Ein gut Gläschen Wein für den *Sopran,* und ein altes braunes Bier, wo es zu haben, für den *Alt,* kann nicht schaden." Kuerzinger, *Getreuer Unterricht,* p. 5.

40. *Ibid.,* p. 52.

41. This is contrary to the usual advice which urges the singer to protect himself from inclement weather. Cf. above, p. 143.

42. Cf. Aubigny, *Briefe,* pp. 199–206.

43. Cf. Lasser, *Vollständige Anleitung,* p. 12.

44. ". . . & particulierement de celuy des femmes, comme Quintilian, & Cornelius Celsus a remarqué." Mersenne, *Harmonie Universelle,* II, 45.

45. Cf. above, pp. 22 f.

46. Cf. Mersenne, *op. cit.,* pp. 45 f.

47. Bacilly, *Remarques,* p. 41.

48. Cf. Carré, *Le Maistre,* pp. 21–24.

49. "Mais pour qu'il soit utile tant pour la voix que pour la santé, il faut que l'on n'eu boive qu'avec modération, sagesse, et discretion." *Loc. cit.*

50. *Op. cit.,* pp. 24 f.

51. "1. De ne se laisser jamais saisir de froid par les pieds, et encore moins par la tête, qu'il faut avoir grand soin de tenir couverte pendant la nuit.

"2. Evites tant que faire se peut les intempéries de l'air sur-tout le trop grand chaud ou le trop grand froid; les rayons du Soleil et de la Lune, la neige, les vents, les brouillards, et le serein tant du soir que du matin, ne s'y promenant jamais; et généralement tout ce qui peut infecter l'air.

"3. Prendre garde de ne pas trop crier, ni parler longtems [*sic*] et avec ardeur.

"4. N'user que le moins que l'on pourra des choses froides et aigus, comme raves, salads, verjus, vinaigre, oranges, citrons, pommes, etc. et en général de toutes sortes de fruites, ou légumes cruds.

"5. Ne se point laver la bouche d'eau par trop froide ni n'en boire, se gardant pareillement de manger de la glace ou de la neige.

"6. S'abstenir tant que l'on peut de manger de l'huile, ou du moins choses où il en entre beaucoup, ou d'en avaler sans nécessité.

"7. S'abstenir de manger des noix et d'user de leur huile ainsi que de celle qui est faite d'olives avant leur maturité.

"8. Ne pas manger d'anguille; parce qu'étant huileuse, gluante, et pituiteuse, elle engendre des obstructions et charge l'estomac.

"9. S'abstenir de la trop grande boisson, parce que la perfection de la voix consiste dans une sécheresse médiocre de ses instrumens: le gosier qui en est un, est pour cette raison composé d'une substance dure et cartilagineuse, afin d'aider l'air poussé par les poumons, à rendre la voix plus claire, plus éclatante, et plus sonore." *Op. cit.,* pp. 25 f.

52. *Loc. cit.*

53. *Op. cit.,* chap. 3, pp. 26–33.

54. ". . . la meilleure est de s'abstenir de toutes sortes d'exces; de toute boisson trop forte; de se garantir de la trop grande chaleur, et du trop grand

froid; du passage trop subit de l'une à l'autre; et de ne chanter ni trop haut, ni trop fort, ni trop longtems [*sic*] de suite." Martini, *Melopée Moderne,* p. 5.

55. Floridio Tomeoni (1757?–1820) was the son of an Italian singer, studied at the Naples Conservatory, came to Paris in 1783 and became famous there as a teacher after the Italian method of singing. His *Théorie de la musique vocale,* Paris, 1799, was highly regarded by Fetis and others.

56. "C'est une jeune plante dont on ne connait point encore la nature on l'espèce, et qu'il faut se contenter d'arroser chaque jour avec sobriété, afin de la laisser croitre et se développer, jusqu'au moment où son caractère reconnu indiquera les procédés de culture que l'on devra suivre alors." Tomeoni, *op. cit.,* pp. 64 f.

57. *Ibid.,* pp. 65 ff.

58. *Ibid.,* p. 108.

59. Cf. Mengozzi, *Méthode de Chant,* pp. 84 f.

60. Cf. Tenducci, *Instruction,* Rules IX, XI, and XVII.

61. Michael Kelly, *Reminiscences,* London, 1862, II, 108 f.

BIBLIOGRAPHY

Wide use has been made of general reference works, as well as the music dictionaries and encyclopedias in the different languages. These are well known and it is not felt necessary to list them.

Adami (da Bolsena), Andrea (1663–1742). Osservazioni per ben regolare il coro de i cantori della Cappella pontificia. Rome, A. deRossi, 1711.

Addison, Joseph. *The Spectator.* June 4, 1712.

Affillard, Michel l'. Principes très-faciles pour bien apprendre la musique, qui conduiront promptement ceux qui ont du naturel pour le chant jusqu'au point de chanter toute sorte de musique proprement, & à livre ouvert; par le Sr. l'Affillard. Amsterdam, E. Roger, 1717 (?).

Agricola, Johann Friedrich. Anleitung zur Singkunst, aus dem Italienischen des Herrn Peter Franz Tosi mit erläuterungen und zusätzen von J. F. Agricola. Berlin, 1757.

Algarotti, Francesco (Conte) (1712–1764). Saggio sopra l'opera in musica. Livonio, M. Coltellini, 1763.

Algier, J. La technique des anciens chanteurs italiens. Paris, Fischbacher, 1918.

Allerup, Albert. Die "Musica Practica" des Johann Andreas Herbst (1588–1666) u. ihre entwicklungsgeschichtliche Bedeutung; ein Beitrag zur Geschichte der deutschen Schulmusik. Kassel, Bärenreiter-Verlag, 1931.

Ambros, August W. Geschichte der Musik. 4 vols. Breslau, 1862–1878.

Andrea di Modena. Canto Harmonico in cinque parti diviso, col quale si puo arrivare alla perfetta cognitione del canto fermo. Modena, 1690.

Aristotle. De Anima transl. by W. S. Hett. Loeb Classical Library. New York, Putnam, 1935.

——— De Audibilibus, in Minor Works, transl. by W. S. Hett. Loeb Classical Library. New York, Putnam, 1936.

——— Poetics, transl. by W. H. Fyfe. Loeb Classical Library. New York, Putnam, 1927.

——— Politics, transl. by H. Rackham. Loeb Classical Library. New York, Putnam, 1932.

——— Problemata, transl. by E. S. Forster, Book XI, "Problems on the Voice," and Book XIX, "Problems connected with Harmony." Loeb Classical Library. New York, Putnam, 1932.

——— Rhetoric, transl. by J. H. Freese. Loeb Classical Library. New York, Putnam, 1929.

Arlberg, Hjalmar (1869–?). Belcanto; der lückenlose Weg zur alt italienischen Gesangstechnik. Ein Wegweiser für Lernende, Lehrende und Dirigenten. Leipzig, B. & H., 1933.

Arteaga, Stefano. Le rivoluzioni del teatro musicale italiano dalla sua origine fino al presente. Venetia, 1785.

Artusi, Giovanni Maria. Delle imperfettioni della Moderna Musica. Venetia, 1600.

——— L'arte del contrapunto. Venetia, 1598.

Aubigny von Engelbrunner (Nina D'). Briefe an Natalie über den Gesang, als Beförderung der häuslichen Glückseligkeit und des geselligen Vergnügens. Leipzig, Voss und Comp., 1803.

Augustine (Saint). De Musica, transl. by R. C. Taliaferro. Annapolis, St. John's Bookstore, 1939.

Avella, Giovanni d'. Regole di musica. Rome, F. Moneta, 1657.

Bach, Albert B. Musical Education & Vocal Culture. London, 1898.

——— The Principles of Singing. London, 1897.

Baci, Adolfo. "Osservazioni sul teatro di musica in Italia," in *Regio Istituto Musicale*. Florence, 1872.

Bacilly, Benigne de (1625?–1690?). Remarques curieuses sur l'art de bien chanter, et particulierement pour ce qui regarde le chant françois. Ouvrage fort utile à ceux qui aspirent à la methode de chanter, sur tout à bien prononcer les paroles avec toute la finesse & toute la force necessaire, & à bien observer la quantité des syllabes, & ne point confondre les longues & les brefves, suivant les regles qui en sont établies dans ce traité. Paris, Chez l'auteur, 1668.

Bailleux, Antoine (d. 1791). Solfeges pour apprendre facilement la musique vocale. 3d ed.; Paris, Chez M. Bailleux, 1760.

Balsamon, Theodorus. Annotations to Canones Sanctorum Patrum qui in Trullo convenerunt. In Migne: Pat. Graeca., vol. CXXXVII, cols. 501–874.

Banchieri, Adriano. Cartella musicale nel canto figurato, fermo et contrapunto. Venice, 1614.

Bauhinus, Caspar. De Larynge Vocis Organo Historia Anatomica. Ferrara, 1600.

Bayly, Anselm (1718[19]–1794). A practical treatise on singing and playing with just expression and real elegance. Being an essay on I. Grammar. II. Pronunciation; or, the art of just speaking. III. Singing—its graces—their application. London, J. Ridley, 1771.

Beattie, James (1735–1803). Essays: on poetry and music. Edinburgh, 1778.

Bedford, Arthur. The Great Abuse of Musick. London, 1711.

Benelli, Antonio Peregrino. Regole per il canto Figurato (in German and Italian). In two parts. Dresden, 1819.

Bérard, Jean Antoine (ca. 1710–1772). L'art du chant. Paris, Dessaint & Saillant, 1775.

Berardi, Angelo (d. 1693?). Ragionamenti musicali. Bologna, G. Monti, 1681.

Berlinische musikalische zeitung. "Historischen und kritischen inhalts." Berlin, 1793–1794.

Bernard (Saint) of Clairvaux. Works. In Migne: Patrologiae Cursus Completus Series Latina, vols. CLXXXII–CLXXXIV.

Bernhard, Christoph (1628–1692). Die Kompositionslehre Heinrich Schützens in der Fassung seines Schülers Christoph Bernhard. Eingeleitet und herausgegeben von Josef Maria Müller-Blattau. Leipzig, B. & H., 1926.

Beroaldus. Commentarius ad Suetonium. London, 1548.

Bertalotti, Angelo Michele (b. 1665). Regole facilissime per apprendre con facilità, e prestezza li canti fermo, e figurato. Bologna, M. Silvani, 1698.

Biaggi, G. A. "Considerazioni della Musica Italiana," in *Regio Istituto Musicale.* Florence, 1865.

——— "Della vita e delle opere di Gioacchino Rossini," in *Regio Istituto Musicale.* Florence, 1869.

——— "Del Melodrama e del Lohengrin di R. Wagner," in *Regio Istituto Musicale.* Florence, 1872.

——— Pietro Romano, and Luigi Casamorata. "Relazione delle commissione," in *Regio Istituto Musicale.* Florence, 1866.

Bianchi, Giovanni Antonio (1686–1758). De i vizj, e de i difetti del moderno teatro e del modo di corregergli. Rome, 1753.

Blanchet, Jean (1724–1778). L'art, ou les principes philosophiques du chant. 2d ed.; Paris, A. M. Lottin, 1756.

Bona, Joannis (1609–1672). Opera Omnia. Antwerp, 1723.

Bonnet, Jacques (1644–1724). Histoire de la musique. 4 vols. in 2. A la Haye & à Francfut sur Meyn, 1743.

Bononcini, Giovanni Maria (1640–1678). Musico prattico. Bologna, G. Monti, 1673.

Bontempi, Giovanni Andrea (1624–1705). Historia Musica. Perugia, 1695.

Bordier, Louis Charles (d. 1764). Nouvelle Méthode de Musique. Paris, Chez des Lauriers, 1760.

Bovicelli, Giovanni Battista. Regole, Passaggi di Musica. Venice, 1594.

Brosses, Le Président de. Lettres Familières Écrités D'Italie en 1739 et 40. 2d authentic edition, 2 vols. Paris, 1858.

Brown, John (1752–1787). Letters upon the poetry and music of the Italian Opera. Edinburgh, 1789.

Bukofzer, M. F. Music in the Baroque Era. New York, Norton, 1947.

Burney, Charles (1726–1814). A General History of Music. New ed. 2 vols. New York, 1935.

Burney, Charles. Memoirs of the life and Writings of the Abate Metastasio. 3 vols. London, 1796.

——— Present State of Music in France and Italy. London, 1771.

——— The Present State of Music in Germany, the Netherlands and United Provinces. 2 vols. London, 1775.

Caccini, Giulio. "Prefazione a L'Euridice (1600)." In Solerti, Angelo: Le Origini del Melodramma. Milan, Fratelli Bocca, 1903.

——— "Dedicatoria e prefazione a Le Nuove Musiche (1601)." In Solerti, Angelo: Le Origini del Melodramma. Milan, Fratelli Bocca, 1903.

——— Le Nuove Musiche. Prefazione a cura di Francesco Vatielli. Rome, Reale accademia d'Italia, 1934. *See also* Playford.

Caffi, Francesco. Storia della Musica Sacra nella gia cappella Ducale di San Marco in Venezia, 1318 al 1797. 2 vols. Venezia, 1854.

Calvisius, Seth. Musicae artis praecepta nova et facilima [*sic:* facilissima?] pro incipientibus conscripta. Jena, 1612. *See also* Forkel: Algemeine Geschichte. II., p. 65.

Campion, Thomas (1567–1620). Campion's Works, ed. P. Vivian. Oxford, 1909.

Canivez, Josephus-Maria. Statuta Capitulorum Generalium Ordinis Cisterciensis ab anno 1116 ad 1786. I, 1116–1120. Louvain, Revue d'histoire ecclesiastique, 1933.

Cannuzio, Pietro de'. Regulae Florum Musicae. Also known as Petrus de Canutiis. Florence, 1510.

Cantus diversi ex Antiphonario Romano Avenione, parts 1 and 2. 1777.

Carissimi Giacomo. Ars cantandi; das ist: Richtiger und ausführlicher weg die Jugend und dem rechten Grund in der Sing-Kunst zu unterrichten; in welscher Sprach aufgesetzt; nunmehro von einem Music-Freund in unsere Mutter-Sprach gebracht. Augspurg, J. Koppmayer, 1696.

Carozzi, G. N. Guida ant' igenica di ginnastica vocale. Milan, 1890.

Carré, R. (b. 1706). Le maistre des novices dans l'art du chanter. Paris, Le Breton, 1744.

Casserius, Julius (1545–1616). De vocis auditusque organis historiae. Ferrara, 1600.

Castiglione, Baldassare (1478–1529). Il Cortegiano. Venice, 1528.

Cattaneo, Giovanni (Conte). La Libertà del cantare. Lucca, Benedini, 1752.

Celani, E. "I Cantori della Cappella Pontificia nei Secoli XVI–XVII." In *Rivista Musicale Italiana,* 1907 (part 1).

Celoni (Pellegrini Celoni), Anna Maria. Grammatica o siano regole di ben cantare. Rome, 1810.

Cerone, Domenico Pietro (1566–1625). El Melopeo y Maestro, tractado le musica teorica y practica. Naples, 1613.

Chrysander, Friedrich. "Lodovici Zacconi als Lehrer des Kunstgesanges," in *V.f.M.W.*, VII (1891), 337–396; IX (1893), 249–310; X (1894), 531–567.

Cicero. Orator, transl. by H. M. Hubbell. Cambridge, Harvard University Press, 1939.

Clément, Jean M. B. (1743–1812). Anecdotes Dramatiques. 3 vols. Paris, 1775.

Coclicus, Adrianus Petit. Compendium Musices. Nuremberg, 1552.

Codronchi, Battista. De vitiis vocis libro duo, in quibus non solum vocis definitio traditur et explicatur, sed ilius differentae, instrumenta et causae aperiuntur; ultimo de vocis conservatione, praeservatione ac vitiorum ejus curatione tractatus. Francofonte, A. Wechelus, C. Marnius et Jo. Aubrius, 1597.

Collier, Joel. *See* Veal, George.

Conforto, Giovanni Lucca (c. 1560–?). Breve et facile maniera d'essercitarsi a far passagi. Rome, 1593 or 1603.

——— Im Faksimile mit Übersetzung hrsg. von Johannes Wolf. Berlin, M. Breslauer, 1922.

Conrad von Zabern (fl. 1470–1500?). De modo bene cantandi choralem cantum. Summarized by Jul. Richter. In *Monatshefte für Musikgeschichte,* XX (1888), 95–106.

Corri, Domenico (1746–1825). The Singers Preceptor, or Corri's treatise on vocal music. London, Chappell & Co., 1811.

Costa, Andrea. Considerazione sopra L'Arte del Canto in Generale. London, 1824.

Coussemaker, E. de. Scriptorum de Musica Aevi Nova Series. 4 vols. Paris, A. Durand, 1864.

Cummings, E. D. Unpublished manuscripts at the New York Academy of Medicine on the History of Castration. Assembled before 1940.

DaGagliano, Marco. "Dedicatoria e prefazione alla Dafne (1608)." In Solerti, Angelo: Le Origini del Melodramma. Milan, Fratelli Bocca, 1903.

D'Arcais, M. Francesco. "Memoria sulla pratica conoscenza della musica." In *Regio Istituto Musicale.* Florence, 1868.

David, François (fl. 1st half of 18th C.) Méthode nouvelle; ou Principes généraux pour apprendre facilement la musique et l'art de chanter. Paris, M. de la Chevardière, ca. 1760.

DeBekker, L. J. Music and Musicians. New York, Nicholas Brown, 1925.

Della Valle, Pietro. "Della musica dell' età nostra che non è punto inferiore anzi è migliore di quella dell' età passata (1640)." In Solerti, Angelo: Le Origini del Melodramma. Milan, Fratelli Bocca, 1903.

Delle-Sedie, E. Arte e Fisiologia del Canto. Milan, 1876.

Dionysius of Halicarnassus. De Compositione Verborum. Transl. and ed. by W. Rhys Roberts. London, Macmillan, 1910.

Diruta, Girolamo. Il Transilvano. 1597 (or 1612, 1625).

Dodart, Denis. "Mémoire sur les causes de la voix de l'Homme," in Mémoires de l'Académie de Sciences. Paris, 1703.

Dolmetsch, Arnold (b. 1858). The interpretation of the music of the XVII & XVIII centuries revealed by contemporary evidence. London, Novello, 1915.

Donati, Ignazio. Madrigali, 1636. Motetti, 1636.

Doni, Giovanni Battista (1593[4]–1647). Compendio del trattato de' generi e de' modi della musica. Rome, 1635.

——— De praestantia musicae veteris libri tres totidem dialogis comprehensi. Florence, 1647.

——— "Descrizione delle opere sulla musica." In Solerti, A.: Le Origini del Melodramma. Milan, Fratelli Bocca, 1903.

Dow, Sabrina H. Artistic Singing. Boston, 1883.

Durante, Ottavio. Arie Devote. Rome, 1608.

Fabricius, Hieronymus (1537–1619). De visione, Voce, Auditu. Venice, 1600. Another edition is entitled: De voce, de gula, de aespiratione et ejus instrumenti. Venice, 1601.

Fantoni, G. Storia universale del canto. Milan, 1873.

Ferrari, Giacomo Gotifredi. Breve trattato di canto Italiano. London, Schulze & Dean, 1818.

——— Giacimo [*sic*] G. Ferrari's celebrated instruction book for the voice, with accompaniment for the piano forte. New York, E. Riley & Co., ca. 1835.

Ferrein, Antoine. "De la Formation de la Voix de l'Homme." In Académie Royale des Sciences, Année 1741, pp. 409 ff. Paris, 1741.

Fetis, F. J. "Examen de l'état actuel de la Musique en France." In *Révue Musicale*. Paris, 1827.

Finck, Hermann. Über die Kunst des Singens, transl. by R. Schecht, *Monatshefte für Musikgeschichte,* XI, 1879, 129–41.

Florino, F. Breve Metodo di Canto. Naples, 1840.

Forkel, Johann Nicolaus (1749–1818). Algemeine Geschichte der Musik. 2 vols. Leipzig, 1788–1801.

——— Allgemeine litteratur der musik. Leipzig, 1792.

Frezza dalle Grotte, Giuseppe. Il cantore ecclesiastico. Padova, Stamperia del Seminario, 1698.

Friderici, Daniel (1584–1638). Die Musica Figuralis des Magister Daniel Friderici. Berlin, R. Gaertner, 1901.

Frosch, Johann (d. 1533). Rerum musicarum opusculum rarum ac insigne. Argentorati, 1535.

Fuchs, Albert. Bel Canto-Arien, Cantatur und Canzonen. Braunschweig, Litolf, 1901.

Galilei, Vincenzo (d. 1591). Dialogo di Vincentio Galilei, nobile fiorentino della musica antica et della moderna. Fiorenza, 1581.

Ganassi, Silvestro. Opera Intitulata Fontegara, Laquale insegna a sonare di flauto. Venice, 1535.

Garcia, Manuel. Hints on Singing. London and New York, 1894.

——— Report by Frederic W. Root on his interview with Garcia. In *The Musical Herald,* August, 1894, p. 229.

——— Memoire sur la voix humaine présenté à l'Académie des sciences en 1840. Réimpression augmentée de quelques observations nouvelles sur les sons simultanés et suivie du rapport de la commission de l'Académie des sciences. Avril, 1841. Paris, E. Duverger, 1847.

Garcia, Manuel del Popolo Vincente, Pere (1775–1832). 340 Exercises composés pour ses Élèves. Paris, 1868.

Gedanken. Über die welschen Tonkünstler. Halberstadt, 1751.

Gerbert, Martin (1720–1793). De cantu et musica sacra. San Blasianis, 1774.

——— Scriptoris Ecclesiastici de Musica Sacra. 3 vols. St. Blasius, 1784.

Giustiniani, Vicenzo. "Discorso sopra la musica de'suoi tempi (1628)." In Solerti, Angelo: Le Origini del Melodramma. Milan, Fratelli Bocca, 1903.

Glareanus, Henricus Loritus. Dodecachordon. Basil, 1547.

Goethe, Johann Wolfgang von. Italiänische Reise. 2 vols. Stuttgart, 1862.

Goldschmidt, Hugo (1859–1920). Die Italiänische Gesangsmethode des 17 Jahrs. Breslau, 1890.

——— Die Lehre von der vokalen Ornamentik. Charlottenburg, Paul Lehsten, 1907.

——— "Verzierungen, Veränderungen u. Passaggien." In *Monatshefte f. Musikgeschichte,* 1891, pp. 110–28.

Gondar, Ange. Le brigandage de la musique Italienne. 1777.

Gretry, André E. M. (1741–1813). Memoires, ou essai sur la musique. 3 vols. Paris, 1789.

Grout, Donald J. A Short History of the Opera. 2 vols. New York, Columbia University Press, 1947.

Guidotti, Alessandro, "Prefazione alla rappresentazione di Anima e Corpo di Emilio de' Cavalieri (1600)." In Solerti, Angelo: Le origini del melodramma. Milan, Fratelli Bocca, 1903.

Haböck, Franz (d. 1921). Die Kastraten und ihre Gesangkunst. Stuttgart, Deutsche Verlags-Anstalt, 1927.

——— "Die Physiologischen Grundlagen der altitalienischen Gesangschule" in *Die Musik,* VIII, September, 1909, pp. 337–47.

Haertinger, Martin, Das Grundgesetz der Stimmbildung für den Kunstgesang. Mainz, 1872.

Hanslick, Eduard. Criticism in *Deutsche Musik-Zeitung.* Vienna, May 12, 1860, p. 60.

Hawkins, (Sir) John (1719–1789). A general history of the science and practice of music. 5 vols. London, 1776.

Henderson, W. J. Early History of Singing. New York, Longmans, Green, 1921.

Hertel, Johann Wilhelm. Sammlung Musikalischer Schriften. Leipzig, 1757–1758.

Hey, Julius. Deutscher Gesangs-Unterricht. 4 parts. Mainz, 1886.

Hiller, Johann Adam (1728–1804). Anweisung zum musikalisch-richtigen Gesange, mit hinlänglichen Exempeln erläutert. Includes 64 pp. of musical examples. Leipzig, J. F. Junius, 1774.

Holmes, Gordon. "History of the Progress of Laryngology from the Earliest Times to the Present." In *The Medical Press.* London, July 15, 1885, p. 49, and subsequent issues to September 9, 1885.

Homer. The Odyssey, transl. by G. H. Palmer. Cambridge, Mass., Houghton, Mifflin, 1929.

Homeric Hymns, transl. by H. G. Evelyn-White. Loeb Classical Library. London, W. Heinemann, 1914.

Isidore (Saint) of Seville. "De Ecclesiasticis Officiis." In Migne: Patrologiae Cursus Completus Series Latina, vol. LXXXIII, col. 737–826.

Jerome (Saint). "Commentaries on the Epistle to the Ephesians." In Migne: Patrologiae Cursus Completus Series Latina, vol. XXVI, col. 439–554.

Jumilhac, Pierre Benoit de (1611–1682). La science et la pratique du plainchant. Paris, 1673.

Kelly, Michael (1762–1826). Reminiscences. 2 vols. London, 1826.

Kempelen, Wolfgang von. Le mécanisme de la parole, Vienna, J. V. Degan, 1791.

Kircher, Athanasius (1602–1680). Magnes: sive de arte magnetica opus tripartium. Rome, 1641.

——— Phonurgia nova; sive, Conjugium mechanico-physicum artis. Campidonae, 1673.

——— Musurgia Universalis sive Ars Magna Consoni et Dissoni in X Libros Digesta. Rome, Corbelletti, 1650.

Kitchener, William (1775–1827). Observations on Vocal Music. London, 1821.

Klein, Hermann (b. 1856). The bel canto with particular reference to the singing of Mozart. London, Oxford University Press, 1923.

Kuerzinger, Ignaz Franz Xaver. Getreuer Unterricht zum singen mit Manieren, und die Violin zu spielen. 3d ed. Augsburg, J. J. Lotter und Sohn, 1793.

Kuhn, Max (b. 1874). Die Verzierung-kunst in der Gesangs-musik des 16–17 Jahrhundert, (1536–1650). Leipzig, B. & H., 1902.

Labat, J. B. "Porpora et ses Elèves." In *Oeuvres Literaires-musicales.* 2 vols., esp. II, pp. 337–355. Paris, 1883.

Lacassagne, Joseph (1720?–1780?). Traité général des élémens du chant. Paris, L'auteur, 1766.

Lach, Robert (b. 1874). Studien zur Entwicklungsgeschichte der ornamentalen Melopöie. Leipzig, C. F. Kahnt, 1913.

Lamperti, Francesco (1811–1892). L'arte del canto. Milan, Ricordi, ca. 1883.

——— Guida teorica-pratica-elementare per lo studio del canto. Milan, Ricordi, 1864.

——— A Treatise on the Art of Singing, transl. by J. C. Griffith. London, Ricordi, 1877.

Lamperti, G. B. (1839–1910). Vocal Wisdom, maxims of G. B. Lamperti, ed. W. E. Brown. New York, W. E. Brown, 1931.

Landshoff, Ludwig. I classici del bel canto. Leipzig, Peters, 1927.

Lanfranco, Giovanni Maria. Scintille di Musica. Brescia, 1533.

Lang, Paul H. Music in Western Civilization. New York, Norton, 1941.

Lanza, Gesualdo (1779–1859). Lanza's Elements of Singing (in the Italian and English styles). 4 vols. London, the Author, 1813.

Lasser, Johann Baptist (1751–1805). Vollständige Anleitung zur Singkunst sowohl für den Sopran, als auch für den Alt. München, Gedruckt mit Hübschmannschen schriften, 1805.

Lavoix, H. Histoire de la Musique. Paris, 1884.

Lecuyer. Principes de l'art du chant, suivant les régles de la langue et de la prosodie françoise. Paris, Chez l'auteur, 1769.

Le Pileur d'Apligny. Traité sur la musique, et sur les moyens d'en perfectionner l'expression. Paris, 1779.

Lessmann, Otto (editor). *Allgemeine Musik-Zeitung.* 1885 and *ad passim.*

Lorente, Andres (1624–1703). El porque de la musica. Alcala de Henares, 1672.

Lyric muse revived in Europe, the, or a critical display of opera in all its revolutions. Anon. London, 1768.

Mace, Thomas (1613?–1709?). Musick's Monument. London, 1676.

Mackenzie, Sir Morell. The Hygiene of the Vocal Organs. 7th ed. London, Macmillan, 1890.

McMurrich, J. Playfair. Leonardo da Vinci, the Anatomist. Baltimore, Williams & Wilkins, 1930.

Maffei, Giovanni Camillo. Discorso della Voce. Naples, 1562.

Magazin der musik, herausgang von Carl F. Cramer. Hamburg, 1783.

Mancini, Giovanni Battista (1716–1800). Riflessioni pratiche sul Canto figurato, terza editione (rivedute, corrette, ed aumentate). Includes musical examples. Milano, Galeazzi, 1777.

——— Practical Reflections on the Figurative Art of Singing, transl. by Pietro Buzzi. Boston, The Gorham Press, 1912.

Manfredini, Vincenzo (1737–1799). Difesa della musica moderna. Bologna, 1788.

——— Regole Armoniche. 2d ed. Venice, 1797.

Mannstein, H. F. *See* Steinmann, Heinrich Ferdinand.

Marcello, Benedetto. Il teatro alla modo. Venice, 1720(?).

Marinelli, Giulio Cesare. Via retta della voce corale. Bologna, 1671.

Marpurg, Friedrich Wilhelm (1718–1795). Anleitung zur Musik überhaupt, und zur Singkunst besonders, mit Uebungsexempeln erläutert. Berlin, A. Wever, 1763.

Martène, Edmond and U. Durand. Thesaurus Novus Anecdotorum. 5 vols. Paris, 1717.

Martini, Jean Paul Egide (1741–1816). Mélopée moderne; ou L'art du chant, réduit en principes. Paris, Chez Naderman, ca. 1792.

Marx, A. B. Gluck und die Oper. Berlin, 1863.

Mastrigli, Leopold. La Decadenza del canto in Italia. Turin, 1897.

Mattheson, Johann (1681–1764). Der Vollkommene Capellmeister. Hamburg, 1739.

——— Mithridat wider den Gift einer welschen Satyr. Hamburg, 1749.

Maugars, André. Sa Biographie suive de sa Response faite à un curieux sur le sentiment de la Musique d'Italie, Escrité à Rome le premier Octobre, 1639, par Ernest Thoinau. Paris, 1865.

Mendelssohn, Felix. Letters from Italy and Switzerland, transl. by Lady Wallace. Philadelphia, 1863.

Mengozzi, B. (1758–1800). Méthode de chant du Conservatoire de Musique, contenant les principes du chant, des exercices pour la voix, des solfèges tires des meilleurs ouvrages anciens et modernes et des airs dans tous les mouvements et les differens caractéres. Paris, 1803.

Mersenne, Marin (1588–1648). Harmonie Universelle. Paris, 1636–1637.

Minoja, Ambrosio (1752–1825). Ueber den Gesang. Sendschreiben an B. Asioli. Leipzig, Breitkopf & Hartel, 1815.

Morley, Thomas (1557–1603). A plaine & easie introduction to practicall musicke. London, 1608.

Müller-Blattau, J. Die Kompositionslehre Heinrich Schützens. Leipzig, 1926.

Mursell, James L. The Psychology of Music. New York, Norton, 1937.

——— and Mabelle Glenn. The Psychology of School Music Teaching. New York, Silver, Burdett Co., 1938.

Nares, James (1715–1783). A concise and easy treatise on singing. London, J. Preston, ca. 1780.

Nassarre, Pablo (b. 1664). Escuela Musica. 2 vols. Zaragoza, 1723–1724.

Nehrlich, C. F. Die Singkunst. 2d ed. Leipzig, 1853.

Northcott, Richard A. (1871–1931). Francesco Algarotti: a reprint of his Essay on opera, and a sketch of his life. London, The Press Printers, Ltd., 1917.

Nouvelle Méthode. Très facile pour apprendre le plein-chant. Rouen, 1719.

Odier, Louis (1748–1817). Epistola physiologica de elementariis musicae sensationibus. Edinburgh, 1770.

Oudoux, Abbe. Méthode nouvelle pour apprendre facilement le plain-chant. Paris, 1776.

Pacchiarotti, Gaspare (1744–1821), with A. Calegari. Modi generali del canto. Milan, 1836.

Penna, Lorenzo (1613–1693). Li primi albori musicali. Bologna, 1684.

Peri, Jacopo. "Dedicatoria e prefazione a L'Euridice (1600)." In Solerti, Angelo: Le origini del melodramma. Milan, Fratelli Bocca, 1903.

Perini, Cesare. "Quale sia il miglior metodo da adottarsi onde il bel canto possa riottenere il suo primato in Italia." In *La Scena.* Trieste, Dec. 14, 21, 28, 1865, nos. 33, 34, 35.

Petri, Johann Samuel (1738–1808). Anleitung zur practischen musik, vor neuangehende Sänger und instrumentspieler. Lauban, J. C. Wirthgen, 1767.

Pizzati, Giuseppe (1732–1803). La scienza de' suoni. Venezia, 1782.

Planelli, Antonio (1747–1803). Dell' opera in musica. Napoli, 1772.

Plato. Laws, transl. by R. G. Bury. Loeb Classical Library. New York, Putnam, 1930.

Playford, John (1623–1686). An Introduction to the Skill of Music in Three Books. 12th ed. London, 1694.

Plutarch. Moralia, transl. by several hands, ed. by W. W. Goodwin. 5 vols. De Musica, I, pp. 102–35. Boston, 1870.

Poisson, Léonard. Traité théorique et pratique du plain-chant. Paris, 1750.

Polidoro, F. I. "Alcuni pensieri sull' insegnamento del canto." In *La Scena.* Trieste, Nov. 22, 1866.

Pollux, Julius. Onomasticon. 5 vols. Leipzig, 1824.

Ponzio, Pietro. Dialogo ove si tratta della theorica e prattica di musica. Parma, 1595.

Praetorius, Michael. Syntagma Musicum, Wolfenbüttel, 1619, reedited by Dr. Eduard Bernoulli, Kahnt. 3 vols. Leipzig, 1916.

Prelleur, Peter (18th C.). An introduction to singing or plain rules and directions whereby any person may in a short time learn to sing any song that is set to music. London, P. Thompson, 175–?.

Printz, Wolfgang Caspar (1641–1717). Musica Modulatoria vocalis, oder manierliche und zierliche Singkunst. Schweidnitz, 1678.

——— Compendium musicae signatoriae & modulatoriae vocalis, oder, Kurzer Begriff aller derjenigen Dinge, so einem, der die Vocal-Musik lernen will, zu wissen von nöthen seyn. Dresden, J. C. Miethen, 1714.

Quintilian. Institutio Oratoria, transl. by H. E. Butler. Loeb Classical Library. London, Heinemann, 1921.

Raguenet, François (1660?–1722). Parallèle des Italiens et des François, en ce qui regarde la musique et les operas. Paris, 1702.

Rameau, Jean Philippe. Code de musique pratique ou Méthodes. Paris, 1760.

Raparlier. Principes de musique, les agréments du chant, et un Essai sur la prononciation, l'articulation et la prosodie de la langue françoise. Lille, 1772.

Raynaldo, Theophilus. Opera Omnia. 19 vols. De Triplici Eunuchismo, XIV, pp. 521–600. London, 1665.

Raynard (Saint). "Instituta Capituli Generalis Ordinis Cisterciensis." In Migne: Pat. Lat., vol. CLXXXI, cols. 1726–1739.

Reese, Gustav. Music in the Middle Ages. New York, Norton, 1940.

Regio Istituto Musicale. Atti dell' Accademia. 3 vols. Firenze, 1863–1892.

Reichardt, Johann Friedrich (1752–1814). Briefe eines aufmerksam reisenden die musik betreffend. 2 vols. Frankfurt und Leipzig, 1774–1776.

——— Geist des Musikalischen Kunstmagazin. Berlin, 1791.

Reisch, Gregor (d. 1525). Margarita Philosophica. 1503.

Rogers, Francis. Discussion of bel canto in Educational Department of *Musical America,* December 25, 1940, p. 35.

——— "The Male Soprano," In *The Musical Quarterly,* vol. V, July, 1919.

——— "What is 'Bel Canto' anyhow?" *The Etude,* vol. LXII, March, April, May, 1944.

Rognoni, Francesco. Selva di varii passaggi secondo l'uso moderno. Milan?, 1620.

Romita, Fiorenzo. Jus Musicae Liturgicae. Mariettus, 1936.

Rosner, Robert. Beniamino Gigli und die Kunst des Belcanto. Wien, C. Haslinger qdm. Tobias, 1929.

Rossetti, Biagio. Libellus de rudimentis musices. Verone, 1529.

Rousseau, Jean (2d half, 17th C.). Méthode claire, certaine et facile, pour apprendre à chanter la musique. Amsterdam, P. & J. Blaeu, 1691.

Rousseau, J. J. Dictionary of Music, transl. by W. Waring. London, 177–?.

Rowley, Christopher E. The Voice; or the physiologist versus the singing master. London, Office of "Music," 1898.

Runciman, Steven. Byzantine Civilization. London, Edward Arnold & Co., 1923.

Sabbatini, Luigi Antonio (1739–1809). Elementi teorici della musica colla pratica de medesimi, in duetti, e terzetti a canone accompagnati del basso, ed eseguibili si a solo, che a piu voci. Rome, 1789–1790.

Salinas, Francisco de (1513–1590). De musica libri septem. Salamanticae, 1577.

Santoro, Fabio Sebastiano (b. 1671). Scola di canto fermo. Napoli, 1715.

Scaletta, Orazio (d. 1630). Scala di musica. Rome, 1656.

Scheibe, Johann Adolph (1708–1776). Critischer Musikus. Leipzig, 1745.

Schelle, Eduard (1816–1882). Die päpstliche sängerschule in Rom gennant die Sixtinische capelle. Wien, 1872.

Schleusingk, Johann Valentin. Musices choralis practicae medulla. Coloniae Agrippinae, P. Metternich, 1657.

Schopenhauer, Arthur. Reisetagebücher. Leipzig, 1923.

Schubart, C. F. D. (d. 1791). Ideen zu einer Aesthetik der Tonkunst, ed. Ludwig S. Schubart. Vienna, 1806.

Sieber, F. Il bel canto. 2 vols. Berlin, ca. 1887.

——— Vollständiges Lehrbuch der Gesangkunst. Berlin, 1858.

Signorelli, Mario. Il tramonto del bel canto in Musica d'oggi. Milano, 1931.

Silva, Giulio. "The Beginnings of the art of 'bel canto'; remarks on the critical history of singing." In *Musical Quarterly,* VIII, no. 1, 53–68. New York, 1922.

Solerti, Angelo. Le origini del melodramma. Milan, Fratelli Bocca, 1903.

Spanuth, A. (1857–1920). "Wagner—Gesang und bel canto." In *Signale,* LXVI, no. 6, pp. 169–74.

Spohr, Louis (1784–1859). Autobiography. 2 vols. London, 1865.

Steele, Sir Richard. *The Tatler,* January 3, 1709.

Steffani, Agostino (1654–1728). Send-schreiben, transl. by A. Werckmeister. Quedlinburg und Aschersleben, 1700.

Steinmann, Heinrich Ferdinand (1806–1872). Geschichte, Geist und Ausübung des Gesanges von Gregor dem Grossen bis auf unsere zeit. Leipzig, Teubner, 1845.

——— Die grosse Italienische Gesangschule. Dresden, 1848.

Sturm, Johannes. Letter to Matthew Stiffelreuter. In Epistolae Classicae, 1565, Book III.

Symmes, Thomas (1678–1725). Utile dulci. Or, a joco-serious dialogue concerning regular singing. Boston, 1723.

Synesius. The Essays and Hymns of Synesius of Cyrene, transl. by Augustine Fitzgerald. 2 vols. London, Oxford University Press, 1930.

——— "in Dionysius Petavius, c. 11. In Migne, J. P.: Patrologiae Cursus Completus, Series Graeca, vol. LXVI, col. 1148.

Taylor, David Clark (b. 1871). New light on the old Italian method; an outline of the historical system of voice culture, with a plea for its revival. New York, H. W. Gray, 1916.

Tenducci, Giusto Ferdinando (ca. 1736–180–?). Instruction of Mr. Tenducci, to his scholars. London, Longman & Broderip, ca. 1785.

Tevo, Zaccaria (b. 1651). Il musico testore. Venetia, 1706.

Thoinau, Ernest. *See* Maugars, André.

Tigrini, Orazio. Il compendio della musica. Venetia, 1588.

Tomeoni, Florido (1755–1820). Le guide musical; ouvrage dont le plan s'étend sur toutes les parties de la musique. Paris, ca. 1800.

———Théorie de la musique vocale. Paris, 1799.

Tosi, Pietro Francesco (c. 1650–c. 1731). Anleitung zur Singkunst. Aus dem italienischen des herrn Peter Franz Tosi mit erläuterungen und zusätzen von Johann Friedrich Agricola. Berlin, 1757.

——— Observations on the Florid Song, transl. by Mr. Galliard. London, J. Wilcox, 1743.

——— Opinioni de cantori antichi e moderni o sieno osservazioni sopra il canto figurato. Bologna, 1723.

Turner, William. Sound anatomized, in a philosophical essay on musick. London, 1724.

Uberti, Grazioso (fl. 1st half, 17th C.). Contrasto Musico. Rome, 1630.

Ulrich, Bernhard (1880–?). Die Grundsätze der Stimmbildung während der a capella-periode und zur zeit des aufkommens der oper, 1474–1640. Leipzig, B. & H., 1912.

——— Die altitalienische gesangsmethode, die schule des belcanto, auf grund der originalschriften zum ersten mal dargestellt. Leipzig, F. Kestner & C. F. W. Siegel, 1933.

Vaccai, Giulio. Vita di Nicola Vaccai. Bologna, 1882.

Vaccai, Nicola (1790–1848). Dodici ariette per camera per l'insegnamento del bel-canto italiano. Milan, ca. 1840.

Vallara, Francesco Maria. Primizie di canto fermo. Parma, 1724.

Veal, George (Joel Collier pseud.). Musical Travels Through England. London, 1785.

Ventura. Review of Lamperti's "Nuova Guida," in *La Scena*. Trieste, May 4, 1865.

Vesalius, Andreas. Icones Anatomicae. New York, New York Academy of Medicine and the University of Munich, 1934.

Vicentino, Nicola (1511–1572). L'antica musica ridotta alla moderna prattica. Rome, 1555.

Vicq-D'Azyr, Felix (1748–1794). Memoire sur la voix. See Memoires de l'Academie royale des sciences de Paris, 1779, pp. 178–206.

Vitali, Filippo. Dedicatoria e prefazione all'Aretusa (1620). In Solerti, Angelo: Le Origini del Melodramma. Milan, Fratelli Bocca, 1903.

Vogler, Georg Joseph (Abbe). Georg Joseph Vogler's Stimmbildungskunst. Mannheim, 1776.

Whistling, C. F. Handbuch der musikalischen Literatur, ed. A. Hofmeister, 3 vols.

Wieck, Friederich (1785–1873). Clavier und Gesang. Leipzig, 1853.

——— Klavier und Gesang. 2d ed.; Leipzig, 1878.

Williams, Watkins. "A dialogue between a Cluniac and a Cistercian." *Journal of Theological Studies,* 1930, pp. 164–175.

Wöchentliche. Nachrichten und anmerkungen die musik betreffend. July, 1766–June, 1768. 2 vols. Leipzig, 1766–68.

Wolf, Ernst Wilhelm (1735–1792). Auch eine Reise. Weimar, 1784.

Woolridge, H. E. The Polyphonic Period, in The Oxford History of Music, Vol. I. London, Oxford University Press, 1929.

Wright, Jonathan. A History of Laryngology and Rhinology. Philadelphia, Lea & Febiger, 1914.

Zabern, Conrad von. De Modo Bene Cantandi Choralem Cantum. Magonza, 1474.

Zacconi, Giulio Cesare (1555–1627). Prattica di Musica. Venetia, 1592.

Zarlino, Gioseffo (d. 1590). Istitutioni Harmoniche. Venetia, 1573.

Ziller, B. "Das Geheimnis des 'bel canto' (schöngesang), einige aufklärende Worte fur Gesangfreunde, Gesangstudierende und Gesanglehrer." In *Allgemeine Musik-Zeitung,* XXXII, no. 32, 33, pp. 534–35; no. 37, pp. 591–92.

INDEX